# THE LESSONS OF PUBLIC ENTERPRISE

# THE LESSONS OF PUBLIC ENTERPRISE

*A FABIAN SOCIETY STUDY*

*edited by*

MICHAEL SHANKS

WITH A FOREWORD BY
ROY JENKINS

JONATHAN CAPE
THIRTY BEDFORD SQUARE LONDON

PRINTED IN GREAT BRITAIN
BY EBENEZER BAYLIS & SON, LIMITED
THE TRINITY PRESS, WORCESTER, AND LONDON
ON PAPER MADE BY JOHN DICKINSON & CO. LTD.
BOUND BY A. W. BAIN & CO. LTD., LONDON

# CONTENTS

FOREWORD BY ROY JENKINS, M.P.                                    7

PREFACE                                                         13

*Part One : Progress Report*

I THE AIMS AND THE PROBLEMS                                     17

II INVESTMENT POLICY                                           34

III PRICES AND PROFITS                                         56

IV WAGES                                                       72

V MINISTERIAL AND PARLIAMENTARY CONTROL                        90
    *by* Austen Albu
        Labour M.P. for Edmonton. Member of Fabian Society
        Executive Committee, 1942–61. Member of Select Committee
        on Nationalized Industries since it was formed. By profession
        an engineer, and at present Chairman of the Parliamentary
        and Scientific Committee.

VI LABOUR RELATIONS                                           113

VII RELATIONS WITH PRIVATE INDUSTRY                           126
    *by* John Hughes
        Tutor in economics and industrial relations at Ruskin College,
        Oxford. Author of Fabian pamphlets on steel nationalization
        (Research Series No. 198) and on nationalized industries
        (Tract No. 328)

VIII COMMERCIAL RELATIONSHIPS IN STATE INDUSTRY              149

IX STAFFING AND RECRUITMENT                                   167

X THE BACKGROUND TO ORGANIZATION                             182
    *by* Arthur Palmer
        A technologist and editor of the *Electrical Power Engineer*.
        Labour M.P. for Wimbledon, 1945–50, and for Cleveland,
        N. Yorks., 1952–9. During his time in the House he spoke
        frequently on fuel and power questions and was for some years
        a member of the Select Committee on Nationalized Industries.

XI STRUCTURES AND THEIR ADAPTATION                           188
    *by* John Hughes

XII STATE INDUSTRY AND THE PUBLIC                            207
    *by* Mark Abrams
        Director of Research at the London Press Exchange. Author
        of *The Condition of the British People, 1911–1945, Social Surveys
        and Social Action*, etc. Former Chairman of the Consumer
        Advisory Council of the British Standards Institution, and for
        five years a member of the Consumers Committees appointed
        under the Marketing Acts for the Agricultural Marketing
        Boards.

5

## Part Two : Looking Ahead

XIII 'ISLANDS OF SOCIALISM'     219

XIV WHO DECIDES THE PUBLIC INTEREST?     227
    *by* Ernest Davies

Labour M.P. for Enfield, 1945–50 and for Enfield East, 1950–1951. Member of Select Committee on Nationalized Industries, 1952–9. Under-Secretary of State for Foreign Affairs, 1950–1. Chairman of Parliamentary Labour Party Transport Group, 1945–50 and 1951–9. Editor of *Traffic Engineering and Control*. Author of *National Enterprise* (1946), *Problems of Public Ownership* (1952), *Transport in Greater London* (1962).

XV NATIONALIZED INDUSTRIES AND ECONOMIC POLICY     248
    *by* J. R. Sargent

Fellow and Lecturer in Economics, Worcester College, Oxford. Author of *British Transport Policy* (1958), and of articles in *Economic Journal*, *Oxford Economic Papers*, *Bulletin of the Oxford Institute of Statistics*, and other publications. Contributor to *The British Economy, 1945–50* (Edited by Worswick and Ady). Other writings include evidence to the Radcliffe Committee, and a report on transport development in British North Borneo (1960).

XVI THE FRONTIERS OF PUBLIC ENTERPRISE     269

XVII LESSONS FROM ABROAD     283
    *by* Peter Lowell

A management consultant who has specialized in questions of organization and control, purchasing and stores. He has a wide experience of industry both in Britain and on the Continent, having spent some years in a senior executive capacity with Volkswagen in Germany.

XVIII THE FUTURE OF PUBLIC ENTERPRISE     300

    BIBLIOGRAPHY     311

# FOREWORD

ONE of the troubles about the debate on public ownership in post-war Britain is that it has so far been carried on largely in the abstract, and largely in ignorance of the facts about the existing public sector of the economy. Attitudes to nationalization have polarized mainly on ideological grounds, not simply between the two major political parties, but also between left and right in the Labour Party itself.

Among the electorate at large, nationalization has become an unattractive label, with highly emotive overtones (witness the very different reaction to the synonym 'public ownership'). This antipathy to 'nationalization' can largely be traced to its identification in the public mind with the problem industries, coal and the railways. Ironically, successful state-run industries tend not to be thought of as 'nationalized' at all. The origins of this ambivalence form one of the main themes of this book.

The authors are entirely non-propagandist in their approach. Naturally, they are all sympathetic to the idea of public ownership. They came together originally as a Fabian Society study group, and many of them either helped to create, or work in, or have specialized knowledge of, one or other of the nationalized industries. This circumstance has been used to establish the facts about the nationalized industries, as shown in the experience of the last ten or twelve years. There are, towards the end of the book, suggestions about the pattern that future extensions of the public sector might assume. But these are not the main purpose of the study.

The book begins, in Chapter 1, with a broad statement of the present predicament of the nationalized industries, and then ranges over all aspects of these industries, their relations with the Government, with the public, with their customers, with their own workers, with each other and with the British economy as a whole. It also takes a close and instructive look at public ownership abroad, and consequently helps to fill one of the largest gaps in the nationalization discussion.

Two interrelated themes recur constantly throughout the book. They represent the two main problems of nationalized industries, to which satisfactory solutions, though clearly indicated here, have yet to be applied in practice. These two themes are the relationship between the nationalized industries and the Government, and the role of these industries in influencing or planning the national economy.

The creators of the nationalized industries in the post-war Labour Government do not seem to have anticipated the uneasy relationship that has grown up between ministers and the chairmen of the boards of the nationalized industries, for which the ministers are responsible. Certainly, there was nothing in the nationalization statutes about the type of behind-the-scenes, backstairs pressure by ministers on board chairmen which has developed.

But in practice (and the practice, it must be admitted, began under Labour), the conception of authority openly conducted and publicly accountable has been stood on its head. Because the relationship between minister and board chairman is loosely defined, it is informal in character. Because it is informal, it is often secret. Because it is secret, it is often unaccountable. The facts emerge, if ever, only when the immediate crisis is over and public judgments, often unjustly hostile to the industry concerned, have been formed.

It is in the sphere of prices that this backstairs pressure has most frequently been used; the best-known example is the 'gentlemen's agreement' whereby the Coal Board consults the Minister of Power before raising its prices. Conservative ministers have on several occasions intervened to prevent price increases which were economically justified, but which might have been electorally unpopular. For this is the crux of the matter. Interference based on some genuine conception of the public interest would be tolerable, even if one disagreed with the conception involved. But, in fact, interference has been largely motivated by short-term political considerations. Neither the long-term public interest, nor the interests of the nationalized industries themselves, have been properly thought out and applied. Partly, of course, this springs from the ambivalence of Conservative ministers and M.P.s towards the nationalized industries for which they are responsible, yet

8

towards which they are politically hostile. This ambivalence has been one of the factors leading to the current financial difficulties of the railways and, to a lesser extent, the mines. Now the air corporations are suffering for the same reason.

Nor is it just chairmen of boards who suffer. At lower levels the ambivalent position of senior officials has seriously weakened morale and efficiency. The half-way status between civil servant and entrepreneur is itself uncomfortable. The lack of clear standards, commercial or social, by which to make decisions, dampens initiative. When, in addition, officials are subject to continual political sniping, to which they cannot by the conventions answer back, then for many the position becomes intolerable. They leave for the higher paid anonymity of private enterprise. Sheer wastage of talent (never in any case very thick on the ground, especially in the railways), has been a major weakening factor in the two problem industries.

The solution is to give the nationalized industries greater freedom of action within a properly planned national policy. Day-to-day interference must end. On the other hand, major policy decisions on, say, the social obligations of the nationalized industries, which at present go by default or are left to the industries themselves to answer by some unsatisfactory rule of thumb, should become the clear responsibility of the Government. The intimate relationship between ministers and board chairmen is, as the authors of this book recognize, inevitable. But it can be brought into the open to a greater degree than at present, partly by tightening the rules governing it, partly by strengthening the position of the board chairmen vis-à-vis the ministers. This is mainly a question of job security, because of the relatively short period for which appointments are made, and the complete ministerial control over renewal.

The other problem that emerges clearly from the analysis contained in this book is that of the function of the nationalized industries in national planning. The mere fact that they are publicly owned means that they are bound to be regarded as instruments for influencing the whole economy, even by Conservative Governments, which have not, until recently, been noticeably enamoured of the concept of planning. In fact, the present administration has tended to use the nationalized industries as a substitute for national planning. Where the Labour Government saw these industries as a means of guiding the economy as a whole, the Conservatives have used them as a compensatory mechanism for checking excessive booms in the private sector. The interests of the public sector have frequently been sacrificed to those of the private.

One of the best instances of the contradictory demands made on the nationalized industries, both by the Conservative administration and by a large part of the electorate, is provided by coalmining. The Coal Board is expected to keep down prices, and to make a profit, and to keep open a large number of uneconomic pits in Scotland, Wales and the North East. The Coal Board is in fact asked to act as a substitute for a proper national employment policy, and at the same time meet commercial criteria.

This is but one aspect of the basic dilemma facing nationalized industries. Presumably, one reason for nationalizing them was that they should operate some services which, in normal commercial practice, would be abandoned or never undertaken. Such uneconomic services are normally paid for by cross-subsidization, that is, by charging more for the remaining services. But this may lead to these industries being undercut in price by private competitors, who have no social obligations to meet.

This has happened in the fields of both energy and transport. The success of both oil and private road transport in attacking the traditional markets of coal and the railways, is due partly to the subsidy factor in the prices charged by the two nationalized industries. Their lack, until recently, of price freedom, with which to counter the challenge to their markets, has also been a handicap.

In short, there is lacking at present a clear conception of how nationalized industries ought to behave in a society where they are minority groups in a predominantly private enterprise economy. Recently, it is true, there has emerged a tentative Tory view of how a nationalized industry should behave. On this view, it should operate like a large private concern. The nationalized industries are being given financial targets to meet, and greater price freedom to help meet them, in an effort to make them as similar as possible to I.C.I., for example – although they will presumably not be encouraged to take each other over.

At the same time, the large private concerns are increasingly having to justify themselves at the bar of public opinion in a way that, until recently, was demanded only of the publicly owned enterprises. There is growing recognition that these giant private firms have more in common with the large state corporations than they have with the small firms in the private sector; and that whatever the form of ownership, the question still to be answered is how to fit undertakings of this size and influence into a controlled or planned national economy. To the extent that this is rendering some of the problems of the nationalized industries technical rather than political, this is all to the good. But it leaves unanswered, as the Conservative view leaves unanswered, the problem of the social obligations of the nationalized industries.

Some form of protection, either by subsidy from the Exchequer or by taxation of competitors (as now with oil), is clearly required. Any protection given should be calculated, as near as may be, to offset losses on those uneconomic activities which a nationalized industry is obliged to continue. If, after this element of protection has been given, the industry is still unable to fend off competitors, then the normal rules should apply. But a clear recognition of the special social obligations of the nationalized industries is essential, if they are to be given a fair chance of prospering.

The Labour Party, the book suggests, needs to think hard about its exact reasons for favouring public ownership. The main arguments for it, as listed in the final chapter, are six. First, the argument of power, the belief that the 'commanding heights' of the economy should be controlled by the state. Second, the role of public ownership in planning the economy. Third, the argument of priorities, on the Galbraithian antithesis of private affluence and public squalor. Fourth, the argument that equality of wealth and incomes is furthered by public ownership. Fifth, the argument of efficiency – that where the performance of an industry or firm is demonstrably inadequate, it should be taken over by the state. Sixth and last, the argument that public funds invested in industry should be accompanied by a measure of public control and accountability.

But none of these arguments (and here the book is entirely in accord with the position of the Labour Party as stated in *Signposts for the Sixties*) is simply an argument for the mammoth public corporation run by what is known as the 'Morrisonian Board'.

Indeed, the book shows that this form of administration was largely dictated by the character of the industries taken over, rather than by any theoretical notion about the proper form of public ownership. Large natural monopolies offered economies of scale and standardization which dictated the shape of the new administrations. But in future, there is little reason why the pattern should be repeated. Individual firms taken over, new industries set up by the state in areas of unemployment, expansion by existing nationalized industries, greater enterprise by the trade unions and the Co-operative movement – all these could add up to a potentially diversified pattern of public ownership.

But before this expansion can be seriously contemplated, the existing public sector must be made to work, and be seen to work by the public. Nationalization, in itself, neither creates nor solves many problems. It is, to quote Mr Shanks, the editor of this book, 'a means whereby great ends can, with wisdom, be achieved'. It is as a contribution to this wisdom that this book is offered.

R.J.

*July* 1962.

# PREFACE

ERHAPS one should begin by saying what this book does *not*
do. It is not concerned, except tentatively in the final chapter
and by implication elsewhere, with the broad question of the
case for and against public ownership as such. It tries to avoid
partisan polemics of all kinds. It does not suggest candidates for
further nationalization. Its aim is the less exciting one of analysing –
as dispassionately, honestly and objectively as we can – the
progress of the nationalized industries in Britain to date, of trying
to find out where, how and why performance has fallen below
promise, and what must be done to enable performance to improve
in the future. We believe that such an examination should be
of assistance to the Labour movement and the nationalized industries themselves, and also to the broader world beyond the Fabian
Society, which will, we venture to hope, find at least some of our
conclusions to be of interest and value.

That at least is what we set out to do. The reader must judge
how far we have succeeded. Our opinions, of course, are our own,
and commit nobody but ourselves. The Fabian Society encouraged
us to begin our work, and helped magnificently in the administrative and secretarial work involved, but it bears no responsibility
for our conclusions.

Of the eighteen chapters in the book, eight are signed by the
contributors, to whom I am extremely grateful. They do not, of
course, necessarily agree with anything that appears in chapters
other than their own. I myself wrote Chapters 1, 13 and 18,
though in the preparation of Chapter 18 I received invaluable
help from Miss Margaret Reid, and she, though not responsible
for the views expressed, *is* responsible for whatever merits the
chapter may have. The remaining seven chapters were originally
drafted by Fabians in or associated with the nationalized industries, who must unfortunately for professional reasons remain
anonymous. To these authors, whose work can receive neither
financial reward – in this sense the book has been a labour of love
for all concerned with it – nor public recognition, I owe a double
debt of gratitude.

13

# PREFACE

The amount of editorial redrafting on these chapters varies from the appreciable to the absolutely minimal. I must record here the invaluable assistance received from Rex Winsbury in the preparation of Chapter 6. It is probably true that this book has involved rather more editorial work than a study of this sort normally does. From the start, all of us who were concerned with it were determined that this should not be a book of unrelated essays, but that it should have a logical sequence of thought and present a reasonably consistent view. Once again, the reader must judge how far this has been achieved. I have not thought it part of my duties as editor to iron out all differences of emphasis or to force all contributors into a monolithic mould. (Specifically, I must in honesty say that I am not fully convinced by the argument for protecting the coal industry in Chapter 16.)

My task as editor would have been an impossible one had it not been for the enthusiastic and devoted co-operation of all the contributors. No editor ever had a better team to work with. Every chapter has been discussed in draft by the entire group, and authors have been remarkably ready to accept criticism from their colleagues. To me at any rate, the working of this group has demonstrated the possibilities of co-operation in a common enterprise in a way which is not always seen in the Labour movement. The group as a whole, and I in particular, owe much to Rex Winsbury for his work as secretary.

There are other debts of gratitude which I am proud to acknowledge. Mrs Shirley Williams and Mrs Gladys Cremer at the Fabian Society were tireless in their help on innumerable occasions. Miss Margaret Cutter gave invaluable secretarial assistance. Many others – too many to mention individually – gave assistance and advice. When so many have given so freely of their time, one can only hope they will feel that, in the end, the results justify their labours.

M.J.S.

PART I

# PROGRESS REPORT

# CHAPTER ONE

# THE AIMS AND THE PROBLEMS

A BELIEF in public ownership has always been one of the
fundamental tenets of the Labour Party. But there has never
been, and there is not now, anything in the way of an official
long-term *strategy* of socialization; either in the sense of a detailed
programme of future take-overs, or of a precise blue-print for the
different forms which public enterprise might take, or even of the
role which public enterprises should play in a mixed economy.
The whole thing has tended, in a typically British manner, to be
*ad hoc.* Industries have been put on, and dropped from, the party's
'shopping list' for nationalization without, in either case, adequate
explanation (or, one suspects, adequate thought). The nationalized industries themselves have been expected to do mutually
contradictory things, and their leaders have been given far too
little guidance on how they should conduct themselves, and what
they should aim for. This air of improvization, this lack of any
detailed guidance on the role of nationalized industries in a predominantly privately-owned economy, has done immense harm.
It has led to loss of public money, it has weakened morale and
initiative inside the nationalized industries, and it has contributed,
among other things, to the electoral misfortunes of the Labour
Party. Whatever anybody may say, in the eyes of the public
nationalization has failed to live up to its promises, and the
Labour Party gets the blame for having nationalized in the first
place.

It is easy to say that this is a grossly unfair reaction – which it is.
By and large, nationalization has in fact been a greater success
than could reasonably have been expected. The coal industry,
despite immense difficulties, has been put on its feet again. Electricity is a successful industry measured by almost any standard.
There is little public complaint against gas or the national air
corporations, or the Atomic Energy Authority (which–significantly
– nobody seems to think of as a nationalized industry at all !). It is

less easy to praise the British Transport Commission, though allowance must be made for the derelict state in which the railways were left by private enterprise and for the extremely unhelpful part played by the Conservative Government ever since 1951.

The unfavourable public image of the nationalized industries is, in fact, based almost entirely on the records of the two problem industries – coal and the railways. To some extent, this may have been an inevitable consequence of the Labour Party's policy of taking first into public ownership the derelict sections of the private economy. But that, unhappily, is far from being the whole story. The Labour Party's dreams for the nationalized industries were never fully thought out and were probably only capable of realization in terms of the planned economy which disappeared after 1951. The disappearance of the Labour Government left the nationalized industries in limbo, survivors of a vanished world trying to adjust themselves to a new environment.

In this task they have had little, if any, support from the Conservative Party or from the Press or private industry. All three have maintained an almost incessant sniping campaign against public enterprise.

The Conservatives bear a heavy responsibility for whatever short-comings the nationalized industries retain. Their attitude has been literally 'two-faced'. In 1951 they accepted public responsibility for the nationalized industries (other than steel and road haulage) which, in opposition, they had done everything they could to discredit. But in the decade since then, they have totally failed, as has the Labour Party, to work out any coherent policy to determine the role and functions of a public sector in a mixed economy.

Only in the last year or so has the outline of a philosophy towards the public sector begun to emerge in Government thinking – namely, that nationalized industries should be made to pay their way as competitive enterprises; in other words, that the public sector should be remade in the image of the private. But even now economic objectives are blurred by political expediency. The prolonged failure to define a policy for the public sector has been the more serious because of the increasing governmental interference in the conduct of the nationalized industries under the Tories, and because of the underlying prejudice against them which still exists in almost all ranks of the party. One feels that if a nationalized industry became too obviously successful it would be an embarrassment to the Government. And outside the Cabinet, back-bench Tory M.P.s quite openly wage a campaign against the very industries which their Government is ultimately responsible for running.

The harm which this continuous sniping does to morale and initiative inside the nationalized industries cannot be over-emphasized. Able men are understandably reluctant to take jobs in public enterprise, where they will be subject to political interference and adverse publicity, without being able (because of the civil service tradition of silence, which – probably wrongly – influences the leaders of most nationalized industries) to defend themselves in public. From their own and the national point of view, it is essential that the nationalized industries should be taken out of politics and allowed to get on unhindered with their industrial job.

It is important for the Labour Party to recognize that it is itself partly to blame for the unfavourable image of the nationalized industries, and that in so far as this has recoiled on to the party it is, like so many of Labour's wounds, self-inflicted. Labour is to blame because it has failed to provide a coherent philosophy or code of conduct for nationalized industries, or to think out what they should be expected to do in the present state of our society. There are many understandable reasons for this failure. To many people on the Left, public ownership is its own justification, and nationalization must be judged on moral and ideological rather than empirical grounds. This is all very well, but it is not much help to a chairman of the National Coal Board whose immediate task is not to propagate socialism, but the more humdrum one of trying to produce and sell coal in a highly competitive market. It is one thing to envisage an economy dominated by public enterprises. It is much harder, but no less important, for a socialist to consider how they can best operate as minority groups in a predominantly private enterprise society.

There is, secondly, understandable reluctance to accept the fact that some of the principles and ideas behind the nationalization measures of 1945–51, which were based on the experiences of the nineteen thirties, have very little relevance to the conditions of the 'fifties and 'sixties and badly need replacing. The Labour Party has in any case had other things to think about. Nevertheless, some new thinking on the role of nationalized industries in present-day society is badly needed, and this book seeks, in part, to provide it. This new thinking is needed not only to help the nationalized industries to become more efficient, but to enable those who believe in nationalization to rebut more easily the many ill-informed criticisms which have been made, and to provide some sort of objective standards by which the barrage of hostile publicity can be judged.

This chapter, therefore, attempts briefly to list the main points at which the high hopes of 1945 have been disappointed – whether through the fault of the nationalized industries themselves or of others. These points will be developed in greater detail in the succeeding chapters of Part I, while Part II deals more generally with future policy.

If we cast our minds back to 1945, it is easy to see how the targets chosen for public ownership, and the form of public ownership chosen for them, were dictated by the industrial and economic circumstances of the 1930s. But it is necessary to remember that the so-called 'Morrisonian' public corporation – in fact invented by the Baldwin administration in the 1920s – is by no means the only possible form of public enterprise, nor is it the most suitable in all circumstances. It is politically unfortunate that our experience of public enterprise in Britain should be so dominated by the use of the Morrisonian corporation[1] that to many people the two appear synonymous; for it seems clear that if public ownership were to be extended to manufacturing rather than service industries a radically different form of organization would be needed. Until recently, too little thought has been given to this by the Labour Party, but there is now a growing awareness of the complexities of the problem and also of the range of organizational possibilities.

Similarly, if the object of nationalization had been to achieve maximum expansion of the public sector at the expense of the private – if the motive had been strategic or ideological – one can think of other targets which might have had a higher priority

[1] The Post Office, Forestry Commission, and the ill-fated Iron and Steel Corporation all represent, of course, in their different ways, alternatives to the Morrisonian corporation.

than those actually chosen. There might then have been a strong case for concentrating on highly profitable industries, or for nationalizing the merchant and joint-stock banks in order to attack the capitalist system at its heart. Instead, the industries taken over were – with the exception of steel – confined to public utilities providing power and transport. In two vital cases – coal and the railways – they were semi-derelict when taken over. So far from weakening private industry, the nationalization of the power and transport undertakings greatly benefited it. Industrialists were supplied with power and rail transport at below-market prices, while the huge expansion programmes of the public corporations provided lush markets for private contractors and equipment manufacturers (though on occasion nationalized industries have been known to exploit their monopoly buying power to good effect).

The reasons for concentrating on the power and transport industries were nevertheless sound ones. In the case of coal and the railways, rescue operations had become essential. But apart from these special cases, the whole thinking of the Labour Party – as of economists generally – was dominated by the fear of a relapse into stagnation and depression, as happened after the 1914–18 war. Hardly anybody foresaw that full employment would remain a permanent feature of the post-war world.

The industries chosen for nationalization had two features in common. They were – or they appeared to be at that time – all natural monopolies, in which the advantages of large-scale operation and centralized control were very great. As a result, the Morrisonian public corporation was peculiarly suitable. At the same time, they were all industries which needed big injections of capital if they were to play their proper part in the economy.

The strictly economic reasons for nationalizing the power and transport industries (apart from the need to redress managerial inadequacy in coal and the railways, and to improve the appallingly bad labour relations in coal-mining) were therefore as follows:

(1) To achieve the economies of large-scale operation and organization. How far this has in fact been realized will be discussed in later chapters. Without doubt, considerable benefits have been reaped, though in some cases (e.g. gas) progress has

been hampered by a markedly decentralized structure. On the other hand, some diseconomies of large-scale have undoubtedly been encountered.

(2) To provide a nucleus for expansion in the economy. In the early years the Government thought of investment in the nationalized industries as a means of countering a recession in private industry. This argument was later stood on its head by the Conservative Government, which tried to regulate the pace of the whole economy by year-to-year adjustments in nationalized industries' capital spending. The idea that nationalized industries' investment plans could be turned on and off like a tap to counterbalance the movement of private investment was finally given an overdue burial in the 1960 White Paper on Public Investment.

Because the industries nationalized were basic services, expansion in their capacity was, of course, a necessary condition for growth in the productive power of the economy as a whole, and this has indeed been largely achieved. Not since 1955 have bottlenecks in the public sector held up the expansion of private industry; the reverse, if anything, has been true.

(3) The third economic argument for nationalization was to ensure that the fruits of this expansion in the capacity of our basic service industries would be enjoyed by private industry and the community as a whole at low prices, and that the benefits of monopoly should be enjoyed without monopoly profits or exploitation. Expansion at low prices was to be achieved partly by eliminating profits, and partly by increasing productivity.

However, more important than the economic advantages expected to accrue from nationalization were the social advantages. First and foremost, there was a feeling that essential public services should be accountable to, and therefore under the control of, the community as a whole. This question of public accountability has dogged the nationalized industries ever since. Is the job to be done by Parliament (limited as it is in time and detailed knowledge), by Governments (who are inclined to put their own political interests before the long-term interests of the nationalized industries), by consumer councils (largely parochial and ineffective, and concerned mainly with keeping prices down), or simply by ensuring that the right men are in charge? It cannot be said that any satisfactory solution has yet been evolved, and it is difficult to resist the conclusion that the Labour Party's thinking on this point was fundamentally rather muddled.

The problem would not, of course, have been anything like so serious if Labour had remained in power. The nationalized industries would then have been ultimately responsible to a Government which wanted them to succeed, which could weigh their interests fairly against those of the economy as a whole. But too little thought was given to the possibility that they might pass under the control of their enemies.

The nationalized industries were also envisaged as an example to the rest of the community, as an advertisement for socialism, as a nucleus from which the public sector would steadily expand. Few people thought in 1945 that the frontier between public and private industry would become rigid, as it has done. The public sector was to demonstrate its superiority partly in its relations with the customer – because it would produce for use and not for profit – partly in its relations with its workers. One has to remember that working conditions in industry as a whole in 1945 were very different from what they have since become. Relations between labour and capital were strained, to say the least. There was little joint consultation, there was little provision for redundancy or for promoting the worker's welfare or enlisting his support in improving productivity and efficiency. By giving their employees a genuine sense of partnership in their public enterprises, the nationalized industries hoped not only to improve the workers' lot – and in the case of coal this in itself was of paramount importance – but to secure their co-operation in reaching new heights of productivity. They were going to demonstrate that industrial democracy pays off.

These hopes were reasonable enough in 1945, and many of them, indeed, have been fulfilled. But, plainly, somewhere along the line, something has gone quite seriously wrong. What is it?

The first obvious misjudgment was in the economic situation. The overriding economic problem since 1945 has not been unemployment, but inflation. This in itself has totally transformed the milieu in which the nationalized industries have had to operate. The labour shortage and the strength of the unions have compelled large sections of private industry to carry out drastic reforms in their own labour relations. As a result, the improvement in the worker's lot, which the nationalized industries were to bring about by deliberate policy, has become a commonplace in much – though by no means all – of private industry also, simply through the operation of supply and demand. Labour has become a scarce commodity throughout industry, and has been able to exact a scarcity price.

Labour relations in the nationalized industries have certainly been no better, in fact in some cases they have been a good deal worse, than in the more advanced privately-owned industries. This has undoubtedly been one reason for the unpopularity of nationalization, both among the workers and the general public. It is clear, in retrospect, that too much was expected to flow from the expropriation of the shareholder. The benefits which would have gone to him under private enterprise have had to be split three ways – in fixed interest compensation payments (a more onerous burden to hard-pressed industries like coal and the railways than dividends would have been), in better wages and conditions for the workers, and in cheap prices to the customer. An expanding industry like electricity can meet all these commitments without too much difficulty. For the National Coal Board and the Transport Commission, with their declining markets, it is another matter. Both bodies have had to go heavily into deficit. Both have had considerable difficulties in labour relations. In the case of the railways, morale and efficiency have suffered badly because the commission has been unable – until the Guillebaud Report in 1960 – to pay competitive wages to its workmen.

There is, in short, a conflict between a nationalized industry's obligations to the consumer and its obligations to its own workers. Both worker and consumer feel that the transfer of ownership gives them rights which they do not claim to enjoy vis-à-vis private industry. A higher standard is demanded of a nationalized industry, and when it does not materialize there is proportionally more resentment – fanned by hostile politicians, the Press and private industry.

This brings us to the second misjudgment underlying the introduction of nationalization – a misjudgment of the human element. Too many people expected too big a change to result from the mere fact of nationalization, and when it did not occur there was corresponding disillusionment. The miners, for example, were given to understand that the mines now belonged to *them* – and were consequently chagrined to find that in many cases they still had to work under the same managers as before, and that improvements in wages and working conditions were not necessarily to be had for the asking. If it was *their* industry, why did they still have to take orders from the bosses? On the other side of the fence, there was genuine bewilderment and disappointment at the workers' reluctance to change their traditional attitudes with the change in ownership. The attitude of the unions was ambivalent. Some union leaders accepted a responsibility for the success of nationalization, and tried their hardest to get their members to co-operate with the new management. Others persisted in regarding the public boards as simply a new set of 'bosses', to be treated, at best, with wary suspicion. Union leaders who took posts in the nationalized industries were too often regarded by their former colleagues, with total lack of logic, as having 'gone over to the other side'. The attitude of the miners' union was, on the whole, better in this respect than that of the railwaymen; but the spirit of co-operation did not always extend to pit level, and there have been marked differences of behaviour between the moderate and Communist wings of the National Union of Mineworkers.

In general, however, nationalization did not produce the change of heart which had been hoped for. There was undoubtedly an improvement in relations, and in the conditions of the workers. Many devoted men on both sides of industry worked hard to remove the bitter legacies of the past. But the revolutionary changes, which many people had hoped for and vaguely expected, were not compatible with the harsh and overriding demands of the national economy. The first requirement was more production. The survival of the economy in those early post-war years rested on the slender foundation of a run-down, demoralized coal industry. In these circumstances it was hardly possible to undertake a complete *bouleversement* of the managerial structure. Change had to be sacrificed to continuity, ideological experiment to industrial efficiency. Existing managerial and technical skills had to be utilized wherever possible, regardless of the effect on the workers.

The difficulties of improvising a vast industrial organization, at a time of tremendous pressure on resources and in the teeth of much organized business opposition, were not fully appreciated before 1945. Once again, the existence of full employment complicated matters. Not only did it increase the urgency of stepping up production and undertaking vast expansion programmes (both the N.C.B. and B.T.C. were extremely short of men capable of planning and carrying out major investment projects), but it also made it more difficult to attract management of the right calibre. Faced with a seller's market for their skills, many able executives preferred to take jobs in private industry. For one thing, the public corporations had difficulty in offering competitive salaries – partly because the salaries of board members were originally fixed relatively too low. Moreover, there was a definite feeling – which still exists in some places today – that a man who took a job in a nationalized industry would encounter considerable prejudice if he ever wanted to get back into private industry.

Full employment had another unfortunate effect on the nationalized industries. It meant that the maintenance of price stability in British industry acquired an importance hardly envisaged before the war. The cost-of-living index came to have an almost mystical significance. This meant that the nationalized industries came under heavy pressure to keep their prices down. For years British industry was, in effect, being subsidized by cheap coal and cheap railway freight charges. This not only complicated matters for the Coal Board and the Transport Commission; it was, almost certainly, economically foolish. At a time when coal was in desperately short supply, industry was given no incentive at all to use it efficiently and economically. The overloaded railway system was allowed to sink further and further into decrepitude, with an increasingly underpaid staff, simply because governments could not face the odium of allowing railway travel to bear its economic cost.

It can be argued that it is in this field of prices and profitability that the biggest mistakes have been made in the treatment of the nationalized industries. Certainly, this is where government interference has been most marked and most mischievous. This interference takes place in different ways in different industries. In the case of coal there is simply an unofficial 'gentlemen's agreement' that the board should seek ministerial approval before putting up prices. This agreement has no statutory force whatever, but it has

26

been an extremely effective weapon in the Government's hand. In 1955 the Coal Board was refused permission to put up prices before the general election, with the result that a much bigger increase had to be sanctioned later. But no knowledge of all this filtered through to the general public at the time. The Government could not be attacked for having refused to sanction a price increase, for officially it had never made such a refusal or even received a request for permission. Officially, the Coal Board is its own master: in fact, the leading strings are firmly in the Government's hands. But since control is exercised entirely behind the scenes, the Government has the best of both worlds. It imposes policies for which it is not apparently accountable; and this applies not only to coal but to the other nationalized industries as well. There is no doubt at all, for example, that the Government has played a big part behind the scenes in recent years in all the major wage negotiations in the nationalized industries, and it has, on more than one occasion, vetoed increases approved by both management and unions. There has also been governmental interference in commercial policy questions – for example, the attempt to compel the nationalized airlines to 'buy British', and the Minister of Power's pressure on the Central Electricity Generating Board first to accelerate and then to slow down the switch-over of power-stations from coal to oil.

In these cases intervention by the Government has been mainly covert and informal. In the case of the railways, the situation has been rather different. The railways inherited certain special obligations from the days when they enjoyed a virtual monopoly of inland commercial haulage. Most important of these was the obligation, as a common carrier, to accept all freight offered to them, however unprofitable. Until 1957 the railways were, moreover, compelled to publish all charges and were forbidden to discriminate between customers. Tariffs were fixed at a standard rate varying with the value of the consignment. The result was that they lost the most profitable traffic to road haulage, and had to carry many goods at unprofitable rates.

In 1957 the railways gained a certain amount of commercial freedom. They no longer had to publish their charges, and were able to discriminate between customers. But the obligation to act as a common carrier remained, and they still had to get approval

27

from a special public body, the Transport Tribunal, for any increase in maximum freight charges or in passenger fares. The Transport Tribunal has only recently been abolished in the provinces, and it still holds sway in London. Moreover, the Government on occasion overruled Transport Tribunal decisions which were in the B.T.C.'s favour. On the railways, therefore, as a legacy of a vanished monopoly, there has been continuous overt public interference in board decisions. While the restraints were justified originally, they were maintained long after the need and justification had vanished.

This raises a number of major issues of policy, which need to be resolved. First, how far is it reasonable for the Government to interfere in the management of nationalized industries, and how should ministerial control be properly exercised? On the one hand, the Government does have an obligation to see that the industries are being run in the public interest – which may not coincide with the commercial interest of the nationalized industry itself. There is a case, for example, for requiring a nationalized industry to undertake an unprofitable service in the public interest – such as stocking coal in a recession, maintaining railway services in remote areas of Scotland, or undertaking rural electrification on an unprofitable basis. There is even a case for trying to use the nationalized industries to influence the movement of prices and wages in the economy – though it is clearly unwise, unfair and impractical to operate a wage 'freeze' in the public sector while wages in private industry are totally unchecked. On the other hand, ministerial intervention does pose grave disadvantages. Running a nationalized industry is not like running a civil service department. Management must be enterprising; it must take day-to-day decisions. It cannot do its job properly if it has to keep running to the minister for approval. There is a serious danger of ministerial 'back-seat driving', which seems to be growing. The unions rightly resent the fact that the chairmen of the nationalized boards with whom they negotiate are not, in effect, free agents when it comes to wages. And there is all the difference between ministerial directives which can be questioned and debated in Parliament, and unofficial pressure exercised in secret.

A Government which believes in planning is plainly justified in using its powers over nationalized industry in furtherance of a long-term economic plan, though such planning can hardly be restricted entirely to the public sector. The use of nationalized industries as strategic agents in a national plan for economic growth has been effectively developed in France, and might have been in this country if a Socialist Government had remained in power after 1951. But the Conservative Governments of the 1950s did not believe in planning, and their interventions have, for the most part, been capricious and, to a large extent, motivated by short-term political considerations.

This raises a second question of at least equal complexity. What yardstick should nationalized boards apply when taking commercial decisions? How far should they put the public interest before their own commercial advantage, and how should they measure the public interest? How should they weigh the competitive claims of their workers and their customers?

On this crucial point, there is almost total confusion in the public mind. If nationalized industries make large profits they are attacked for exploiting the community (and by the trade unions for not paying their workers enough); if they make losses they are attacked for inefficiency and for conspiring with the unions to pay uneconomic wages at the taxpayer's expense. It is difficult to deal effectively with these arguments because of the lack of any generally agreed rationale of how a nationalized industry *should* behave. Certainly, a nationalized industry should not simply seek to maximize profits to the exclusion of other considerations. On the other hand, how is it to assess the efficiency of its operations except by regard to the profit earned on them? A nationalized industry is required by statute at least to break even, 'taking one year with another'. This must surely imply that unprofitable services must be offset by the profits earned on the others, and that an unprofitable service should not be undertaken without some definite justification. But in such cases, is it the responsibility of the nationalized industry to assess the social value of unprofitable services, or should it be the responsibility of the Government? Again, all the nationalized industries have big expansion programmes in hand. How far should these be financed out of internal resources (which means profits), how far by borrowing from the Treasury? (Or, for that matter, why not directly from the public?)

These issues become, of course, much more acute when the nationalized industry is in deficit, and is having to compete with private enterprises which lack any of the inhibitions and divided loyalties which beset the entrepreneurs of the public sector. This is pre-eminently the case with coal and the railways. In each case the nationalized industry was prevented from earning the profit which its near-monopoly position in a seller's market would normally have earned it during the early post-war years. During that time, the Coal Board and the Transport Commission were both treated as monopolies which needed to be kept under restraint in the public interest. As a result, when their monopoly position was lost and they came under intense competition from oil and road transport – developments which again were not fully foreseen on nationalization (though in the case of the Transport Commission, the denationalization of road haulage, of course, aggravated the problems) – these industries found it extremely difficult to compete. They lacked any accumulated surplus which could be used to sustain price competition or a sales campaign. They were denied the normal commercial freedom to discriminate between customers, or raise charges swiftly where the traffic would bear it. These limitations were not fully appreciated by the public, who took the difficulties of the N.C.B. and B.T.C. as proof of the latent incapacity of public enterprise.

The results have been little short of disastrous. The B.T.C. became a pensioner of the Government, since only by Government subsidy could it afford to carry out the modernization programme on which the survival of the railways depends. As a result, effective control passed from the commission itself to Whitehall, with serious consequences for managerial morale, efficiency of operations and harmony of labour relations. Yet, despite their enormous deficit, the railways still had to run hopelessly unprofitable services, pay capital charges to compensate the original shareholders, and seek permission from the Transport Tribunal to raise fares on those few routes where they retained some degree of monopoly power. Eventually the whole system became unworkable. Most of the railways' debts had to be written off, the commission itself abolished in a sweeping decentralization programme, overall control vested in the Minister of Transport, and the chance of an integrated public transport system lost, perhaps for ever. All this might have been avoided if the railways had been given a normal degree of commercial freedom before the frightening slide into deficit began.

In coal the situation is not, as yet, quite so serious. But the symptoms are there, too. Because of its deficit, the N.C.B. is prevented from paying its workers enough money to stop them from moving into other industries; labour shortage is consequently having a serious effect on productivity in many areas. Economies are in some cases endangering future efficiency. If the Board had entered the recent recession with an accumulated surplus instead of a deficit, it would have been much better placed to fight competition both at home and abroad by price-cutting, and it might have been more successful in its policy of stockpiling surplus coal. But that deficit stemmed directly from the 'gentlemen's agreement'.

Clearly, therefore, a major reason for the public's disenchantment with nationalization has been the unexpected emergence of intense competition in the energy and transport fields, and the refusal to allow the N.C.B. and the B.T.C. the degree of commercial freedom which would have enabled them to meet this competition. An important part of this commercial freedom is the right to earn profits. To some sections of the Labour Party, for whom 'profit' is still almost a dirty word, this may be a hard saying. And yet to a socialist it is surely preferable that money should flow from the private to the public sector, rather than the other way round!

There is, therefore, a serious need to unravel the relationships between ministers and nationalized boards, especially in the field of prices, profits and wages where ministerial intervention has been most pronounced. At the same time, it is important to consider afresh the role of the public sector in the economy – its expansion programmes, its relations with its workers, with the trade unions and with private industry. These issues will form the subject-matter of the next six chapters. Here they have only been touched on, as matters which have contributed to dissatisfaction with, and in, the nationalized industries.

But there is another side to the picture. Could the nationalized industries not do more themselves, both to improve their internal structures and operating efficiency, and secondly, to improve their

relations with the public? The questions of staffing, decentralization, and relations with the consumer are considered in Chapters
9, 10, 11 and 12. Chapter 8 deals with the specific question of the
relations between the nationalized industries themselves. This is
an important issue which has received very little public attention.
The nationalized industries all face common problems. Could they
not with advantage seek to meet them in co-operation rather than
competition?

Co-operation could perhaps take the form of combined advertising or public relations campaigns, to explain the problems and
achievements of the nationalized industries to the public. There
might also be scope for operating a combined 'nationalized industries lobby' in Parliament. This would, no doubt, be highly un-
welcome to the Ministers of Power and Transport, but it is
arguable that one of the main defects of the nationalized industries
up to now has been that board chairmen have been unduly
deferential to the wishes of ministers.

This deference has undoubtedly been increased by the lack of
security of tenure of board members, who are normally appointed
for three or five years and whose re-appointment rests with the
minister. A man who has made his entire career in a particular
nationalized industry will naturally be reluctant to cross swords
too frequently with a minister who is also his effective employer –
especially as there are no 'golden handshakes' or 'top hat' office
pension schemes for nationalized industry board members. This
becomes particularly important when long-term investment plans
are under consideration, which cannot reach fruition until after
the period of office of the board members taking the decision has
expired (an example would be B.O.A.C. ordering a new jet air-
liner from the drawing-board). In such cases, it would be a bold
board member who would stake his career on defying his minister
if he thought his policy was wrong, since he would be likely to be
out of a job before he knew whether his stand was justified or not!
The question of security of tenure for board members needs to be
looked at again, together with the question of salaries and conditions, especially in view of the anomalies which have arisen in
this field.

How much, if anything, has been done to explore the possibilities of combining facilities for research, training and recruit-

ment? Why not, for example, a Nationalized Industries' Staff College? Would a regular interchange of staff help – especially in closely related industries like coal, gas and electricity? And in these industries is there no possibility of working out a joint *de facto* fuel policy, if the Government will not do it? Is it in the national interest that coal, gas and electricity should meet only as competitors?

There would indeed seem to be considerable scope for self-help by the nationalized industries, which at the moment is hardly being exploited at all. To develop this would demand a more aggressive spirit at the head of the boards, and a willingness to incur ministerial wrath. But there is little doubt that if those at the top showed more of this spirit, the morale of those lower down would be greatly raised; and of all the needs of the nationalized industries today, better morale is perhaps the most urgent.

# CHAPTER TWO

# INVESTMENT POLICY

ONE feature common to nearly all the nationalized industries is the major part played by investment in new capital equipment. Throughout the 1950s more than a third of the nation's total fixed capital formation took place in the public sector, and of this nearly a half was in the nationalized industries (including the Post Office). In the early years of the decade, in fact, public investment actually exceeded the total of private investment. Even now, with our economy distorted in favour of private consumption, and essential public services in many cases neglected, public sector investment is plainly of considerable weight and importance. In the financial year 1962–3, for example, the nationalized industries are scheduled to spend some £930,000,000 on capital investment. There are not many private firms where investment is of such major importance in the scheme of things.

This is no accident. Indeed, the need for major new development and re-equipment was one of the main reasons for taking each of the present nationalized concerns into public ownership. When the original prototype of the modern national industrial public corporation – the Central Electricity Board – was set up in 1926, the aim was not so much to take over or amalgamate the activities of existing undertakings, as to pool electricity supplies throughout the country. This required a major new piece of capital construction on a national scale – the building of the grid. When the Electricity Act, 1926, was given its second reading in the House of Commons, Colonel Ashley (Minister of Transport in the Conservative Government of Stanley Baldwin) justified it on these grounds. A rather similar situation resulted in the London Passenger Transport act of 1933 – again under a predominantly Conservative Government.[1] This made possible a pooling of

[1] The Act originated partly from the initiative of Herbert Morrison in the previous Labour Government, and partly from the desire of the predominant

resources, not only by those undertakings incorporated in the new board, but also by co-operation between the board and the main-line railway companies. Previous amalgamations and agreements among London transport undertakings, when privately owned, had similar purposes; and both these earlier amalgamations and the setting up of the London Passenger Transport Board were followed by large programmes of new capital investment – new railway lines and new fleets of buses.

The various nationalization Acts passed since the war have usually been discussed and defended or attacked outside Parliament on political grounds, but when we look at the actual second reading debates in Parliament in each case, and particularly at the minister's speeches, we see that they were to a very large extent justified as measures of reorganization preliminary to major capital redevelopment. The reorganizations, in turn, were justified as consequences of earlier technical developments and on the basis of reports of independent committees.

The same applies to the subsequent steps taken by Conservative Governments to reorganize these industries. In all cases a great deal of the argument on both sides of the House has turned on how effective the measures would be in making possible major extension and re-equipment, which was agreed on all sides to be urgently necessary. For instance, the McGowan Committee before the war had recommended further co-ordination of the development of electricity supply over wider areas, and the Electricity Act of 1947 was justified on the ground that it made this possible. Again, the Electricity Act of 1957 was specifically commended to the House by the then Minister of Power on the ground that, by establishing a separate generating board, as proposed by the Herbert Committee, it would make possible the speedier and more efficient planning and construction of power-stations. Similarly, under the war-time Coalition Government the Reid Committee had pointed to the very serious state of technical backwardness in the coal industry and recommended general introduction of more modern methods, such as 'horizon mining', wholesale mechanization and 'an extensive and national co-ordinated programme of searching and boring for coal'. The committee, composed of

transport interests to eliminate wasteful competition. The 1933 Act differed in important aspects from the Morrison Bill.

managing directors or managers of large colliery companies, concluded that, to enable their proposals to be carried out, there would have to be 'an Authority' which could supervise the reorganization of the industry 'on a coalfield basis rather than mine by mine'. The main reason given for the nationalization of the railways, when the Transport Act of 1947 was before Parliament, was the need to co-ordinate the overtaking of vast arrears of capital expenditure.

The main difference between the railways and the fuel and power industries has been that the major post-war capital redevelopment made possible by the reorganization of the railways was, in fact, delayed for more than a decade. The first five years' delay under the Labour Government may have been unavoidable owing to the post-war scarcity of resources and the even greater needs of the fuel and power and exporting industries. But it is hard to make similar excuses for the meagreness of subsequent achievements. A fallacious belief seems to have persisted through the early years of the Conservative Government that the major problems of the industry were to be solved through organizational and economic change rather than by physical investment. Railway management itself was not fully aware of its own technical backwardness. It is startling to find that, at a time when steam traction was clearly in decline in every other advanced industrial country, the development resources of the newly-nationalized British Railways were devoted to the development of a wide range of standard steam locomotives large and small.

Indeed, almost every measure for bringing an existing industry under public control or setting up a new public industrial organization (both before and after the war) has been justified, at least to a considerable extent, on the ground of a need for major new capital development. The North of Scotland Hydro-Electric Board was set up during the war, following the report of the Cooper Committee, almost entirely to carry out major new construction, and took over hardly any existing resources.

When we look at the particular kinds of capital investment which the nationalized industries have undertaken and the place of this function among their other activities, we see a marked contrast to most privately-owned industrial organizations except the largest and newest, both in absolute terms and in proportion to the size of each undertaking. The investment programmes of the nationalized industries are enormous. The electricity supply industry invests well over £300,000,000 each year – over half through the Central Electricity Generating Board – against total fixed assets of something under £2,000,000,000. The coal industry and the railways invest about £100,000,000 and £175,000,000 a year respectively, while around £50,000,000 a year is spent by the gas industry on capital expansion.

From the point of view of the organization, functioning and internal management of these industries, however, what is much more important and in greater contrast with most private industries is the *continuity* of investment programmes. In relation to the national economy as a whole, they have been maintaining investment programmes of this order of magnitude for over a decade. Large-scale capital investment, therefore, must be a major (often the outstanding) preoccupation of the top management of all the major nationalized industries, not only on special occasions, but continuously. Moreover, it seems unlikely that this situation will change in the foreseeable future.

Although continuity is a common feature, the particular purposes of these enormous investments differ in each case. In electricity supply, the main need has been to keep pace with an ever-growing demand. Ever since the first world war, there has been a steady increase in consumption of electricity both in this and in other advanced countries, and demand is currently doubling itself – or even more – each decade. There is an element of obsolescence as generating plant design gets strikingly more efficient, but a great deal of old plant is kept for use at peak periods. On the whole, transforming and switching plants have long lives and cables have almost indefinite ones. The industry has been profitable and has not suffered, but rather gained, from competition with others. Its history, therefore, has been (and is likely to continue to be) one of expansion coupled with a steadily increasing efficiency on the generating side.

The coal industry, often regarded as declining, needs continuous and massive new capital investment. The immediate need after the war was for modern mining methods and mechanization on a very large scale, but this did not mean simply re-equipping existing installations. In a coal-mine it is very hard to draw a clear distinction between current and capital expenditure. The productive unit is not, as in a factory, a fixed piece of man-made equipment to which materials are brought from elsewhere; the raw material is fixed and the man-made capital equipment moves. The largest single element in the permanent capital equipment is the main tunnelling, but tunnelling is also the chief element in the process of current production. As the tunnelling moves forward, some mines become exhausted as far as profitable production goes. But profitable production itself cannot be defined absolutely. The most easily worked seams are exhausted first, and as they are exhausted others have to be tackled – seams which would not have been regarded as worth while at an earlier stage. Technical methods must be improved to compete with worsening geological conditions. Any mining industry needs a high and continuous rate of investment to maintain its current level of production – quite apart from expansion. Like the Red Queen in *Alice in Wonderland*, it must keep running very fast merely in order to remain in the same position.

With railways, we find a rather similar situation – a need for massive new investment, to make up for the long years of neglect both before and after the war, resulting from sheer shortage of money. A massive programme of re-equipment was needed to overtake the lag in technical development that had been growing ever since the first world war. With the coming of the Conservative Government, wedded to theories of road/rail competition, modernization, to increase the railways' competitive power, became the more urgent. It may be that, if this process of re-equipment continues for another decade or so, it need not be continuous thereafter, though further technical development by both the railways and their competitors may modify this possibility. With London Transport, which before the war had reasonably modern technical methods and has reached saturation point with its traffic, the amount of investment justifiable on normal financial grounds is proportionately much smaller than on other railways, and is indeed confined primarily to the replacement of worn-out equipment. Social considerations however, undoubtedly justify further expenditure – notably the Victoria Tube line, approved after much delay but unlikely ever to pay its way commercially. The investments of the air corporations are large, but their purpose is mainly to keep pace with obsolescence, though in doing so they have, in fact, greatly increased their capacity. The gas industry, on the other hand, has to work desperately hard and invest desperately hard in order to avoid being overwhelmed by competition from the electricity industry.

In order to consider the problems of both policy and management that these major investment programmes present, we need to look a little more closely into just what sort of things they actually comprise. One must consider in each case both the size and the physical and technical nature of the projects; how like they are to one another, how long it actually takes to plan them and get them carried out, and how far the industries concerned can complete them with their own resources, or alternatively how far they have to rely wholly or partly on the resources of other industries.

About ninety per cent of the annual investment of the Coal Board consists of colliery works. The rest is carbonization equipment (not now any complete new plants), and various large workshops, stores and a few offices. Colliery works may be either complete new mines or major reconstruction schemes, or all kinds of small projects, mechanical re-equipment and so on. Of course, the most important projects and the most difficult to plan and carry out are complete new mines, or reconstructions which are so large as to be comparable with new mines. The typical size of a colliery, whether measured in bulk or cost, has increased enormously since the war. For instance, the average book value of the eight hundred-odd existing collieries in the Coal Board's balance-sheet is about £600,000 each, but this includes many very old pits. The modern mine is something quite different and may, with all its associated and ancillary works above and below ground, cost something between £10,000,000 and £15,000,000. A little less than half of this may be incurred above ground, not only in the buildings and equipment actually forming part of the mine, but also in railway sidings and the coal preparation plant (which is to be found at practically every large new mine and which may cost nearer £1,000,000 than £500,000). In the underground works, over £2,000,000 may be spent on actual tunnelling, nearly as much on mechanical plant and equipment, and the remainder on shaft sinking. The point of mentioning these proportions is that the underground tunnelling work is normally carried out directly by the Coal Board's own labour and, of course, entirely under Coal Board design and supervision. Indeed, there are statutory requirements, as well as considerations of management, which make it essential for such work to be carried out under the direction of a regular, qualified colliery manager. If the scheme is a major reconstruction – that is, something which may double the size and capacity of an existing mine – this same colliery manager will also be responsible for current production in other parts of the mine. The two processes of current production and new capital development, as far as tunnelling is concerned, are closely interlocked, and there may well be competition between the two for scarce resources of labour, supervision, control and equipment – and even for use of the shafts. The other parts of the whole scheme of constructing a new mine consist, of course, of contract work – either work on the site (including shaft sinking), or by manufacture elsewhere. There are a considerable number and variety of quite separate civil, mechanical and electrical engineering contracts. Normally the responsibility for overall design and, above all, for general co-ordination (as well as detailed design of certain parts) rests with the Coal Board's own staff, and not with outside contractors or consultants. There have been some exceptions, but this is the broad picture. It follows that the whole process of capital development in the colliery field imposes a far greater strain on the management of the user organization than capital development projects in most other fields – including, for instance, the construction of carbonization plants under other departments of the Coal Board.

A carbonization plant, which may be nearly as extensive and complex as a new coal-mine, will generally be provided under a single main contract by one of the only two or three British firms capable of handling such work. These firms, subject only to fairly broad specifications and consultations with the board's engineers, will provide all the types of equipment and constructional work, and nearly all the services of design, planning and co-ordination. The reason for the difference, of course, is that such firms are used to providing somewhat similar plant for the gas and steel industries – and neither the Coal Board, the Gas Boards nor any of the steel firms has a continuing demand for such a large number of carbonization plants as to warrant setting up complete design staffs of their own. For complete collieries, on the other hand, there are obviously no other British purchasers. Contractors who provide their own equipment and design their own methods of working may be employed for shaft sinking – because relatively few such jobs have to be done – and methods employed abroad can be, and have been, successfully employed in this country. Within the Coal Board's organizations, therefore, we see a distinction between two broad types of capital project. One is carried out largely by the user organization – that is, the Coal Board itself – because there is a continuing programme of somewhat similar projects, and because the work of construction is very closely linked with the current operations. The other type of project is purchased more or less complete in an outside market.

In the electricity industry we find variations on these two themes. The laying of local cables is generally carried out by the Area Electricity Board's own labour in conjunction with the day-to-day processes of maintenance. Larger cables and the grid are generally laid or constructed by contract, but subject to design and supervision by the Electricity Board's own professional staffs. The major capital projects in the electricity supply industry are, of course, power-stations – indeed, they are the largest capital projects of any of the nationalized industries, and among the largest of any British industries. A major conventional power-station (coal or oil-fired) now costs over £40,000,000, and a nuclear power-station perhaps £50,000,000 or £60,000,000. For each there has, of course, to be a major overall plan and design, and within that a number of very large subsidiary projects of design and manufacture, involving different industries and professions. Generally, for a single coal- or oil-fired station, the Central Electricity Generating Board will place some forty separate contracts itself, retaining responsibility for co-ordination between the contractors. Broadly, out of the £40,000,000-odd cost of the whole station, something between £25,000,000 and £30,000,000 will go on mechanical engineering contracts. There is relatively little building or architectural work in the traditional sense but, including all the site works and structures and associated buildings, there may be civil engineering contracts amounting to £10,000,000 while the remainder of the cost will go on electrical engineering works and design costs.

The pre-war electricity undertakings (whether local authorities or companies) generally commissioned main consultants to design entire power-stations for them, and these main consultants would commission other specialist consultants and deal (directly or through them) with the various contractors. The new British (later Central) Electricity Authority, set up in 1947, largely continued this practice, although its own engineering staffs seem to have taken an increasingly active part in the general design. The Central Electricity Generating Board, which succeeded the C.E.A. in 1957, has now very largely dispensed with main consultants and with mechanical and electrical engineering consultants and replaced them by permanent design staff of its own, while still to a large extent relying on civil consultants. The arguments for employing consultants in any field are presumably the advantage of getting both completely independent professional advice and also experience based on comparable work elsewhere. These arguments apply to a much lesser degree now that there is one authority controlling such a very large and continuing volume of construction. It is a little hard to see why the arguments for consultants are still held to apply in the civil field, although not in the electrical or mechanical. Presumably there is more value to be gained from experience in other types of civil project.

For the nuclear stations we find a completely different system. Each station is constructed under a single contract by a 'consortium' of leading electrical, civil and mechanical engineering firms. Each has its own design staff and contracts to produce a complete station. The C.E.G.B., however, plays a considerably larger part in the control of design and construction of nuclear power-stations than the N.C.B. appears to in the field of carbonization plants. It employs, for instance, a very large staff of site engineers as well as its own design specialists. It also gets advice and help from the Atomic Energy Authority. In this special field, of course, the volume of scientific manpower is naturally limited and for this reason at least the 'consortia' may be regarded as somewhat artificial creations. No doubt the idea was that, having accumulated experience in constructing at least one nuclear station in England, they would be in a good position to compete for similar contracts abroad, but so far the prospects of such work have turned out to be very much more limited than at one time appeared.

In one particular section of the electricity supply industry we find a complete contrast to the general practice of the Electricity Boards. Although the North of Scotland Hydro-Electric Board has new capital construction as a very much larger proportion of its responsibilities and its expenditure than perhaps any other nationalized industry, it relies probably more than any other on outside consultants, as well as contractors, in the civil, electrical and mechanical fields.

Although it is virtually the only concern in Great Britain constructing hydro-electric schemes, its design and planning engineers assigned to such work are very thin on the ground indeed.[1] This apparently, is deliberate policy; but one doubts its wisdom when one looks at the record of the very long times taken to get its major schemes carried out, and the way in which costs have risen above estimates by as much as twenty and forty per cent in real terms – far greater amounts than could possibly have been explained by monetary inflation.[2] The board's whole method of dealing with manufacturers and contractors seems to have been weak.

A prominent feature of the major capital projects of larger nationalized industries is not only their immense cost and bulk and the size of the organization needed to administer them, but also the very long time that they take to come to fruition. Indeed, the failure to appreciate these immense time scales is perhaps one of the most serious of the many general misconceptions about the nationalized industries. Let us take the two most outstanding and important examples. The construction of a large coal-mine, including shaft sinking and all the works above and below ground, takes about four or five years before any significant amount of coal is produced, but it will be a further year or two before all the working tunnelling has been so developed that the maximum

[1] According to the article by H. A. Clegg and T. E. Chester on 'The North of Scotland Hydro-Electric Board' in *Public Administration*, vol. XXXI, Autumn 1953, the board's headquarters staff comprised eighteen in the chief electrical and mechanical engineers' department and eight in the chief hydraulic and civil engineers' department. By 1961 the figures had risen to twenty-six and twelve respectively.

[2] The Fabian pamphlet 'Nationalized Industries in the Mixed Economy' by John Hughes, pp. 21–2, makes a detailed analysis of the rise in cost of certain hydro-electric schemes on the basis of figures in the Select Committee of Nationalized Industries Report, 1957, p. 197, Annex C, appendix H.

level of production has been reached. This, of course, is not the limit of the time scale – a further two or three years must be allowed for deciding upon and planning the whole project in out-line, for designing it in detail, and for manufacturing the equip-ment. Even this is not the whole story. The development of modern coal-mining, as described for instance in the Reid Report, involves not merely the setting up and working of a number of independent units, but a strategy of exploiting entire coal seams and coalfields in the most economical way. Indeed, it is a grand strategy of exploiting the coalfields of Britain as a whole, on a long-term plan providing for the most efficient and economical production of a balanced supply of various types of coal over a long period of years. This is why, from its earliest days, the Coal Board has made, and published, ten-year plans in considerable detail.

Electricity generation is – and has been since the 1920s – even more a matter of closely interlinked national planning. Ever since the grid was constructed, each power-station could be regarded as an addition to a total pool of generating capacity, and the con-struction of successive stations has been planned accordingly, together with the planning of inter-connecting grid routes. As their design has become more efficient, power-stations have been getting bigger and fewer, and their individual planning, as well as the overall national planning, has become a more and more com-plex matter. In addition to the processes of planning, design and manufacture, for which there are very broad parallels in the coal industry, a very considerable period has to be allowed, in most cases, for arguments about the site. The Central Electricity Authority, in the decade following the war, had a rather complex system for planning and constructing power-stations, which allowed a total of eight years for the whole process. This was roundly criticized by the Herbert Committee, which demanded that the whole process should be streamlined and speeded up – without making any very practical suggestions as to how this should be done. The Central Electricity Generating Board claim to be making efforts to this end and some shortening in construc-tion periods does seem to be in sight. New power-stations (coal-fired, oil-fired, and nuclear) have to be sited in more and more remote areas, largely because most urban sites with sufficient water are now taken up – quite apart from the deliberate policy of putting nuclear stations in less populous areas. The result is that a period of at least two years has been occupied up to now in controversies, public inquiries, and so forth, about siting and local amenities, even where the owners of the land will agree to sell, and when no one suggests that there is really any effective alternative site. The further elaboration of public inquiry procedures as a result of the Franks Report may be expected, if anything, to lengthen this process even more. (The same sort of thing may happen in the case of new grid routes.) Such is the result of the present-day pressures in favour of private property rights against public needs, and the pressures of the legal profession for the formalizing and elaboration of procedures of this kind. Similar time scales apply to railway investment schemes. In the provision of diesel locomotives, for example, the proper sequence would be, (1) the construction of a variety of prototypes, (2) their testing in service over a fairly lengthy period, and (3) the production of those types proved to be the best. Such a programme might well have taken eight years or so to produce any extensive results. Because of the Government pressure to produce early results, these steps were telescoped in the railway modernization programme. Batches of locomotives have been ordered without the amount of prototype-testing ideally required, and a greater variety of types have been ordered than was desirable, simply to keep all manufacturers employed, and to test on the basis of general experiences. As a result of the shortcomings resulting from this process, the full economies which should derive from the change in methods of mechanization are certainly not being achieved as yet.

Similarly lengthy time scales apply to railway electrification. The period required for electrification of the London–Birmingham–Lancashire complex would probably have been about eight years, even without the delays occasioned by the Minister of Transport; and except on minor routes, a scheme of this type represents about the smallest main line development which can be economically justifiable.

Long-term planning is obviously not only desirable, but absolutely essential for all industries, public or private, which have to undertake a series of major capital projects of the order we have described. The electricity supply industry has, indeed, been undertaking regular long-term planning since some years before the war, and the Coal Board almost from its earliest beginnings. So has the gas industry. The long-term plans of the railways, except for particular types of investment such as London Transport rolling stock, were, until 1955, in very vague and general terms. Practically all this planning, however – whether in detailed or general terms – has been a matter of statements of intention by the industries themselves and not of definite financial provision, which in the case of nationalized industries can only be authorized by the Government. In the White Papers which the Government has published on the subject of capital investment in the fuel and power industries, and in Government statements about railway modernization, there has never been anything firm and definite going more than a year or two ahead – although more vague and general Government approval has sometimes been expressed (and then withdrawn or amended) for longer-term plans such as that for nuclear power. There appears to be a similar general lack of long-term planning in privately-owned British industry – in marked contrast to American industry and American-owned firms in this country.

More recently the Government has started to move towards the idea of five-year planning for the nationalized industries. This is a step in the right direction. But is it enough? If a coal-mine project takes seven to ten years to get into full production from the time it is first conceived, and five to eight years from the time major contracts begin to be placed, it is quite futile to talk about five-year planning as '*long-term* planning'. It is also quite futile to try to restrict the activities of the Coal Board and the Central Electricity Generating Board by limiting their borrowing powers to periods of two or three years, when in fact for all their major projects they are bound to be committed for *at least* five years ahead. Of course the great length of construction times in the nationalized industries is a source of inflexibility and weakness, and it would be a great help if it could be shortened, but the scope for doing this is limited. Meanwhile it is not sufficient for planning and budgeting to extend merely up to the first year in which any capital project starts to be fully productive. To make a proper financial assessment of a project before embarking on it, one needs to know what its total life is going to be, and what the demands for production are going to be over that period. This, in effect, means at least twenty-year planning and preferably fifty-year planning – something which few, if any, institutions in British industry, public or private, have so far attempted. In practice, of course, any form of capital construction on the scale of the major projects we have described inevitably involves, at least by implication, very long-term commitments indeed – even if such commitments are undertaken with little or no conscious 'planning'. The short-term financial restrictions which are imposed on paper are largely illusory. When any serious attempt is made to enforce them it simply means a virtual cessation of minor investment projects, such as minor buildings, vehicles and small plant replacements, which can in effect be cut because they take only a short time to provide. But relatively these small projects may produce just as worthwhile results as the major uncuttable projects, and their termination may, in any case, make little substantial difference to the nationalized industry's total capital commitment. And yet despite all this the White Paper on public investment of 1960 can describe as follows, 'How public investment is *controlled*' (sic): 'Each summer the Government considers the proposals for expenditure on public investment *in the following financial year* ... This review is the *focal point* in the control of public investment' (our italics). What, if anything, is done to influence programmes further ahead is not described, but how the Treasury's fiddling about with a few figures can help after practically all the contracts concerned have already been let, is beyond comprehension or comment!

The 1961 White Paper, 'The Financial and Economic Obligations of the Nationalized Industries', does seem to represent at least one step forward. The Government will now 'each year discuss with the (nationalized) undertaking and approve the general lines of its plans for development and capital expenditure for the next five years ahead and be ready to agree to long-term commitments as appropriate'. *Eppur si muove!*

There is another aspect of long-term planning which the major nationalized industries have been slow to undertake: that is, the development of the internal resources necessary for the outline planning, design, and carrying through of major projects. The National Coal Board took over the coal industry when it was almost completely denuded of young graduate mining-engineers capable of planning major new schemes. Large numbers of qualified engineers were required for positions of general management and for current production, and in its first few years the board described in successive annual reports how capital development was being held back through lack of suitable engineers. Yet it was not until after the Fleck Report in 1955 that the board set up a really strong central staff department, and there was even more delay before this department made plans on a national scale to recruit the many various types of qualified engineers who were required over a long period, both for capital planning and current production. Recruitment and training schemes had been instituted, but the board was working to a large extent in the dark until it really knew what men it wanted, and when and where. It was not only a matter of men, but of internal organization, of planning and management. At a fairly early stage, the board took the important decision of setting up in all areas with large new capital construction projects a planning staff quite separate from that responsible for current production. Yet the obvious corollary of this, the setting up of a separate reconstruction department at national headquarters, did not follow until after the Fleck Report. (Unlike the staff department, this proposal was not made by the Fleck Committee, and it has since been reversed!)

However, this contrast in organizational structures between areas on the one hand, and divisions and national headquarters on the other, does not tell the whole story. In fact in the early years headquarters and divisional officials were probably much more capital-development-minded than most area general managers.

In electricity generating, major new construction was not completely separated from current operations until the first decade after the war, and the Herbert Committee in 1955 described and rather ridiculed the somewhat complex organization, partly centralized and partly regional, for planning new power-stations. The Herbert Committee had a doctrinaire obsession with decentralization and recommended that the work of planning and construction of most power-stations should be delegated to the twelve generating divisions of the C.E.A. It overlooked the fact that even at the time when it reported, the power-stations were getting so much bigger and fewer, that it would soon have been unlikely that any of the twelve divisions would have had either a sufficient load of work to justify the highly specialized planning and design staff required for modern power-stations, or would have been able to accumulate the necessary experience. The then Minister of Fuel and Power, Mr Aubrey Jones, introducing the Electricity Act, 1957, which implemented the Herbert Committee's recommendation, rather rashly went out of his way specifically to commend this recommendation about new power-station construction to the new generating board.[1] The new board, however, under the chairmanship of Sir Christopher Hinton (who must have had a unique experience of planning major units in the Atomic Energy Authority), in fact adopted an almost diametrically opposite solution to that of the Herbert Committee. It has taken the whole of the new responsibility for power-station planning and construction away from the divisions, and also separated it completely from the departments concerned with current operations at headquarters. It now has a headquarters planning department for the long-term national planning, and a headquarters design and construction department which deals with major questions of design and manufacture and some of the largest items of equipment. For the actual control, detailed design, and carrying through of power-station construction, however, completely new units of management have been set up – the three project groups. These rather high-powered organizations are concerned with nothing but power-station construction and are able to employ specialists on every aspect of their work, particularly on highly developed systems of progress control and co-ordination. British Railways, again, has no separate department devoted to reconstruction. Modernization, as such, is in some cases the responsibility of individuals. For example, in some regions an assistant general manager supported by a planning office is mainly or wholly concerned with modernization. From the executive point of view, it may be argued that railway reconstruction is too intimately linked with day-to-day operations to be handed over to reconstruction teams, but the experiment might, nevertheless, be worth trying.

It is one thing, of course, to have an organization in control of planning, design and construction in the sense of keeping things moving and co-ordinated. It is much more difficult, while not discouraging such movement and expansion, to be in complete control, in terms of precise costs and times. In fact, it seems to be a

[1] Hansard 1956–7, vol. 562, col. 942.

common experience of all organizations, public and private, undertaking really large capital schemes, that they cost very much more money and take very much more time than was expected. The worst examples of this are to be found probably in the North of Scotland Hydro-Electric Board, which, as we have seen, keeps its own headquarters staff to the smallest possible numbers. But in its early years the Coal Board also had great difficulties in this respect. Now, however, with its strong technical and finance departments it probably leads the field, at least in the soundness of its basic systems of time and cost control. One of the essential features of this is a standard form of detailed financial assessment with a full calculation of return on capital for every project at a fairly early stage, and – also at an early stage – the making of a detailed time-table for each section of the work. This is, of course, done by many other concerns, but the Coal Board has instruments for making its planning realistic through a quite elaborate system of checks, during and after construction, in the form of reports made to headquarters on the comparison between actual results and original estimates in terms of time, cost, and production achieved. The Central Electricity Generating Board and most other electricity boards also have fairly detailed systems of financial assessment and time-table controls. Without such control systems any form of long-term planning can easily become purely theoretical; costs can run right away from estimates and the resulting panic financial cuts at the last moment can, of course, easily produce chaos.

The impression left by reading the 1960 Report of the Select Committee on the Nationalized Industries is that situations of this sort have arisen in British Railways only too frequently. Certainly, costs have run away from estimates on the grand scale, though the extent to which the electrification programme represents technical pioneering, and the difficulties of estimating for the reconstruction of century-old installations rather than for new constructions, are, perhaps, mitigating factors.

A sound system of financial appraisal for each project has two advantages. It assists in deciding both whether to embark on capital projects at all, and also in what order of priority to take them. 'Assists', however, is the operative word. It is not possible in real life to make such decisions about priorities solely on the basis of the percentage return on the capital invested. In an integrated public service like electricity supply or railways, once it has been decided to provide a certain type or standard of service over wide areas, or over the country as a whole, it is not always possible to make so many local variations in charges that a profit results from every little bit of the system.

Although a coal industry is not a public utility service like gas or water or electricity supply, it shares certain characteristics with them, in sharp contrast to manufacturing industry. This is particularly true when it is run on a nationalized basis under policies such as those applied by successive governments since the last war. Broadly, the Labour Government – rightly at the time – gave priority to maximum production, and the Conservative Governments – wrongly – to low prices, both at the expense of profitability. The policy as to profits has been to 'break even' over a period of years and over the country as a whole, but this has been sacrificed to these other objectives. If you can scarcely 'break even' over the country as a whole, and conditions vary, you must in some places make a loss. The then Deputy Chairman of the Coal Board explained this tactfully, but unanswerably, to the Select Committee on Nationalized Industries in 1958. Nor is it always possible to isolate the financial effect of a particular improvement in one part of the system. Certain types of installation or equipment, such as passenger stations or offices or stores depots, can hardly be expected to show a financially measurable profit. Nevertheless, even when a full calculation of return on capital cannot be made, it should always be possible to make some financial appraisal in terms of net increase or decrease in ascertainable annual charges – even when this does not represent the whole extent of the advantages to be gained. It is understood that the Coal Board invariably requires this to be done for *all* types of project, and the Central Electricity Generating Board for all types of project where any real choice exists; for instance an improved workshop, but not a cable scheme needed to meet the demands of existing consumers for more electricity. (A power-station and its main component parts can be assessed on the basis of £1 per kilowatt capacity.)

Clearly, working over the whole range of capital projects in the nationalized industries, and indeed other public services like those of local authorities, there will be different categories from the point of view of assessing priority:

(a) Where profitability is calculable and should be the basis of priority.
(b) Where profitability cannot be fully calculated in isolation because one project interlocks with others in a national system or network, or because the effects – such as attraction of more traffic – are not precisely predictable.
(c) Where other considerations such as public service and public safety outweigh considerations of profitability.

This emphatically does not mean that because there are so many factors all efforts at a logical assessment of priorities should be abandoned, or that public bodies should live from hand to mouth doing the easiest jobs first – although that is what one suspects some of them often do! The point is rather that the more difficult the business of assessing priorities is, the more important it is to have a proper system for it.[1]

To sum up, to carry out a major continuing programme of capital investment, it is necessary to have really long-term plans, based on long-term assessments of demand for products or services, and on assessments of priorities of particular schemes in relation to the satisfaction of these demands and the return on capital. Such plans need to include long-term assessments of the availability and cost of resources, human and material, natural and manufactured, internal and external. The plans must be in realistic detail and must on completion be checked against results. Partly because the industries belong to the whole community, and partly because liaison and proper understanding with so many people inside and outside is necessary, they should be published in some detail.

In practice, planning of this kind is most needed in the coal and

[1] The Royal Institute of Public Administration Study Group report, 'Budgeting in Public Authorities', pp. 201–5, compares the method of assessing total needs in order of priority and that of seeing what projects can be fitted into a predetermined budget figure. The programmes for Post Office buildings and Ministry of Transport roads are cited respectively as examples of these two contrasting methods. For contrast see the account of the vague methods of assessing capital projects in at least some sectors of private enterprise in Tibor Barna's *Investment and Growth Policies of British Industrial Firms*, 1952.

gas industries and in electricity generating and main transmission – in all of which much has been done already on these lines. It is also needed in railways, where it has been applied, at least until fairly recently, very much more vaguely and sketchily – perhaps because of lack of assurance of continuing resources and Government support. In local electricity distribution detailed long-term planning need only be carried up to about five years ahead, and on this basis it seems, on the whole, to have been fairly well and thoroughly done. However, in most electricity areas there has been less publication of detailed plans than in the case of generation.

The making of plans by one industry alone, however, is not sufficient. Each is dependent on both suppliers and customers in other industries and public services. The extent to which plans are actually based on consultation with such suppliers and customers has varied – to put it mildly. There is for instance an all-important triangle of interdependence between the electricity supply, coal, and railway industries. It seems that the two former are the best, both in their own planning and in their liaison with one another – although some liaison machinery on the third side of the triangle also exists. But liaison machinery is surely not enough. In matters like the siting of power-stations, or the choice between coal or oil or nuclear heating for them, or methods of railway traction or gas production, it is not sufficient for each nationalized industry – or even any pair of such industries jointly – simply to plan and calculate on the basis of information supplied by other publicly-owned industries or services or public authorities. As all are owned by the whole community, each should surely act in the interests of the public as a whole. Energy can be taken from the coalfields to the people who want it in the form of electricity by grid line, or in the form of coal by railway – according to where the power-stations are sited. The power-stations can use coal (and water) which is locally available, or oil which has to be imported. Should the choice be made on the basis of profits in one bit of the nationalized industrial system, even if this produces counter-balancing financial losses or other disadvantages in another part? Probably in practice no such simple choice will be open. But the important point is that *we do not really know, because the necessary overall calculations simply are not made* – or if they have been made, the public have not been told about them. (The point can be applied not only to electricity generation but to coal and gas manufacture, railway electrification, air, rail or road transport of goods, passengers, mail and so on.)

Many people would say that such considerations would lead to an unanswerable case for the national planning of the activities of all major industries, including those in private or local ownership. But, however that may be, it is surely incomprehensible to take industries into national public ownership and then not take full advantage of the opportunities for integrated long-term planning. It is quite possible that privately owned groups of industrial companies achieve more internal co-operation with one another than do some of the nationalized industries and Government departments.

The major public industries and their suppliers of capital equipment also need to co-ordinate their long-term planning more closely. Yet if the suppliers are in private ownership, this must not be done in such a way as to prevent an adequate degree of competition. There must be a fair balance between standardization of design (or at least specification) and scope for experiment – an adequate control of priorities and streamlining of supply systems without excessive centralization. Full advantage must be taken of whatever scope for control of manufacture and supply already exists. This includes the making of bulk and long-term contracts as well as the voluntary or compulsory purchase of manufacturing firms. Such plans, if flexibly applied, could be to the advantage of the manufacturing interests as well as their customers. It seems that the Coal Board has now made very great progress with co-ordination and standardization of its supplies, although in its first five years or more, areas operated very largely independently of, and even in competition with, one another. Area Electricity Boards still carry on their stores and purchasing organizations entirely independently of one another and have no standard designs, although there are standard *specifications* for the bulk of their equipment. The Electricity Boards and London Transport are still hampered by statutory restrictions on their ability to manufacture equipment for themselves – restrictions not imposed on their private enterprise predecessors.

In short, one can see that, although the major nationalized in-

54

dustries have considerable achievements in the planning and execution of new capital development to their credit, they have by no means solved all basic problems of organization involved, nor taken full advantage of the scope public ownership gives for really major long-term overall planning and co-ordination. The achievements have probably been most outstanding in the fields of electricity generating (all along) and coal-mining (in recent years), and the failures most marked in the railways. A heavy share of responsibility for the failures must ultimately be laid at the door not of the industries but of the Government, which has failed to provide them with coherent policy guidance or adequate financial support. In a Government fundamentally out of sympathy with public ownership and (despite some recent conversions) national planning, this is, of course, hardly surprising.

# CHAPTER THREE

# PRICES AND PROFITS

NATIONALIZED industries charge high prices, yet they also incur heavy losses which have to be met by the taxpayer. That might be described as the most popular version of the anti-nationalization viewpoint, though it is worth noticing that something very like its opposite occasionally gains currency. For example, the surpluses of the electricity supply industry have on occasion been under attack from both trade unions and consumers' representatives who felt they ought to be diverted to higher wages or lower prices; and the road haulage industry frequently complains about the low freight rates charged by British Railways under the 1953 Act.

Indeed, the complaint about prices is very far from being generally justified. For example, in the years 1952–9 British Railways' receipts per passenger mile rose by fifteen per cent compared with a rise in retail prices of about twenty-seven per cent. A more rapid rate of increase in 1960 brought it to twenty-eight per cent, which more or less corresponded to the rise in retail prices; but a glance at the freight figures shows an even more modest rise. There the increase in receipts per net ton mile, 1952–60, was only eighteen per cent. The level of charges fell in 1958, 1959 and 1960, and is now little higher than it was in 1956.

These movements are in part explained by pressures of competition. There are other cases, however, of less than proportionate increases, where such considerations do not apply to any great extent. From 1948, when nationalized electricity began operations, up to 1960, the overall cost of electricity to all consumers had gone up just under twenty-eight per cent and the cost to domestic consumers by twenty per cent, compared with an overall increase in retail prices of some fifty-seven per cent. Other industries – notably coal – have, admittedly, recorded more than average price increases. But over most of the post-war period, coal has been too cheap rather than too expensive, with the result that the nation's power resources have not been used to the best advantage.

That there is an overall deficit in the operations of the nationalized industries is, however, an undoubted fact. The Government White Paper, 'The Financial and Economic Obligations of the Nationalized Industries', published in April 1961 (Cmd. 1337), gives figures which may roughly be described as the cumulative surplus or deficit for the nine main publicly-owned industries with commercial transactions. These figures show a combined cumulative deficit at the end of 1959 of about £220,000,000.

This figure requires a good deal of examination. Firstly, of course, it is in no sense comparable with the profit or loss of a private firm. The surpluses or deficits are calculated after interest has been paid. The picture would be entirely different if the operating surplus or deficit before payment of interest were taken. Even the B.T.C.'s accumulated deficit of £350,000,000 would be, instead, a surplus of nearly £200,000,000. But it would still be the case, as the White Paper shows, that the return on capital is very much less in the public than in the private sector.

Setting aside the question of interest payments, however, there are certain other respects in which the total deficit of £220,000,000 needs to be qualified. It needs to be reduced, firstly, in respect of an obligation which is peculiar to publicly-owned enterprise, namely, to provide for the ultimate redemption of capital. This has the aim, analogous with municipal undertakings, of providing ultimately a 'debt-free' undertaking. But it is a constantly receding goal, as long as the industry is raising fresh funds; it cannot be justified on the grounds of 'euthanasia of the *rentier*', since the stock is repaid in full. (In fact the sums set aside are frequently reinvested temporarily in the industry, and we shall see later on that there is much to be said for more financing of investment from within the nationalized industries.) The only possible justification of redemption is that it relieves the industries of the 'burden' of compensation. But there is no reason why this burden, resulting from the political necessities of the past, should be borne in extra measure by the present in order to reduce the compensation payments (though not, be it noted, to redistribute the wealth) of the future.

The size of the redemption provisions is not inconsiderable. Those of coal, transport and electricity are currently running together at over £20,000,000. But they are far more than counterbalanced by the fact that, in general, the nationalized industries make provision for depreciation at historic cost and not at replacement cost. This underprovision probably involves an understatement of the true deficit by something like £100,000,000 a year, and is the key factor in the assessment of the deficit. It cannot be given an exact figure, but it might well treble the £220,000,000 of the White Paper.

To turn from the overall figure to the contribution of the various industries to it, the effect of the B.T.C. with an accumulated deficit of £350,000,000 is overwhelming. It is often forgotten that, after initial losses in 1948–50, the commission achieved a modest surplus totalling £8,800,000 in the years 1951–3. This trend might well have continued but for the 1953 Transport Act, and the loss of much of the profitable road haulage undertaking and the depression of many rail freight rates that followed it. Further, the whole picture of public sector profitability would have been entirely different but for the denationalization of the iron and steel industry. A large part of the overall deficit can thus be attributed to denationalization rather than to nationalization. But for the disposal of these profitable and relatively easily transferred sections of the economy, the nationalized industries might well show a surplus on their existing basis of accounting.

The nationalization statutes were open-ended. They laid down that receipts, taking one year with another, should not be less than outgoings, but did not prohibit a surplus. But it is fairly clear that no cumulative surplus was intended. Good years were expected along with the bad years. But these good and bad years would be the good and bad years of the economy as a whole. In good years there would be a surplus and this would be an anti-inflationary influence at a time when inflation was a danger. Similarly, deficits in bad years, when the level of activity generally was low, would constitute a part of the Government's deficit financing, which would help to reflate the economy on orthodox Keynesian lines. What actually happened, that certain industries incurred continuing deficits at a time when the economy generally was still buoyant, was not part of the plan.

The 1961 Government White Paper initiated a new policy on the overall financing of the nationalized industries. In the first place, instead of the indefinite 'taking one year with another', it laid down that a break-even over a period of five years was to be required. This appears to be a purely administrative convenience – a long enough period for an industry to correct a deficit which is, *ipso facto*, regarded as a bad thing. There is, however, nothing economically sacrosanct about a five-year period, despite Soviet precedent, and the period of years now appears to have no special significance or importance. Indeed, it is difficult to take it very seriously. It obviously cannot be made to apply to British Railways even after the writing-off of capital, and it is fairly obvious that no Government would adhere to it slavishly if economic considerations dictated otherwise. On the other hand, it does clearly impose a degree of discipline which may in certain circumstances prove salutary.

Secondly, provision for depreciation is to be made at replacement cost price levels. This is, no doubt, sound in principle, but it may be tricky to apply, and it should be noted that, as the years go by and the fact that past underprovision is excluded becomes of lesser importance, it is liable to give the knife-edge economies of some industries an additional financial instability. Suppose, for example, that in the last year of a piece of equipment's life, there is a substantial rise in prices. At present, the additional cost of replacement would, in effect, be a matter of increasing the supply of capital. In future, the underprovision that had been going on over the years would all have to come, presumably, out of revenue in that one year. A fall in prices could lead to equally fortuitous and, perhaps, embarrassing surpluses.

Thirdly, adequate general reserves are to be established to contribute towards capital development and safeguard against obsolescence and contingencies. This is certainly much needed. The absence of reserves means recourse to emergency measures to meet even a transitory crisis; and the nationalized industries have, in general, an even greater need for contingency reserves than private industry, since they are, in general, unable to reduce risk by diversifying their activities to any material extent. They cannot offset a declining market in one field by entering another – even, perhaps, a related one. Even where legally entitled to do so, they have, on occasion, been prevented by the Government. The refusal to allow the B.T.C. to acquire an interest in a cross-Channel airline of a type that could obviously be closely co-ordinated with British Railways is a case in point.

As to the financing of investment from funds already held by the industries, most of the boards appear to feel that some self-financing is desirable; and those with the resources to do it have, by and large, done it.

The Electricity Boards, for example, increased the proportion of capital provided from within the industry to nearly a half in the year 1959–60, and the Coal Board, to judge from evidence given to the Select Committee, would like to do the same if it could.

The desirability of self-financing has been the subject of debate. In general, to finance investment for the future, whether in public or private industry, out of the surpluses earned on current operations, is to raise capital by forced savings from the industry's customers, who may not be either the most willing or the best able members of the community to make this contribution. The most extreme and discriminatory form of this argument against self-financing comes from the Herbert Committee. In a travesty of the actual position, it argued that profits ploughed back in the competitive world of private enterprise are 'the prize of success' whereas, in sheltered nationalized monopolies, they would merely be the result of extortion. Certainly, at the moment, the nationalized industries are out of line with private industry in this respect. The White Paper showed an excess of capital formation over saving in the Public Corporations and the Post Office of £640,000,000 in 1959. In the company sector of the economy, on the other hand, there was an excess of saving over capital formation of £580,000,000. This position is the outcome of a large increase in investment in the nationalized industries in the years 1954–9, combined with a small increase in savings. The White Paper gives the Government's view that there are powerful grounds for requiring nationalized industries to make a substantial contribution to capital development out of their own earnings, without, however, actually saying what these grounds are.

It can, of course, be argued that by not following private industry's example in respect of self-financing, the nationalized industries have kept their prices relatively low in relation to private industry (which we have already seen to be the case to a significant extent), thus maintaining a high level of demand and causing the capacity required to meet demand – and so the volume of investment – to be higher than it otherwise need have been.

This seems a purely theoretical argument. Nationalized industries' investment plans since the war have been limited, not by the volume of investment indicated by demand at a particular level of prices, but by the amount the Treasury has been able to allocate to each industry. Even if higher prices had restricted demand quite substantially, many industries would still have been able to use as much capital as they were, in the event, able to get. Moreover, it should be recalled that we are dealing here with basic industries, on the adequacy of whose physical structure depends the whole fabric of industrial production.

It is probably true, though it may not be entirely logical, that the position of a nationalized industry that is proposing to spend its own money on capital projects is stronger vis-à-vis the Treasury than one which is dependent on borrowing. Lacking any sort of intelligent overall planning of investment in both public and private sectors, we have had the situation in which private investment schemes, once started, can run their course unchecked, whereas nationalized industries are subject to a series of stops and starts according to the direction of the economic wind. From the point of view of the steady development of the nationalized industries in present circumstances, it is reasonable to hope that self-financing would overcome, to some extent, this disability.

Self-financing means higher prices and so may appear to weaken the advantages of nationalization. But the basic fact is that the industries need the funds, from whatever source, and there is, moreover, a good socialist reason why a part of them, at any rate, should be supplied from within the industry. So long as capital development is financed through the issue of stock, the nationalized industries are making no contribution to the redistribution of wealth. The increase in public assets is simply matched by an increase in public indebtedness to the private sector. But financing from the surpluses of the industry is different. It involves a real increase in the total of public compared to private property, unmatched by indebtedness, and therefore a genuine redistribution of wealth. Wealth has, in the past, proved even more resistant to redistribution by fiscal means than has income, and it will be of value if a practice is being established, for whatever reasons, which could become an effective agent in the redistribution of wealth under a Labour Government.

How far is Government policy likely to make it possible for nationalized industries to earn the much larger surpluses implied by the White Paper? Certainly, policy will have to be very different from what it has been over the last decade, if there is to be any hope of achieving them.

Selective denationalization has been mentioned as one of the causes of deficits. Another has been the repeated refusal of Governments to sanction price increases on the scale required to meet increased costs. There have been isolated instances of this in gas and electricity supply, but it is in coal and transport, the principal deficit industries, that it has been most evident. In coal, apart from frequent delays in sanctioning increases, there have been several occasions when considerably less than the increase asked for was granted, and one when it was refused altogether. This, be it noted, applied to an industry which never attempted to reap monopoly profits from a situation where, over a long period of years, the demand for its products continuously exceeded supply.

The Transport Commission has been in an even worse predicament in respect of price increases. Firstly, the machinery of the Transport Tribunal ensured, almost inevitably, that losses must be made in a period of inflation. An application to the tribunal could only be based on increases in costs that had actually taken place. But the machinery of application and public hearing ensured that the increases took six to nine months to implement, and might not even then be approved in full by the tribunal or authorized to take effect all at once. Even if the tribunal approved an increase, the Government might still block it. Sometimes this took the form of 'advice' to the commission – advice with which the commission, generally speaking, was not in a strong enough position to argue. But in 1952 there was a celebrated case where the Government referred a more than proportionate increase in substandard London fares, already approved by the tribunal, to the Transport Users Consultative Committee, only to find that it too endorsed the increase. The Government, however, still refused to permit it. The political furore surrounding this episode was in no small measure responsible for the 1953 Transport Act.

This widespread and deliberate limitation or delay in approving price increases was, generally speaking, conducted in the name of fighting inflation. Prudently, though somewhat unfairly, the Government in the 1961 White Paper shifted to public opinion its own responsibility for this pressure on prices. For the anti-inflation argument is fallacious. An increase in prices may be inflationary to the extent that it is passed on through the economy; but it is not passed on fully. Consuming industries will be impelled to increase efficiency to counteract it; it will squeeze some profits; and it will, to some extent, decrease consumption by the individual. But if the nationalized industries are allowed to run into debt to the community, by being prevented from earning the extra money to recoup cost increases, this *is* inflationary.

Genuine anti-inflationary measures might have been practicable if the Government had at the same time been pursuing a progressive rather than a regressive policy in other directions. But, of course, it was not, and the nationalized industries were forced, in the name of fighting inflation, to acquiesce in policies that had the reverse effect.

Turning from the general level of prices to the price structures of the individual industries, we find hardly any guidance in the Acts as to the policies to be followed. The instructions – to produce at prices and in quantities that were in the public interest – have been interpreted, no doubt correctly, as an injunction against making profits through the deliberate restriction of the market. But there are at least two other major questions on which, in practice, decisions have to be made. The first is how far, within the limits imposed by the Acts, an industry can indulge in marginal pricing of its individual products. The second is how far the costs of various products should be averaged in arriving at the prices to be charged for them, with the dual effect, generally speaking, of simplifying the price structures and cross-subsidizing one product by another.

There has been much abstruse economic argument on the first of these questions – that of marginal prices; but the general principle is both simple and attractive. The marginal user – the one who may just be persuaded to use the service or buy the product – should pay what it costs to provide that unit of the service of product, neither more nor less, if the optimum output of the industry is to be achieved.

Complications arise, however, from the fact that, generally speaking, if the marginal user pays this price, so must the other users. The Coal Board, forced for a number of years to work high-cost pits in an attempt to satisfy demand, should, according to marginal theory, have charged high prices during that time and so made an astronomic surplus. The Transport Commission, with surplus capacity on its express freight trains, should charge on the basis of the small additional cost required to run an additional wagon. In doing so it would increase demand, but by generalizing these rates it would also produce an enormous loss.

Both these policies have been rejected in general. The deliberate loss in which the Transport Commission would be involved is clearly contrary to its statutory duties, particularly in view of the involuntary deficit arising from other causes. Theoretically, it could recoup these losses by the further application of marginal pricing in cases where capacity is strained to the limit, for example the London passenger peak. But, in practice, these are just the areas where the limitations imposed by the Transport Tribunal, even now, limit and delay very much more modest increases than would be involved by the revolutionary doctrine of marginal cost pricing.

The large surplus that the Coal Board would have made over a number of years would not indeed have been contrary to statute. It would have had a variety of economic effects, some desirable and some undesirable. For example, it would have encouraged the more efficient use of coal and produced a large financial surplus; but it would also have weighed heavily on the poorer section of the community. In fact, to carry out the policy in either industry would have involved the Government in unpopular policies – higher prices for coal or larger deficits from transport (there is not much political gain to be got from lowering transport rates in the cases where there is spare capacity), and it has not been seriously considered.

Only where one can discriminate between consumers is it possible to move towards marginal pricing without extreme financial unbalance. This is to some extent possible where undisclosed bargains can be struck and where an industry's competitive position varies from customer to customer. It thus applies, to some extent, to the Coal Board in respect of contract prices for industrial coal which the board now negotiates, and to rail freight charges under the powers of the 1953 Act, where the charge to the marginal user can be raised – for example to the firm which is for some reason tied to rail. An interesting experimental variant of this is the two-part tariff for freight carriage. A fixed annual charge is combined with a low rate per ton mile, with the effect that the revenue from tied traffic is preserved, while a competitive rate is offered for traffic subject to competition. No doubt these private rates rarely, if ever, rise or fall to the level of marginal cost in circumstances of excess demand or capacity. But they do move in that direction.

As to averaging, there are no injunctions in the Acts to restrain cross-subsidization of one product by another, even when these products differ widely in character. This, in fact, has gone on widely ever since nationalization. Within the broad divisions under which the boards analyse their published working results, there is no obligation on them to find out, let alone to publish or to relate in any way, the costs and prices of individual products. Averaging of costs, in the first instance, was accepted, or even approved. The Minister of Transport responsible for the 1947 Act gave his explicit approval to the principle of cross-subsidization; and in one of the few specific references to pricing policy contained in the Acts the Electricity Boards were enjoined to 'simplify' tariffs. Presumably what was in mind was the removal of purely arbitrary variations in system, which were to be expected in any industry previously consisting of a large number of separate undertakings. But it could also be interpreted as an injunction to refrain from variations in other directions. It certainly meant this to the Herbert Committee, which recommended the removal of the obligation to simplify, primarily in order that the boards might vary their supply prices between peak and off-peak periods; this variation in price would reflect the immense variation in cost caused by the need to keep in being generating-stations with high running costs, overheads and interest charges, which are only needed to meet brief periods of peak demand. The introduction of cheap night rates for domestic heating does, in fact, represent a small step in this direction.

Not only in the recommendations of the Herbert Committee but elsewhere the tide has been running against averaging of costs. The Coal Board, for example, started out, while it was still without any serious marketing problems, to produce a price structure which was related to the relative values of the grades of coal to the consumer, assessed on a technical basis. The system involves some heavy averaging of transport costs through the use of the zonal pricing system, which averages transport costs over wide areas on the basis of standard rail rates. But, in practice, the widespread use of road transport for coal even over fairly long distances, and the large number of reduced private rates which have been introduced by the railways to meet this competition, must have gone far towards destroying the degree of averaging implied by zonal prices, while commercial considerations have largely taken over from technical assessment in determining the price of coal.

The Transport Commission inherited, amongst other deficiencies, a great deficiency of information on the relative costs and profitability of its various rail services. As the Select Committee discovered, one of its greatest problems has been to identify where the whole of the deficit has actually arisen. When Dr Beeching took over the chairmanship of the commission early in 1961, his first move was to try to collect the necessary information on which to base commercial decisions – and we are now starting to experience the results. It is rather deplorable that this should still have been necessary in 1961.

The 1953 Transport Act brought with it, firstly, a new maximum charges scheme which was related in a very broad manner to probable costs, and secondly, the power to charge substantially less than the maximum permitted rates on a purely private basis, for which purpose the relation of costs and charges in the case of individual flows of traffic was obviously essential. However, partly because of still fairly large, though rapidly decreasing, areas of monopoly, partly through the important part which generalized scales of charges still play, for example, for parcels, small consignments of goods and ordinary passenger fares, and partly because costs, on a system for the most part either still physically out of date or in the process of reconstruction, may be

66

so far out of line with those of competitors as to be commercially impracticable, a substantial amount of cross-subsidization still exists. It is true to say, for example, that holiday travellers, short-distance commuters (particularly on steam services), forwarders of small consignments of general merchandise, country dwellers, and Scotland generally, are subsidized by coal users, city dwellers, travelling businessmen and long-distance commuters; and of course, at present by the taxpayer.

Opinion is swinging generally against cross-subsidization. The economists (or most of them) have always been against it. The Herbert Committee was against it. The Select Committee was against it, when for example it recommended a specific subsidy to B.E.A. for the 'Highlands and Islands' services that operate at a loss in North-West Scotland.[1] It also opposed it in recommending that services provided at a loss by British Railways, but which were considered socially necessary, should be subsidized from public funds, and not from other rail users – from whom, in any case, it was no longer possible to make monopoly profits on any considerable scale.

On the other hand, it has been argued that the whole question of cross-subsidization is an unnecessary academic refinement introduced by economists, but happily ignored by most of private industry. Oil firms, chain-stores, and so on maintain their nation-wide retail prices, and the fact that their costs of transport and retailing must vary widely is accepted without complaint by them and the public. But this is to miss the point. The nearest competitor to an oil firm is another oil firm, operating to the same convention and tacitly agreeing to limit its competition by so doing. By contrast the nationalized industries, where they impinge on each other or on private industry, are in contact with widely differing pricing policies, and the potential misdirection of demand at such points can indeed be the cause of serious distortions of the industries concerned. In the case of electricity supply, generating capacity has been enlarged to meet a peak demand which, if charged with its full costs, would be transferred in large part to other and (in this particular context) more economical fuels, or would have spread itself across the off-peak hours, for example, by the use of more highly insulated, lower-powered immersion heaters

[1] A recommendation which B.E.A. endorsed in October 1962.

than are normal in this country (but not in others where more time/price differentials exist). Another example, recently before the public gaze, lies in the relationship between rail and air fares between London and Scotland. There can be no doubt that the programme of investment in greatly increased capacity on which B.E.A. has embarked is based, in essence, on the abstraction of a large volume of existing railway business by reduction of fares, at any rate at off-peak times, to or below the level of rail fares. No doubt this can be done, given the present rail fares. But suppose, as is probable, that Anglo-Scottish passenger business could still be profitable to British Railways at a fare level far below the present one? In that case one of two things must happen. Either British Railways must reduce fares, thus increasing their overall deficit, but still continuing to carry this particular traffic at a reduced level of profit, in which case B.E.A.'s investment would prove to have been misplaced; or British Railways must abandon the whole traffic to B.E.A. B.E.A.'s investment decisions are justified, but the net revenue of British Railways is decreased even further, and the public is denied the low, but still economic, fares which it could have enjoyed by rail if a purely commercial policy had been pursued. It looks very much as if assumptions on the permanency of cross-subsidization have gone very deep into investment planning here.[1]

In favour of average cost pricing are the following points. Firstly, it is popular. It appears to be fair, even when it is not, to charge the same price per ton for coal over a wide area, or the same rate per mile for passenger fares in the north of Scotland as between London and Brighton. Secondly, as has already been mentioned, it is by no means confined to nationalized industries. It is an odd world in which average cost pricing is being attacked in the public sector at the same time as the enforcement of resale price maintenance is being made legal in the private sector. Thirdly, it is a matter on which the Government has so far persistently refused to take effective action. The 1961 White Paper says that commercially unprofitable activities will be taken into account in setting the financial standards for each undertaking – financial standards which, it has already been noted, are much more rigorous than those that have obtained in the past. This may

[1] This question is further discussed in Chapter 15.

be a practicable solution in the case, for example, of the Post Office. Loss-making activities such as the telegraph service or the provision of call-boxes in rural areas may be considered socially desirable. The losses can be balanced by monopoly profits on other services. But what of the industry which, while involved in the provision of socially necessary but unprofitable services, is in competition with other agencies, public or private, over the rest of its field, so that it has no chance of making monopoly profits on other services? This is already the position of most of the public transport industry, and in so far as the Coal Board may be considered to have an obligation to maintain overall productive capacity or employment in declining coalfields, it may also be the position of coal. The specific subsidy, which the Government has so far refused to accept and which is not favoured by the Transport Commission – the organization most likely to benefit from it financially – appears inevitable.

The point of policy here is essentially simple. If a nationalized industry wishes to abandon a particular service or project which it cannot justify on commercial lines, and which it cannot finance from profits earned elsewhere, it is surely up to the Government to find the money to keep the service going, if it thinks it desirable for social or other reasons. The obvious method is for the nationalized industry to operate the service under contract to the Government – or it might be to the local authority concerned. Of course, there would be complications. The Government would have to take awkward decisions – to subsidize or not to subsidize – which at present can be sloughed off on to the nationalized boards. One can imagine the embarrassment of a minister caught between the cross-fires of the Treasury and a powerful local lobby. But the decision whether to run air and rail services to the Scottish Highlands and Islands is, after all, a political and not a commercial one – and there are other cases less dramatic, but equally cogent.

But this does not mean that as a general rule cross-subsidization – for example, between two services within a profitable enterprise – must always be avoided. It is true that distortions of pricing policy have produced some real misallocation of resources over the past ten years. A different pricing policy for domestic fuels would probably have kept us just as warm in the years since the war, while enabling some of the expenditure on power-stations to be postponed a year or two. Higher coal prices ten years ago would have meant more investment in efficient coal-consuming equipment and, as a result, a market more solidly tied to coal than it is today. We have also seen some of the dangers that can arise from averaging rail fares but not domestic air fares. We should, in fact, be on our guard against cross-subsidization wherever it is liable to influence major investment decisions.

But on the other hand we cannot possibly hope to charge the economically correct price all the time, everywhere. There are, in fact, two things to be said in favour of averaging. The first is simplicity. Simplicity is a virtue in itself and one for which we should be prepared to pay a certain, though not an excessive, price. The individual does not want to be eternally weighing halfpence and economists pay him no compliment in assuming that it is his natural function to do so. There are products produced by nationalized industries which one may well want to turn into free public services where payment is virtually unrelated to cost. The social undesirability of private cars in large cities may prove so great as to make it desirable to provide urban transport free (i.e. financed through the fiscal system). In such a case, discussion about relative prices is a barren exercise. Further, there are practical limits to the extent to which we can go in relating prices to costs. A really thoroughgoing application of specific costings could turn a cross-country journey by train into a nightmare of rebookings, surcharges and general uncertainty. When one reflects that transport, communication and power-supply costs vary not only from place to place but for every hour of the day and every day of the year, it is obvious that we cannot afford to be too nice about their application.

Finally, we should remember that a good deal of this cross-subsidization has been introduced deliberately over the years and that it has often been introduced for social reasons. One should not assume that the 'law of the market place' will always produce the best possible allocation of resources – indeed, in many cases, it demonstrably will not.[1] The licensing system used for provincial bus services, for example, has been deliberately designed to ensure that monopoly profits earned in thickly populated areas are used

[1] The role of deliberate cross-subsidization by nationalized industries is dealt with more fully in Chapter 15.

to subsidize services in rural areas. Even where these transfers are not deliberate they may not be entirely bad. What socialist would worry, for example, if he suspected that pink gins on the Midland Pullman went some way towards subsidizing trips to the sea for those who could not afford a car of their own? Would he not rather feel that pricing was carrying on the good work that his direct taxation system had either failed to carry far enough or had abdicated completely? There is nothing to be said for the destruction of socially useful cross-subsidization when the Government in power is at the same time taking socially regressive measures. Even a Labour Government would not be so well equipped with the economic instruments necesssary to create an egalitarian society that it could ignore the part the nationalized industries' pricing policies could play towards that end – provided that in so doing the nationalized industries were not jeopardizing their financial stability or distorting their investment policies.

# CHAPTER FOUR

# WAGES

How relevant is the fact of nationalization to the wages policies, levels and structure in the industries concerned? Does it really make a significant difference?

The instinctive answer from both ends of the political spectrum would undoubtedly be an emphatic 'yes'. On the Left, though with ever diminishing confidence, it has been asserted that nationalization, by eliminating private profit, makes it possible to attain higher wage standards than can be wrung from capitalist firms. More realistically, the nationalized industries are credited with a freedom from sectional jealousies, a lack of addiction to individualist economic philosophies, and a consciousness of public responsibility and accountability, which make them seek the accolade of the 'good employer' and influence them in the direction of coherent wages policies and fair and consistent wages structures. Finally it is argued that the publicly-owned sector of industry can be used to facilitate in the field of wages policy – as in other respects – the application of measures of overall economic planning.

These views are mirrored on the Right. Admittedly the contention that wages levels have risen more rapidly in the publicly-owned sector than elsewhere has proved increasingly difficult to maintain in face of the mounting evidence, culminating in the Guillebaud Report, of the failure of wage rates on the railways to keep pace with those elsewhere – and, more recently, of the loss by the miners of their traditional post-war leadership in the earnings league. But if the Right cannot, with any assurance, claim that wages rise fastest in the nationalized industries, they can – and do – fall back on a second line of argument: namely, that the increases in the nationalized industries, if no bigger than anywhere else, come first in each 'wage round' and thus set the pattern for the whole economy. A powerful mythology has been erected around this theme in recent years. Time and time again, the gallant captains of private industry have found their flank turned in the ceaseless struggle against wage inflation by the weak-kneed board of some public corporation. That the board in question may be actively in league with the trade unions in this goes without saying; that from time to time it appears to be aided and abetted by Conservative ministers of the crown provides only an ironical comment upon the sad times in which we live.[1]

How much evidence is there for the view either that wages have risen exceptionally rapidly in nationalized industry, or exceptionally early in each 'wage round'? The *Guardian* Index of Weekly Wage Rates, which covers rather more than a hundred industries, shows for July 1962, for all industries (men's rates), a value of 194·2 (1948=100). For industries within the nationalized sector the figures are:

| | |
|---|---|
| Coal Mining | 193·9 |
| Gas | 202·0 |
| Electricity | 201·4 |
| Railways | 189·0 |
| London Transport Buses | 185·3 |
| British Road Services | 185·7 |
| Inland Waterways | 183·8 |
| Post Office | 212·0 |

Only in the Post Office and in the nationalized public utilities of gas and electricity has the rate of increase been markedly more rapid than in industry as a whole, and this is balanced by the significantly slower rate of increase in the nationalized transport sector, with coal-mining close to the average. The position of the railways is interesting. The substantial adjustments made in railway wages following the Guilleband Report in 1960 resulted for a time in a marginally higher index figure than for industry as a whole. But this was exceptional – for most of the post-war period, railways have lagged well behind the field, and after Guilleband they started to fall back again. Index figures of this kind will, of course, be influenced both by the base period selected and by the timing of recent increases in the industries concerned. Thus, for example, the choice of 1948 as base year means that the figure for

[1] For an example of this mythology at work in one celebrated instance, see Clegg and Adams, *The Employers' Challenge* (Blackwell, 1957).

coal-mining excludes the large post-nationalization increase of November, 1947. (Nor does the index take into account changes in piece-rates in coal-mining, a substantial factor in the industry.)

The Post Office does not show a particularly rapid rate of increase in wage rates compared with the leading private industries. Six industries in the private sector – furniture, envelope making, general printing (Scotland), printing and bookbinding, civil engineering construction and electrical installation – precede it. A further sixteen industries in the private sector (excluding water, municipal buses, local authority services, and police and fire services, which have also done well) have indices exceeding 200·0, and these include such relative heavyweights as pig iron, constructional engineering, flour milling, brewing, saw-milling, rubber manufacture, company buses, and coal and coke distribution.

The conclusion must be that wage rates have risen, in general, no more quickly in the nationalized sector than elsewhere. The Post Office, gas and electricity have done well, coal has more or less kept pace with the field, and nationalized transport has fallen some way behind. The man who handles coal on the colliery surface has seen his wages rise more slowly than those of the man who delivers coal to the consumer, electricity supply has done worse than electrical installation, and even selling stamps and delivering letters to the door has attracted a smaller percentage increase in remuneration than making the envelopes which carry both. This, moreover, is in terms of wage rates. As is well known, however, stricter and more formal wage structures exist in the nationalized sector (with a few exceptions, like the piece-working coal-face miners), and this means that the disparity between rates and earnings is less than elsewhere. The Ministry of Labour's six-montly earnings inquiry for April 1962 showed that the average weekly earnings of men in all industries covered was £15 12. 10d., or 159·1 per cent higher than the (roughly) corresponding figure for October 1946. Of the nationalized industries covered, for which similar data are available, only electricity shows a higher percentage increase (163·3 per cent). For gas the figure is 141·7 per cent, and for coal-mining 146·7 per cent (despite the piece-workers!), although the basis may not be wholly comparable. For the railway conciliation grades comparison is more difficult, but the evidence would suggest a figure of about 140 per cent.[1]

The facts about wage rounds are much more difficult to interpret. K. G. J. C. Knowles and E. M. F. Thorne, whose recent article[2] is the first thorough investigation of post-war British data bearing on this question, point out that the attribution of leadership to an industry in wage rounds can mean at least five different things:

(1) That the industry is a 'key' industry, a recognized pattern-setter, to whose settlements those in a number of related industries will broadly correspond;

(2) That the industry is the first to grant a substantial increase after a period of relative calm on the wages front;

(3) That the industry concedes an increase of a monetary amount which becomes characteristic of a large number of subsequent settlements, even in quite unrelated industries;

(4) As in (3), but with the characteristic increase defined in percentage terms;

(5) That the industry's wage increases occur at an early point in a 'complete cycle' of wage increases, i.e. one embracing a significant sample of major industries.

The first type of 'wage leadership' is not particularly relevant in the present context, since it depends upon more or less permanent institutional factors which determine the boundaries of the more important 'clusters' of related industries. None of the nationalized industries enjoys any particular pre-eminence in this regard. 'Automatic linkage' with railway and coal-mining settlements is confined to increases affecting smaller groups of employees of the British Transport Commission and the National Coal Board respectively. Settlements in gas and electricity interweave with those in other public utility employments, such as those affecting manual workers in water, local government and the health service, but the links are not automatic, and leadership varies from round to round. Civil aviation is itself a member of a cluster whose leadership lies with the private enterprise engineering industry.

---

[1] Railwaymen won an increase of about 6 per cent in November 1962, which of course does not appear in these figures.

[2] K. G. J. C. Knowles and E. M. F. Thorne, 'Wage Rounds 1948–59' (*Oxford Institute of Statistics Bulletin*, vol. 23, no. 1, February 1961).

This is, in fact, the most important 'natural cluster' of all, embracing also shipbuilding, Government industrial establishments and railway workshops, and maintenance workers in a variety of industries on whose behalf the Confederation of Shipbuilding and Engineering Unions conducts negotiations.

As wage-leaders in terms of their second test, Knowles and Thorne cite road haulage, road passenger transport, railways, retail co-operatives, and multiple groceries. (One might well also include agriculture as being at least a consistent 'early starter'.) Among industries which set the pattern in monetary terms – the third test – electricity supply, London Transport buses and, again, retail co-operatives are the most prominent, but company and municipal buses, gas, electrical contracting, railways, and occasionally engineering also appear. Percentage-wise the pattern-setters are electricity supply and London Transport buses, with railways, retail co-operatives and engineering closely behind. Finally, Knowles and Thorne, in their analysis of 'complete cycles', ascribe leadership in the early years of their period to electrical contracting, and more latterly to agriculture, with retail co-operatives coming second throughout among the ten major industries considered.

There is some evidence here of wage leadership by the nationalized industries. Electricity supply, railways and London Transport buses are particularly prominent, while road haulage (not wholly nationalized) and gas also put in an appearance. Are the public corporations, after all, the villains of the piece?

All the industries mentioned, however, have one other common characteristic, whose significance is more obviously relevant in this regard than is their form of ownership. They are all 'standard rate' industries, situated outside the complex of manufacturing industry, and offering relatively few opportunities in their internal wage structure for augmenting negotiated rates by piece-work, bonus systems and other forms of plus payment. A glance at the complete list of 'wage leaders', as described by Knowles and Thorne, will show that this is also true of most of the non-nationalized industries mentioned – the ubiquitous retail co-operatives, company and municipal buses, multiple groceries, and agriculture, for example. The nationalized industries, moreover, exhibit this characteristic in an exaggerated fashion, since to the relative absence of opportunities for plus payments, typical of public utilities and service trades, they add the more uniform and strictly controlled application of nationally agreed standard rates which single ownership makes possible.

The truth of the matter is that the size of the pay-packet can be increased in either, or both, of two ways: by way of nationally-agreed additions to standard or minimum rates, or by way of that familiar and much-discussed phenomenon, the 'earnings drift'. Those industries in which there is considerable scope for 'earnings drift' can keep their wages more or less in step with the general trend, even between bouts of national negotiation – or, indeed, push yet further ahead by means of locally determined premium rates, piece-rates, output bonuses, merit increments and the like. Is it surprising that the 'standard rate' industries, conscious of the increasing gap between their wages and those of their competitors in the labour market (or, seen from the worker's point of view, between his wages and those of his neighbours), and dependent upon national negotiations as the means of closing it, are the first to concede industry-wide increases? It may be noted that coal-mining, whose national wage structure ends with the time-worker, and whose large piece-working element in its labour force presents it with both the headaches and the benefits of the 'earnings drift' to an extent exceptional in the public sector, has never figured in the post-war period as a 'wage leader'. It may admittedly at times have given, by its settlements, an upward twist to an already existing spiral, but then what major industry has not?

Their relative absence of 'earnings drift' offers the main explanation why increases in wage rates in the nationalized industries have at times appeared to be comparatively large (though there is, in fact, little substance in that charge) and, with more justice, to have occurred comparatively early within each 'wage round'. There is no need to labour the point. The British Employers Confederation themselves have used the selfsame argument in advising their members that the size of the increases conceded by publicly-owned industries cannot always legitimately be cited as a reason why they should follow suit.[1]

Why, in the face of all the evidence, has the legend persisted

[1] 'B.E.C. Bulletin', October 5th, 1960, p. 1 : 'The factor of competition between employers helping to drive up rates offered locally, above the nationally

that the nationalized industries adopt a particularly 'soft' attitude towards wage claims? Part of the explanation lies in what is little more than the rationalization of political prejudices. The argument runs something like this: nationalized industries are socialist creations; people of socialist inclination or with a trade union background (like Dr Beeching?) are prominent on their governing bodies and among their staffs, especially on the labour relations side; therefore they are sympathetic to trade union claims, or even in league with the unions to exploit the consumer. Moreover – a point which has a particular appeal when the industry concerned is in deficit – the national boards are not spending their own money, at least not in the same sense as the private employer, and accordingly are more inclined to give way to wage pressure. Political prejudice not only offers 'explanations' of this sort for the ease with which nationalized industries are alleged to concede wage increases, but in itself provides an explanation why increases in these industries arouse a particular resentment among wide sections of the Press and the public.

This sort of argument – especially in view of the statistical evidence cited above – is really too silly to merit serious examination. But there is a more important reason for the exceptional public concern shown over wage settlements in the nationalized industries – the extent to which the Government itself becomes involved in them.

In theory, the level of wages in the nationalized industries is determined by free collective bargaining between the managements of those industries and the trade unions through the negotiating machinery (buttressed by the provisions, of a more or less

negotiated rates, has been commented on many times in the "Bulletin". The position has now been reached that in many important industries, earnings are found to have risen, between one wage settlement and the next, sometimes by as much as twice the last negotiated increase. The effect of overtime can explain only a small part of this, and it is becoming increasingly obvious over a wide range of industries that the nationally negotiated basic wage rate plays a decreasing part in determining the amount of the industrial wage packet.

'In public employment, to a much greater extent than in many forms of private employment, the basic rates negotiated nationally are closely adhered to and the feature just described is of far less significance in such forms of employment. A wage increase in public employment does not justify a corresponding increase elsewhere.'

automatic and binding character – depending upon the industry – for the reference of unsettled questions to arbitration) which the boards were by statute obliged to establish in agreement with the organizations which appear to them to be representative of their workers. In practice, the settlements made have by no means always been reached independently of the views expressed, and pressures exerted, by the Government of the day.

There are, broadly, four sorts of reasons why this has happened. Where an industry is in deficit, a substantial projected wage increase may raise the question of an extension of its borrowing powers, or perhaps even of more direct and drastic forms of subvention. Secondly, whether the industry is in deficit or not, it may wish to meet the cost of a wage increase by an increase in prices. Formally, or by convention, this may require governmental consent. Thirdly – and even if the industry is able, without a price increase or extended borrowing, itself to finance the increase proposed – the increase may be of an order, or of a timing, which conflicts with the Government's ideas of what is appropriate in the light of its general attitude to wages at the time. Finally, even if none of these things apply, the habit of informal consultation between ministers and board chairmen is so ingrained that the latter cannot fail to be aware of – and being aware, to be influenced by – whatever views ministers may express.

The process has been well described by Mr Aubrey Jones, M.P., a former Minister of Fuel and Power, in an article in the *Guardian* of September 22nd, 1960. 'The pattern of intervention on wages', he writes, 'is now well known. Here is Government concerned over the inflationary effect of the competitive race in incomes. To indulge in general pleas for restraint to the whole of industry seems an anodyne procedure; how much more tempting to seek to appear forceful in the sector which is its own – the public sector. And so, on the first appearance of a wage claim, it whispers to the nationalized undertaking to stand firm – even though the undertaking may think that some concession may well be reasonable. The fact that the undertaking is not speaking with its own voice but is merely the echo of another's soon becomes known. The indignation of the trade union mounts; there is the threat of a strike; Government, which fears a strike more than the nationalized undertaking, sounds the call for retreat; and amid paeans of praise for everybody's wisdom in choosing the path of peace the claim is settled – more generously than it could have been in the first place.'

Government intervention clearly goes further than the exercise of the conciliation functions of the Ministry of Labour, which would certainly be used to the utmost in the face of a strike threat in any of these basic industries whether they were nationalized or not. Indeed, it may be the case, as Mr Jones asserts, that the active character of Government intervention in the wages affairs of the nationalized industries has helped to undermine trade union faith in the conciliation machinery of the Ministry of Labour, and perhaps even in independent arbitration generally.

The process described by Mr Jones is not, however, wholly typical. The threat, or reality, of an industry-wide strike has, in the nationalized sector, occurred only on the railways and London Transport, except during the 1961 pay 'pause' when there were similar developments in electricity supply and the Post Office. On the railways, however, the experience has been a frequent one. Elsewhere the procedures of determining wages and conditions of service, and for settling disputes have culminated, as until recently in coal, in an automatic and binding form of arbitration, or, as in electricity, gas, civil aviation, and British Road Services, in something only a degree less stringent – binding arbitration at the request of either party.[1] These arrangements have not, in practice, operated with quite the full and precise formality prescribed in the relevant agreements, but, nevertheless, their existence, in reserve if necessary, has been sufficient to ensure the avoidance of official strikes.

On the railways, however, arbitration awards are not binding, and there have been a succession of incidents in which a national strike has been avoided only at the eleventh hour, and as the result of more or less open intervention by the Government. These incidents, in which the Government has advised or facilitated concessions, have attracted a great deal of publicity, but it is not certain

[1] The position in coal-mining was changed in the summer of 1961 by an amendment under which 'national' questions do not proceed to arbitration if either side objects. Arbitration awards, when given, remain binding however, and arbitration continues to be automatic on 'district' and 'pit' questions. It is too early to assess the effects of the change.

that they have been more important than the cumulative effect of 'the whispers to stand firm', necessarily undocumentable, to which Mr Jones refers, and which have certainly not been confined to the railways.

Is such intervention defensible? When its origin lies in Government control over borrowing or prices, criticism, where valid, must primarily attach either to that control itself, or to whatever aspect of their arrangements (for example, insufficient opportunity or encouragement to accumulate reserves) makes it impossible for the nationalized undertakings concerned to meet major wage claims without resort to these expedients. Once ministerial control over borrowing and/or prices, and associated aspects of the relationship between the Government and the boards, are accepted, the minister's advisory responsibility with regard to wage negotiations can scarcely be denied. Even in such cases, however, the board's judgment on the consequences of making an inadequate offer – whether on manpower or on morale – should also weigh heavily in the balance. Increases in prices or in deficits may sometimes be the lesser evil!

Criticism has even more justification where the intervention is founded upon general concern about wage inflation. What is at issue here is the tendency of Governments to enforce with especial severity in the public sector, where their influence can most directly be exercised, policies whose frame of reference should properly be the economy as a whole. The temptation is great – perhaps, indeed, not least to a Labour Government, since socialist arguments for nationalization have usually included the very point that the existence of a large public sector facilitates the operation of general measures of economic planning. Nevertheless, it is a temptation which should be recognized, and in general resisted. 'Discriminatory planning' of this kind has affected more than wages, and in a variety of fields its effects have been unfortunate. It has, for example, played havoc with investment programmes in the public sector. Similarly, the application of discriminatory planning in the sphere of wages, in the form in which it has usually been exercised, can only intensify manpower difficulties and exacerbate relations by exciting trade union suspicions of the genuine character of negotiations, of the impartiality of arbitrators, and of the intentions behind governmental mediation.

A Government would, of course, be placed in an indefensible position if a policy it was successfully implementing elsewhere were to be flouted within the public sector itself. Intervention in such a case, however, is not discriminatory. 'Discriminatory planning' itself can, moreover, be justified where it has 'multiplier' effects of an order which ensures that the whole economy is significantly affected, even though the initial action is confined to the public sector. (This is the argument for a large public sector investment programme as an anti-recession measure.) But what is indefensible is for the nationalized industries to be subject, in the name of a general economic policy, to restraints which are applied elsewhere ineffectively, if at all, and whose initial discriminatory application has no 'multiplier' effect. In the present instance, intervention would appear defensible only if the nationalized undertakings persistently exhibited a desire to make wage settlements which exceeded the general run of such settlements, without being able, in justification, to point to any exceptional circumstances in their own manpower position. It is difficult to believe that this is, or has been, the situation. On the contrary, the purpose of this type of intervention seems to have been to get the nationalized sector to 'set an example' by being 'sticky' beyond the average in its attitude to claims. Had the example been generally followed, this would have been a defensible tactic – there is little evidence that it has.

If, then, the Right-wing critics, who feared that wages would 'run away' in the nationalized sector (and who, in some cases perhaps, still think their fears were well founded), have been wrong, so have those on the Left who hoped either that nationalization would provide a horn of plenty for the wage-earner, or that it would facilitate the operation of some kind of 'national wages policy'. Nevertheless, if exaggerated fears and high hopes have alike been disappointed, it is noteworthy that the nationalized industries, despite their deficits, despite the acute and special problems of transport and coal, and despite their particular exposure to governmental 'whispers to stand firm' have, by and large, roughly kept pace with the movement of wage rates in the economy generally. In part, this may reflect the strength of the unions; in part it may be an illusion, disguising a less marked degree of success if the comparison is conducted instead in terms of earnings. But three special factors have undoubtedly played a major role. Whatever the general experience within the public sector, electricity supply, the Post Office, and to a lesser extent gas, have been profitable and able to afford the position of relative 'wage-leaders'. Secondly, coal-mining has been confronted, almost throughout the whole period, with the problem of at least localized manpower shortages, and these have justified wage advances which might otherwise have been discouraged. Thirdly, in the most unhappy of all the nationalized industries, the railways, has occurred the most significant development of what might appear to be an appropriate 'wage doctrine' for the whole public sector, that of 'comparable wages for comparable work'.

This doctrine was first explicitly stated in the trenchant words of the Interim Report of the 1955 Court of Inquiry presided over by Sir John (later Lord) Cameron:

> The nation has provided by statute that there shall be a nationalized system of railway transport which must therefore be regarded as a public utility of the first importance. Having willed the end, the nation must will the means. This implies that employees of such a national service should receive a fair and adequate wage, and that in broad terms, the railwayman should be in no worse case than his colleague in comparable industry.[1]

The Final Report spelled out the argument in these words:

> Where (as in the case of the Commission), the employer is bound to keep his business going and can neither show a working profit, nor shift the scene of his operations, nor reorganize his capital structure, nor be wound up by his creditors, then the factors which are understood by all as affecting the wage rates in normal industry are absent. The conditions in his business are, commercially speaking, artificial and it therefore becomes necessary to fall back on the expedient of relating the wages he should pay to those paid in such comparable industries as may be found.[2]

[1] Cmd. 9352, 'Interim Report of a Court of Inquiry into a Dispute between the B.T.C. and the National Union of Railwaymen', para. 10.

[2] Cmd. 9372, 'Final Report of a Court of Inquiry into a Dispute between the B.T.C. and the National Union of Railwaymen', para. 62.

There is a straight line of descent from Cameron to Guillebaud. The Railway Pay Committee of Inquiry, under the chairmanship of Mr C. W. Guillebaud, which reported in March 1960, was established in 1958 by agreement between the B.T.C. and the three railway unions 'to conduct an investigation into the relativity of pay' of railway staff 'with the pay of staff in other Nationalized Industries, Public Services and appropriate Private Undertakings ... where reasonable and useful comparisons can be made.'[1] Job comparability was to be taken into account in any such comparisons.

This concept of a kind of inter-industry job evaluation has been much criticized as ignoring the economic criteria which should influence wage determination, and no doubt its general adoption would lead to difficulties in the mobility and optimum development of labour. But it can be defended as peculiarly suited to the circumstances of a nationalized industry in heavy deficit, to which many of the normal economic criteria influencing wage determination could only have a nonsensical application. What is important for our purpose at the moment is, however, that the adoption of this concept on the railways has been an important additional factor making for the general parity which now exists between the nationalized and non-nationalized sectors in their rates of wage increases since the early post-war years. Had the pre-Guillebaud position on the railways still obtained, the non-nationalized sector would have enjoyed a clear lead.

Nationalization has had then no marked observable influence, one way or the other, on the level of wages in the industries concerned.[2] Moreover, in so far as nationalization has facilitated the application of general governmental wage policies, the effects would seem largely to be limited to the publicly-owned sector itself, and to have done at least as much harm there as good. Is nationalization then wholly irrelevant to the wages question?

There are three aspects of the internal wages arrangements of the nationalized industries which would contradict such a verdict.

[1] Report of Railway Pay Committee of Inquiry, March 2nd, 1960, para. 3.
[2] This means only that wage levels have moved at much the same rate within the nationalized sector as elsewhere. Without nationalization, of course, wage levels may have been either lower or higher in the industries concerned than has in fact been the case. But there is no way of determining which.

To the first – the comprehensive nature of the arrangements for negotiation and arbitration – reference has already been made. It is true that a number of reservations must accompany a favourable judgment here. In the majority of instances, the procedures in question have largely been taken over from those which operated in the same industries under private ownership, though here and there improvements have been made. The most 'compulsory' in character of the arbitration provisions, those in coal-mining, have been amended at the request of the National Union of Mineworkers, who wished to have the right, on national issues, to prevent a reference to arbitration. Finally, while the arrangements made have been successful, over the greater part of the public sector, in avoiding official strikes, unofficial strikes have been numerous – especially in coal. Nevertheless, these strikes have only occasionally been connected with national wage negotiations, and it remains the case that the public sector provides, throughout the whole range of its employment, an orderly, comprehensive and generally pacific system of wage determination, founded upon full trade union recognition, which goes beyond the general level of outside arrangements.

More controversial is the second aspect of the internal wages arrangements of the nationalized undertakings. As sole employers, they have inevitably tended to introduce throughout the industries in which they operate uniform 'wage structures', based broadly on the principle of the 'rate for the job' and taking little account of differences in the productivity or profitability of individual units or districts, or of the relative intensity of competition in different local labour markets.

The apparent rigidity of these structures has aroused criticism, both within and outside the nationalized industries themselves, on a number of counts. These criticisms can be divided roughly into two main groups. First is the 'economic' criticism which draws attention, in particular, to the difficulties experienced by nationalized industries when faced by widely differing manpower situations in different parts of the country. Region A may have a relatively high level of unemployment with manpower easy to obtain; region B may be an area of over-full employment, where desirable projects are held back by shortage of labour. Yet the nationalized concern is inhibited by its own wages structure from offering differential rates in the two places. Secondly, there is the 'industrial relations' criticism. There is a growing school of thought among students of industrial relations in favour of 'plant bargaining' as against 'industry-wide bargaining'. Largely inspired by American examples, this school of thought contends, first, that 'plant bargaining', with its associated control over wages and working conditions through comprehensive local collective contracts, offers a means of revivifying the flagging branch life of the trade unions; and, secondly, that it permits a more realistic type of wage negotiation, avoiding a situation in which only minimum rates are effectively within the control of trade union negotiators.

The economic criticism is formidable. It does not, however, necessarily call for the abandonment of industry-wide wage structures, but merely for greater flexibility in their design and operation. Any wage structure which is more than the application of a single uniform wage rate must recognize a number of factors whose existence justifies variations in rates. Theoretically, at least, there is no reason why one such factor should not be that of locality. Indeed, some of the existing wage structures (and salary structures) in nationalized industry do incorporate district differentials, although usually along the lines of recognizing regional differences in living costs (e.g. London differentials) rather than differences in labour market competition.

The introduction of regional differentials within a national wage structure is, then, unobjectionable in principle, and their economic attraction is undeniable. The difficulties presented by such a course within the service of a single undertaking, especially one confronted by a single trade union or a small and closely-knit group of unions, are, however, considerable. In these circumstances, the pressures of 'equitable comparison' are so strong that the establishment of regional differentials may well lead, in the relatively short term, to the raising of all rates to the new premium level. The fact that the 'labour shortage' areas within a particular industry are likely next year, or the year after, to be slightly different from what they are now will reinforce this tendency, since no area is likely ever to be deleted from the 'high-rate group', while new ones will from time to time have to be added. After all, the gradual disappearance of regional differentials has been the common experience of industry-wide negotiations in the private sector. That they could survive the stronger pressure towards uniformity within the nationalized industries seems unfortunately rather improbable.

Moreover, to be effective in influencing the recruitment and wastage of labour, the regional differentials would have to be large. The incorporation of large – and if necessary, reversible – regional differentials within the wages structure of a single undertaking is administratively a daunting proposition, whatever its theoretical attractions.

The industrial relations criticism, in so far as it parallels or repeats the economic, can be dealt with in the same way. The argument that national negotiations mean concentration upon minimum rates alone appears to stem from the obsession of its proponents with engineering, admittedly Britain's largest, but by no means its only, industry. It is singularly inappropriate in its application to the comprehensive and detailed wage structures of the nationalized industries, where negotiations relate to a wide variety of grade rates (standard, not minimum), and to the grading of the individual jobs to which these rates apply.

More serious is the contention that the centralization of negotiations, which national wage structures imply, has meant a lack of virility in the life of the trade unions at local level. Again, however, full account must be taken of the institutional environment. The formal decentralization of negotiations cannot disguise the fact of a single organization on the employers' side and of nationally-organized trade unions on the other. Neither the national boards nor the unions' national executives will permit local negotiations to escape their control; local managements and trade union branches may formally conduct independent negotiations, but their autonomy is more apparent than real. The negotiation of piece-workers' price lists in the coal-mining industry is highly decentralized in form – generally on a pit-by-pit basis – but in practice the pressures towards uniformity, at least within single coalfields, are strong on both sides of the table, and are limited in their pervasive effects only by the bewildering variety of physical conditions encountered below ground. It is difficult to escape the conclusion that decentralization of wages negotiations, however desirable, must wait upon the decentralization of management.

On the credit side, uniform wage structures have much in their favour. The 'rate for the job' is a principle of equity which has powerful appeal, not least to the trade union mind. The practical value as a 'morale builder' of the sense of fairness which this principle satisfies cannot be assessed, but is not negligible. There are, moreover, more tangible practical benefits. The 'escalating' of wage rates by competitive up-bidding between districts is avoided. Again, the scope and effect of changes in rates, introduced to achieve some particular object of policy, can accurately be assessed. Where wage rates are relatively unstructured, such changes can easily fail to achieve their objectives, or can even have a boomerang effect.

The outstanding achievement in the creation of more rational wage structures has been in coal-mining, where the initial diversity was probably greatest. To a ramshackle structure of wage rates and an impressive variety of jobs was added an even greater variety of traditional local names for jobs – more than six thousand in all. By a process which might be described as that of 'common-sense job evaluation', these were reduced to four hundred-odd national occupations, each with an associated description of its main content. These national occupations were, in their turn, divided among thirteen grades, for which sixteen standard grade rates were negotiated.[1] This process, completed in 1955, means that the principle of the 'rate for the job' now applies to virtually the whole of the industry's 300,000 day-wage workers.[2] Whatever blemishes the structure may have, it clearly represents a major advance, when compared with the anomalies of its predecessor or the 'structures' of such large private industries as engineering. Here is an achievement of the first order in the direction of more orderly wages arrangements, which would have been quite impossible without the single ownership and management which nationalization has brought. But even here, success has been far from complete. Attempts to achieve a similar national structure for piece-rates have proved unavailing.

The third province in which nationalization has certainly not

[1] Separate underground and surface rates were established for the three craftsmen's grades. The number of grades has now been increased to fifteen, and the number of grade rates to nineteen.

[2] A later structure applies to the weekly-paid staff of the industry.

been irrelevant belongs more properly to the chapter on labour relations. In terms of money wages the nationalized industries have not been able to act as pacemakers. But they have been, to a large extent, pacemakers in respect of such non-wage benefits as pension, sickness and accidents pay schemes, security of employment, redundancy compensation and welfare facilities. While individual private firms may do as well, or better, in one or more of these directions, the nationalized undertakings provide them on a comprehensive and industry-wide scale which only single ownership makes possible.

The opening of a new medical centre or an increase in an industry's pension rates may attract limited publicity in comparison with a major advance in wages, but the importance of these things to the quality of the relationship existing between an undertaking and its workers can scarcely be exaggerated.[1] That such provisions have been widely made in the nationalized industries is a measure not only of the opportunities which single ownership has brought, but of the will to use these opportunities which is engendered by that facet of the public service ethos which seeks to promote the image of the 'good employer'. If, within the field of wages narrowly defined, that will has to any extent been blunted either by the exigencies of Government policies, or of the profit and loss accounts of the undertakings concerned, the fault lies not with public ownership, but with its method of operation so far. Only through the removal of the general financial limitations to which they have been subject can the nationalized industries hope to dispense with the useful, but minimum, protection which the Cameron-Guillebaud doctrine provides.

---

[1] This applies even more strongly to policies designed to safeguard employment, such as those which the coal industry adopted in the face of the declining demand of 1957–9 – stocking, cessation of Saturday working, restrictions on recruitment, compulsory retirement of older workers, run-down in opencast, etc.

# CHAPTER FIVE

# MINISTERIAL AND PARLIAMENTARY CONTROL

*by*

AUSTEN ALBU

THE attitude of the Labour Party to the nationalized industries has always been ambivalent. On the one hand they were to be instruments of national economic and social policy; on the other they were to be enterprising and largely independent commercial undertakings. Obviously, the degree to which they would be subject to Government control and parliamentary questioning would be determined by which view was taken of them. By 1945 the choice appeared to have been made, in the case of the group of industries then to be nationalized, by the decision to use the form of the public corporation. It was thought that this would ensure the industries' freedom from day-to-day ministerial or parliamentary interference and guarantee a sufficient degree of managerial independence to be sure that their boards were enterprising and efficient. The attempt to translate this concept into legislation has not, in practice, worked well; the industries have been the victims of the dilemma, in which all Governments found themselves, between the risk that too much control would interfere with good management, and the desire to use the industries to assist in the planning of national investment or to control inflation. Conservative Governments have even not been above interfering, for instance in railway fares, for political advantage at times of election. This chapter examines the statutory position, compares it with the reality of control exercised by minister and Parliament, and draws some conclusions for future policy.

The concept of the public corporation is chiefly associated with the name of Lord Morrison. In his book *The Socialization of Transport*, he insisted that a minister should only have such duties in regard to a nationalized undertaking as are imposed on him by the statute creating the corporation, and should have no right to interfere with its work. At the same time he thought it perfectly proper that there should be contacts between minister and board, which 'would work much better if allowed to evolve on the basis of good sense and tradition; rather than if embodied in formal law or regulations'. This view has been strongly supported by the trade unions in the industries concerned, who have generally allied themselves with the boards to resist ministerial and parliamentary control. Ministers, on the other hand, with the tacit approval of Labour ex-ministers, have increasingly practised a system of private arm-twisting of board chairmen, while resisting parliamentary questioning and any serious degree of parliamentary control. In fact, the Labour Party in Parliament, pressed by the T.U.C., even opposed the setting up of the Select Committee on Nationalized Industries, though this had been recommended unanimously by a Select Committee which included five Labour Members, one an ex-minister and two of them ex-Parliamentary Secretaries. Conservative ministers, although responsible for the setting up of the Select Committee, gave it at first such restricted terms of reference that it could not operate, and have strongly resisted pressure from a group of their own back-benchers to provide opportunities for more detailed control of the industries' investment policies. Ministers on both sides have obviously wanted ministerial control without too much parliamentary accountability.

The difficulties of this system were already becoming obvious in 1949 when Mr Gaitskell, as Minister of Fuel and Power, opened the first debate on the report and accounts of a nationalized industry, those of the National Coal Board. He referred to the confusion that existed on the constitutional position, that is to say about the relationship of Parliament and the minister to the board. After pointing out that the Acts limited the minister's powers pretty severely, he went on: 'If the board in the exercise of their statutory functions were to proceed on lines which the minister thought were contrary to the national interest, he would give them directions of a general character. Thus the minister must accept responsibility for the general lines on which the boards are carrying out their functions. He must accept responsibility for ... the general success or failure of the enterprise.' This is taking the responsibility of the minister rather far, and it would appear that it was not easy to carry out, for Mr Gaitskell said: 'It does not necessarily follow that the present position in which the minister's powers are limited is necessarily the most attractive and easy for the minister'. It was well known, in fact, that there were serious conflicts of view between the minister and Lord Citrine, who was chairman of the Electricity Authority, and, by virtue of his previous position as General Secretary of the T.U.C., a powerful figure in Labour politics.

It was at this time that the custom grew up of regular meetings between ministers and board chairmen, often over lunch or dinner, at which the minister's views were made known. Meanwhile, the minister was kept informed of what the boards were doing by the regular contact between their officials and those of the minister's department. In this way, actions apparently taken freely by the boards had in fact often originated with the minister. Naturally, this process was easier when the chairman had himself been a civil servant, and the extent to which it was used varied with the personalities of ministers. There is no doubt, however, that it has been carried on and extended by Conservative ministers, whose interference in the policy of the boards would seem to have increased. This interference has naturally led to criticism from Labour Members of Parliament interested in particular industries; but the right to interfere was strongly supported by Mr Aneurin Bevan in the debates on the resignation of Mr Hardie, the chairman of the Iron and Steel Corporation, because of a disagreement about steel prices. Mr Bevan said:

> The responsibility of deciding what is in the overriding interests of the nation rests with the minister, because only by resting with him can it rest here. Once we deny to the Minister of Supply, or to any other minister responsible for a great national undertaking, the right to determine what he thinks to be in the national interest, then we are erecting a species of the corporate society more familiar to Italian Fascist principles than to the British democratic constitution. I have always denied the right of great corporations to decide such issues.

It is not surprising that Parliament became more and more disturbed at the growing evidence of ministerial interference with the policy of the industries which found no expression in formal directions or even reports, because it meant that ministers were taking policy decisions for which they could not be made answerable in Parliament, and for which the boards themselves were unable publicly to disclaim responsibility. The vested interests at play here are obvious, but were they inevitable, and could the situation have been different? This is a question that can only be answered after an examination of the statutory powers of ministers and Parliament and of the subjects on which ministers have exercised control and the methods they have, in practice, used. Whatever party leaders may think of the Select Committee on Nationalized Industries, the facts on these matters are now available for public discussion and criticism in a way that they never were before its formation.

## The Power of the Minister

The most powerful statutory power possessed by a minister responsible for a nationalized industry is that under which he appoints – and, perhaps even more important, re-appoints – the members of the national and, in the case of electricity and gas, the area boards. It is from this, far more than from the little-used power to give directions in the national interest, that he derives the powerful personal influence which every minister has over all aspects of the policies of the boards. The second most powerful statutory power is that of approving plans of reorganization and development involving substantial capital expenditure; a power which, strangely enough, does not apply in the case of the air corporations. This power, it should be noted, applies only to long-term overall plans and does not itself include any power to determine the annual rate of expenditure. On the other hand, ministry consent and Treasury approval had always to be obtained for borrowing or the issue of stock; a provision rendered temporarily obsolete by the more direct control exercised since the Treasury became the sole source of finance for all the nationalized industries in 1956. In the case of the British Transport Commission, the minister had power, under the 1947 Act, to approve the acquisition of railway, harbour, inland waterway, tramcar or trolley vehicle undertakings, and to direct the commission to discontinue

93

any activities, dispose of any part of its undertakings or securities, call in any loan or exercise any power it might possess to revoke any guarantee which it had given. Under the 1953 Act the minister was given the power to approve, amend or revoke, after appropriate consultation, schemes of reorganization. It was under this power that the area boards were created.

Over prices no statutory powers exist, although the Minister of Transport may require the Transport Tribunal to review the operation of any charges scheme. The Minister of Power may direct the National Coal Board to remedy a defect in its general arrangements for the production, sale or supply of coal, coke or manufactured fuel reported to him by either the Industrial or Domestic Consumers' Council. Ministers have power to make regulations for pensions schemes and must give their approval to programmes of training, education and research. Apart from certain regulatory powers inherited from the days when most of the industries were statutory monopolies, the only other important statutory powers are those which require the publication of annual reports and accounts and other periodical statistics and the approval of the auditors and the scheme of audit. The ministers must lay the reports and accounts before Parliament.

It may seem that these are formidable enough powers, but in practice the control exercised by ministers is far greater and of a much more day-to-day nature than would appear to be possible if the boards were to insist on their legal rights. So far, there has been no test case of the meaning of the 'national interest' and, in fact, very few formal directions have ever been given by a minister to a board.

In spite of the lack of specific authority to control prices or charges, ministerial interference has taken place in nearly every one of the industries. One of the earliest examples was the pressure exerted on the Electricity Authority to introduce a differential between summer and winter prices (the Clow differential) in 1948. The retail price of coal was controlled under Defence Regulations until 1958: but the pit-head price has remained subject to a 'gentlemen's agreement' continuing a wartime arrangement which gave the minister the right to approve charges. In 1957 two Gas Boards were prevented from raising tariffs to the extent they thought desirable, with consequent losses of revenue. Successive

Ministers of Transport have intervened to prevent or delay an increase in railway fares, even though these have been within the level approved by the Transport Tribunal, and their delay has involved the Transport Commission in heavy losses. International air fares are subject to regulation and agreement by the International Air Transport Association. Negotiations within the association are not operative until approved by Governments, whose authority derives from the fact that the right to carry traffic between countries depends on bilateral agreements between Governments. Cabotage fares are not so regulated, but this has not stopped ministers interfering with them. In spite of the absence of statutory powers the Government has now made specific its interests in prices and fares in the White Paper on 'The Financial and Economic Obligations of Nationalized Industries' (Cmd. 1337.)

Whether the minister directly intervenes or not, the close relationship between his officials and those both in the industries themselves and in the Ministry of Labour undoubtedly exercises a strong influence on their wages policy. Direct intervention is perhaps rare and has taken place chiefly on the railways. Perhaps not surprisingly the two known cases, prior to the introduction of the pay 'pause' in 1961, were both concerned with wage increases: Mr Bevan's instruction to the British Transport Commission to raise wages in 1951, and the Conservative Government's approval to the recommendations of the Guillebaud Committee on Railways Pay in 1960. It may be thought that these interventions are the inevitable result of the financial difficulties of the British Transport Commission, but there is no doubt that ministerial pressure has been exerted on the boards of nationalized industries, generally to restrain or postpone wage increases at times of inflationary tendency, since the days of the White Paper on wages and income issued by Sir Stafford Cripps in 1948, during the period of post-war industrial reconstruction. In fact, such pressures have rarely been supported by arguments which distinguished between the financial position of a particular industry and the general state of the economy.

Perhaps the industry over whose activities the Government has exercised the largest measure of control without statutory authority is air transport. So much is this so that the Select

Committee commented that, 'faced with the total extent of the minister's non-statutory powers, they are bound to ask if these do not add up to a degree of control far in excess of that envisaged by the statute under which B.O.A.C. and B.E.A. were created, and so lead to an undesirable diminution in the authority of the chairmen and boards of the corporations, and in their feeling of responsibility'. Although the Minister of Aviation has no statutory authority for the general development plans of the air corporations, the fact that the Treasury provides the capital for them means that, in practice, a strict control over capital expenditure is exercised. As eighty per cent of such expenditure is for new aircraft, this has led to considerable Government influence over the types of aircraft which the corporations fly. Government approval is needed for the purchase of American aircraft, but on the whole the corporations have agreed with the Government that they have a duty to help develop British aircraft. They told the Select Committee that there are advantages in being first in the air with a new type, although they thought that they should receive a subsidy to cover the high development cost involved. Government influence is very strong, not only in resisting dollar expenditure on aircraft, but also, through the Ministry of Supply (now the Ministry of Aviation), in influencing the corporations to place their orders with particular firms. There was a six months' delay in getting started on the De Havilland D.H. 121 for B.E.A. because the Ministry of Supply wanted the order placed with another firm. In an industry in which so much Government money is involved in research and development, in which development for civil and military purposes is sometimes indistinguishable, and in which the Government itself has exercised so much influence over the structure of the manufacturing companies themselves, it is no doubt inevitable that a very strong control should be exercised by the minister concerned over the types of aircraft purchased, even though the final decisions are taken by the boards themselves.

The Government's control over routes partly arises out of the need for the negotiation of traffic rights: but the corporations were persuaded in 1952 not to operate any new routes without first obtaining the minister's permission. This was done in order to give greater opportunity for the independent companies, and today all applications for new routes by both public and private airlines

96

are subject to approval by the Air Transport Licensing Board set up under the Act of 1960.

The corporations have also been forbidden by the Government to retain aircraft specifically for charter work, a restriction admitted by the ministry to have no statutory basis. On the other hand it is presumably Government policy that B.E.A. should continue to operate its unprofitable services to the Scottish Highlands and Islands without subsidy. The corporations may not invest in foreign airlines without ministry and Treasury approval, but B.O.A.C. were persuaded against their will to invest in Kuwait Airways for reasons purely of foreign policy.

In view of the responsibility of ministers and the Chancellor of the Exchequer to Parliament for the raising and appropriation of supply, it is not surprising that when exchequer finance is needed, or is likely to be needed, to cover a revenue deficit, the independence of the board disappears. This was made clear by the Permanent Secretary to the Ministry of Transport in his evidence to the Select Committee when he said that, 'when the financial situation gets worse it does create a new situation in which the ministry has to consider whether it must not ask more detailed questions than it has perhaps asked in the past'. This reply dealt with investment plans on the railways, but there is no doubt it would apply equally to other proposals likely to lead to a substantial rise in expenditure.

Although ministers have no statutory powers to determine the annual level of capital expenditure within an approved long-term plan, in fact the control over such expenditure has become one of the major weapons in the economic armoury of the Treasury. In this they have no doubt been assisted by the change introduced by the Conservative Government in 1956 under which the Treasury became the sole external financier of all the nationalized industries instead of being merely their guarantor. Some Conservative members have expressed doubt over this control, preferring Government control to be exercised solely as banker by the extent of finance which it makes available to the industries.

This view was put by the chairman of the Select Committee, Sir Toby Low, in a debate on public investment in November 1960. It is difficult to see what practical difference this would make or in what way it would differ, in practice, from the present arrangements. No Government is likely to give up the useful weapon of annual control – even though, as Mr Selwyn Lloyd admitted when he was Chancellor of the Exchequer, in practice only marginal adjustments can be made in annual investment expenditure already planned; in one way or another, Governments will continue to use it.

In some ways ministerial control is quite inadequate. Under the 1947 Act co-ordination of transport policy was to be the duty of the British Transport Commission. Its power to do this was removed when a large part of its road haulage undertaking was denationalized in 1953. With the abolition of the commission this duty falls on the Minister of Transport, but so far his department has not had the resources or, apparently, the will for the task. The Minister of Power, by the Act of 1945, has the 'general duty of securing the effective and co-ordinated development of coal, petroleum, and other minerals and sources of fuel and power in Great Britain ... and of promoting economy and efficiency in the supply, distribution and consumption of fuel and power, whether produced in Great Britain or not'. Such duties require a far larger degree of policy planning than has ever been exercised by any minister responsible for the fuel and power industries; but it has not prevented the minister interfering with them in matters for which he has no statutory powers in the nationalization Acts. For instance, in the gas industry, where a big development involves a new process – as in the case of the Lurgi plants – or involves the making of gas from oil instead of coal, it is subject to specific approval. Other examples are schemes for a national grid or underground storage transcending the boundaries of a particular area board. The Minister also takes it as part of his responsibility to see that there is an adequate supply of solid smokeless fuel – a matter that one would have thought could have been left to the judgment and initiative of the area boards. In these cases the functions and responsibilities of the minister go a good deal wider than the specific duties defined in the statute. The truth is that his duties under the Act setting up the ministry, and his powers under the nationalization Acts, are in conflict. What is ironical is that the ministry has so far done little in the way of planned co-ordination; while it interferes in matters, sometimes of a comparatively minor nature, as if it had. In the case of the British

Transport Commission, and in particular the railways, ministerial interference – both statutory and non-statutory – has in recent years become almost continuous. What is particularly serious in this case is that successive proposals for the reorganization of the commission, from the denationalization of a large part of British Road Services in 1953, to the decision of the Prime Minister to give the advisory group in 1960 terms of reference which were based on the breaking up of the railway system into autonomous regions, appear to have been made without any detailed prior inquiry, and against the advice of members of the commission themselves. Such continuous meddling smacks of ministerial irresponsibility and undoubtedly undermined the authority of the commission.

*Parliamentary Control*

Parliamentary control of the nationalized industries has been a bone of contention for more Conservative than Labour members, and for different reasons. Doctrinal prejudice and the difficulties faced, particularly by coal and the railways, led at first to attacks on management and demands for examination of the efficiency of operation. More recently, there have been attempts to control the annual level of investment permitted by the minister. Trade union members have, from time to time, felt annoyance at their inability to raise matters of local management, but, since the advent of a Conservative Government, the main frustration felt by Labour Members has been the inability to question ministers about policies which, they suspected, were being imposed on the boards without disclosure.

Members of Parliament, of course, receive complaints from their constituents as consumers. As these are matters of day-to-day administration, they are not accepted by ministers as subjects for parliamentary questions, even though they may raise matters of some importance, such as the closing of branch railway lines. These matters are dealt with directly by correspondence with the board chairman; but there are a number of opportunities to ventilate them in debate. The first Select Committee, which was set up in December, 1951, 'to consider the present methods by which the House of Commons is informed of affairs of the nationalized industries', and to suggest what changes were desirable, only considered questions to ministers and came down virtually in favour of no change. Its main reason for doing so was that the industries were not subject to any direct control by ministers in individual matters of detail, and as the basic feature of a parliamentary question is that of the responsibility of the minister to whom it is directed, it would not be appropriate for him to be questioned on such matters. The question of what is or is not a matter of detail is entirely at the discretion of the minister, who can agree or refuse to answer a question. Once a question has been refused, all subsequent questions of the same nature would be refused by the clerks at the table. However, in 1948 the then Speaker said that he would exercise his discretion to allow questions on matters of day-to-day administration, even though information on them had been previously refused, if they were matters of sufficient public importance.

The Second Committee, set up with the same terms of reference in 1952, listed the opportunities that Members of Parliament had to obtain information about the industries. They comprised the following:

1. *Debate motions*
   (a) Motions specifically concerning one or more of the industries, either moved by a minister or by some other Member when the Government have given time for the debate;
   (b) 'Ballot Motions' in Private Members' time;
   (c) Debate on the address in reply to the Queen's speech;
   (d) The daily half-hour adjournment at the close of the sitting;
   (e) Adjournment motions moved by a minister for the purpose of debating a particular subject.
2. *Debate in Committee of Supply* or on an amendment to a motion 'That Mr Speaker do now leave the chair'.
3. *Debate on Bills* whether public or private dealing with one or more of the industries.
4. *Debate on motions to approve or annul orders* or other statutory instruments made by ministers under the various Nationalization Acts.

5. *The annual reports and accounts* of the various boards and commissions, which are laid before Parliament.
6. *Questions of Ministers.*

The opportunities for debate may seem extensive, but it must be borne in mind that 1(a), 1(e), and 3 (as far as it concerns public Bills) are all occasions which form part of Government business; while 2, as far as it relates to debates in Committee of Supply, is an occasion when the choice of subject rests with the official Opposition. On the other hand, the opportunity for back-bench initiative under 1(b) and 1(e) is subject to the whims of a ballot or, for daily adjournments, partly to the Speaker's choice. At the present time, the Government, which has almost complete control of business in the House of Commons outside supply days and the twenty days divided between Private Members' Bills and motions, normally gives three days for debate on the reports and accounts of most of the corporations; in 1961 it also introduced a general debate on public investment. In the House of Lords, whose arrangements for business are much more flexible, there are more opportunities for back-bench Members; but not, of course, supply days.

The committee recommended the appointment of a sessional committee to inspect the reports and accounts and to obtain further information as to the general policy and practice of the industries, with the object of informing Parliament about their aims, activities and problems, but not of controlling their work. They recommended that the staff of the committee should include an officer of the status of the Comptroller and Auditor General and at least one professional accountant. They also recommended that the statutory auditors of the corporations should, in preparing their annual reports, give such information, in addition to that now provided by them, as might be of use to the committee and of interest to Parliament. As the subsequent debate showed, although there was unanimous support among members of the committee for the recommendation to set up a sessional committee, the recommendations on staff went further than all Members of the House were prepared to accept.

Not until 1955 did the Government finally move; a Select Committee was then set up, but its deliberations were interrupted by the general election. The subsequent committee reported that its terms of reference were so restricted that it was unable to do anything at all. It was forbidden to inquire into matters which were the responsibility of ministers; which concerned wages and conditions of employment; which were the subject of formal machinery established by statute or were matters of day-to-day administration. Finally a committee was appointed in November 1956, with virtually unrestricted terms of reference; but it was, nevertheless, warned not to deal with matters of ministerial responsibility, of day-to-day administration or, normally, the subject of negotiation between employers and trade unions. It was given no staff except the usual committee clerk. There is no doubt that this committee, which has continued to be appointed every session, interpreted its terms of reference very broadly and has performed a most useful function; proving unjustified the fears of most members of the Labour Party and of some board chairmen that it would be a hostile and partisan inquisition, and even converting some organs of the 'establishment' Press which had pontificated against its formation. So far, it has had two chairmen, both from the Government side, who have succeeded in getting the committee to produce unanimous reports on nearly every matter that they have investigated. Like most Select Committees, it has operated with the minimum of party conflict and has succeeded in establishing a relationship of confidence with the boards, who recognize the value of the informed presentation of their problems to Parliament which the committee has made possible.

After their third report, the committee produced a special report in which the problem of whether they should be provided with additional staff was considered. They agreed on three general principles: that any staff working for them should clearly be servants of Parliament and not of the Executive; that any change in staff should not lead to interference in the working of the industries; and that it was important that the industries themselves should have full confidence in the staff. They examined a number of proposals after first turning down the original proposal for an officer of the status of the Comptroller and Auditor General as likely to lead to a 'grand inquisition' into the nationalized industries. Nor did they think it wise to impose on the statutory auditors any duties other than those normally carried out in commercial companies. A Treasury witness, Mr R. A. Butler, at that time Leader of the House, suggested that Treasury officials might be seconded to work for the committee. They were turned down on sound constitutional principle. Whatever the original intention of those who set up the committee, in practice it had found itself exposing the relationship between the boards and the Government, and in many cases calling in question the effect on the boards of Government decisions or actions. In these decisions the Treasury might itself have taken part. Further, the committee feared that the Executive might, by an official acting on the committee's behalf, be brought into closer contact with the operations of the industries in areas from which it was excluded by statute and convention. There is the further point, not mentioned by the committee, that Treasury officials acting for the committee might try to influence the committee's view against a department, thereby attempting to use Members of Parliament in a dispute between ministers which should properly be settled in the Cabinet.

This report disclosed the inadequacy of the facilities available to M.P.s. The House of Commons' librarian, who is responsible for the very limited research service, told the committee that it would be difficult to fit an extra man of high enough qualifications into the normal work of the library, because he would be unable to take part in the customary circulation around the department and might find difficulty in getting promotion. The committee thought these difficulties could be overcome and that perhaps someone could be appointed from a university on a temporary basis. They agreed that their clerk should be their principal officer, but that he should serve five or six sessions so as to gain experience; and they asked for a second clerk who would, in addition to providing greater assistance, assure continuity of experience. As a result of this report, the next committee was provided with a second clerk but no other changes were made.

The committees so far appointed have not had power to take evidence outside the House of Commons; although this does not prevent individual members from paying unofficial visits to any of the establishments of the industries they are examining. Although in their first inquiry they took evidence from interested M.P.s, they have since established a tradition that they normally only take evidence from the sponsoring Government department, from the Treasury and from the board chairmen, accompanied by such of their colleagues or officers as they care to bring with them. The committee which examined the gas industry also took evidence from the chairman of the National Coal Board. They have, however, on occasion asked for memoranda from outside experts. One suggestion that had been examined in the Special Report was the use of an outside assessor, as had been done in the case of the Select Committee on the Telephone Service in 1921. The committee had particularly in mind the employment of a chartered accountant or economist. Although the Leader of the House, after at first opposing it, changed his mind on this suggestion, no such appointment has yet been made. On the whole, the committee undoubtedly have preferred that any additional help they receive should come from within the House, and this view was strongly supported in evidence by the Leader of the Opposition, Mr Gaitskell. There is no doubt that the research facilities provided in the House ought to be of sufficient quality and quantity to be able to provide such general assistance as any committee would be likely to require in examining the accounts and statistical material.

On the other hand, the experience of the committee has been that a Clerk of the House, recruited in much the same way as an administrative class civil servant, is perfectly capable of becoming proficient at assisting the committee by breaking down and presenting statistical material, and at assisting the chairman in extracting from the reports and memoranda the main lines of useful inquiry, provided he remains with the committee for a number of sessions. What has perhaps been missing is any expert assistance in interpreting the accounts, on the need for which there have been differences of opinion between the two sides of the committee. The committee has never sought assistance on the purely technical aspects of the industries' operations. This is clearly right, as a parliamentary committee, carrying out its work at meetings lasting a couple of hours once or twice a week during a session, is obviously a quite unsuitable body to judge detailed expert evidence on highly complicated matters. For the same reason it cannot, except by inference, pass judgment on the efficiency of an industry's operations, whether in the managerial, commercial or operational sphere. It has been suggested, for instance, by Lord Morrison, that the industries should be subject to regular efficiency audits. More recently, Professor Robson has suggested that this should be done by an audit commission which should report to the Select Committee.

This suggestion, or any similar suggestion for operational research or the use of outside consultants, overlooks an essential feature of such inquiries. They can only be successful if they are carried out with the goodwill of the management of the organization in which they are operating, and this is unlikely to be forthcoming if they are undertaken at the request of an outside, and potentially hostile, body to whom they are to report. Furthermore, such inquiries, when they are successful, involve continuous association between the consultants or researchers and the management staff, and nearly always lead, during the course of the inquiry, to changes in organization or methods. It would be much harder to get improvements accepted by management at all levels if the inquiry were being conducted on behalf of a body not itself responsible for carrying out the changes required, and among whose members there might be some not averse to using the disclosure of any faults for partisan and propaganda purposes.

## The Impact of the Select Committee

It may well be asked what effect the Select Committee has had on the industries into which they have inquired, on Government policy towards them or on the attitude of Parliament. Unlike the established tradition for the Select Committee on Estimates, by which the department replies to the committee's recommendations and the replies are issued as a report by the committee, no rule has yet been established about the form of reply to the committee's reports. In the case of two of the earlier reports, on the North of Scotland Hydro-Electric Board and the National Coal Board, replies were made by the appropriate ministers in debates, and each board published its own answers in its next annual report.

In the former case, the board accepted the committee's recommendations for competitive tendering for generating plant and fixed price contracts, and agreed to explain how depreciation costs were calculated, and to publish details of costs of schemes compared with the estimates for them. The Coal Board's replies to various suggestions made by the committee, none of a major nature, were in general non-committal. On one point – that the minister should have statutory power to give the board specific directions on prices, but that otherwise the board, having consulted the ministers as to the public interest, should take full responsibility for the decision – it reported that the Government did not accept the recommendation and with this it was in agreement. The ministry accepted the committee's view that the board should provide the ministry with fuller details of its less profitable projects.

In the case of the air corporations, although replies had already been given in the House of Commons by the minister, full replies, together with the comments of the Minister of Aviation, were later received by the committee and published. This report covered the supply of new aircraft, fares, routes, operations, maintenance, subsidiary and associated companies, competition with the independent airlines, and relationships between the corporations and between them and the Ministry of Transport and Civil Aviation. It included comparative operating figures for other airlines, and it made some criticism of maintenance costs of both airlines. The committee's views on the competition from the independents were cautious; but it expressed the opinion that an arbitrary division of traffic between B.O.A.C. and the independent companies, based on a definite percentage of the traffic, would hinder the efforts of B.O.A.C. to improve the efficiency of the service and to expand its activities. On the controversial recommendation that the corporations should receive subsidies for routes operated for social or political reasons, the corporations indicated their support, but the minister turned it down. The other main recommendation was also directed at the minister and was intended to reduce the degree of non-statutory control which he exercised, by ensuring that when he wished to override the commercial judgment of a board, he should do so by directive, which should be published. The minister's reply, while maintaining the need to keep ministerial responsibility for a number of matters, failed to make any reference to the point that this responsibility was exercised without statutory authority.

Perhaps the most influential report so far has been that on British Railways. This was because it took place at a time when the Government was considering a major reorganization of the

British Transport Commission, and for this purpose appointed an advisory panel of businessmen to study the means of doing so. The Prime Minister, at the time of their appointment, had said that their task was to break up the railway system into autonomous regions. The Select Committee, with a Conservative majority, unanimously reported in terms hostile to this proposal, and the fact that its chairman was an ex-minister and Deputy Chairman of the Conservative Party gave powerful support to its views. As a result, the subsequent proposals of the Government were far less drastic than they might otherwise have been.

The committee dealt at length with the structure of the British Transport Commission and its relationship with the Ministry of Transport, with its finances, with the plans for rationalization and modernization of the railway system, with productivity and technical resources, and with performance. It was extremely critical of the manner in which approval for substantial schemes in the modernization programmes had been given without any agreed basis of calculation of the financial return on them, and without adequate comparison of their economics with those of possible alternatives. It drew attention to the late introduction of an improved costing system; but while recognizing the value of regional accounting, refused to commit itself on its practicability. It also criticized the commission's attitude to the serious shortage of qualified engineers. But again the committee's main recommendations concerned the powers exercised by the minister and the responsibility for unprofitable services.

The B.T.C. and the Ministry of Transport sent their comments on the report to the committee in March 1961. The commission replied at length to the suggestions made by the committee, with many of which it was in agreement; but on the controversial question of unprofitable services it emphasized the technical difficulties of identifying them. The ministry replied that the Government must reserve their views on the subject, as the question affected other nationalized undertakings.

It will be seen that the most significant feature of most of the reports so far has been to direct attention to the extent of the powers exercised by the minister, and the responsibility for deciding when services are provided or decisions taken 'in the national interest'. In fact, the committee has almost established the doctrine that boards should, except in minor cases of cross-sub-sidization, operate on commercial principles, unless instructed to do otherwise by a directive for which the minister can be held responsible. The Government has gone so far to meet the views of the committee as to state in the White Paper on financial and economic obligations that when a board modifies its proposals because of ministerial pressure it should be entitled to a written statement of the minister's views which could be published. The Government has also admitted that unprofitable activities should be taken into account when fixing the financial objectives of the boards. The committee has been careful to carry out the injunction not to trespass on matters normally the subject of collective bar-gaining. This has made it tread warily on such matters as the cost of B.O.A.C.'s maintenance, and work study on British Railways; on both of which, however, it reported.

On the former, where it exposed a bad situation, it has been criticized for not hearing trade union views; which it could not do in view of its decision not to hear evidence other than from the boards. There is no reason to believe, however, that the views it expressed – which did not purport to allocate blame for the situation – would have been significantly affected if it had.

The need, from time to time, to introduce legislation to increase the borrowing powers of the boards has provided one of the oppor-tunities for parliamentary criticism. A group of otherwise not very influential Conservative Members, who would like to see Parlia-ment in control of the boards' annual rate of investment, have used these occasions to extract a number of concessions from the Government.

The method of sanctioning the amount which a board may borrow is by a Bill which raises the existing limit on outstanding advances made by the minister and, in the case of the N.C.B., specifies the limit of the amount which can be borrowed in any one year. The latter figure can be raised by order, not requiring the affirmative approval of the House of Commons. The first con-cession was made in 1956 on the occasion of a Bill to increase the N.C.B.'s borrowing powers for a period of ten years. The period was reduced in committee to five years. A more significant amend-ment was moved by Mr Nabarro, the leader of the group of Tory rebels which was carrying on the campaign for the control of the nationalized industries' rate of investment. This would have had the effect of compelling the minister to introduce a Statutory Order, requiring affirmation by a resolution of the House of Commons, to cover each year's rate of borrowing. This was turned down, but during the debate the minister promised to publish an annual White Paper on 'Investment in the Fuel and Power Industries'.

This has now been expanded into the White Paper on 'Public Investment'. Some further concession towards the critics' point of view was made during the passage of the Electricity Borrowing Powers Bill of 1959. The minister then responsible introduced amendments to reduce the total amount that could be borrowed from £2,300,000,000 to £1,800,000,000. Any further amount within the ceiling of the higher figure was to require a Statutory Order, subject to affirmative resolution by the House of Commons. This change reduced the period within which the minister would have to come to the House for further authority for the Electricity Council to borrow, and so ensure further debate. In January 1960, the Minister of Power accepted an amendment to reduce the annual borrowing power of the N.C.B. from £75,000,000 to £50,000,000, with the probable effect of providing one extra debate on the coal industry in the then current Parliament.

## Control Mechanisms Reconsidered

It is clear that the boards of the nationalized industries are subject to strong and continuous control by Government over a large field of policy-making. This control is exercised in the first place by the appropriate minister, partly in what he conceives to be the national interest, and partly under pressure from M.P.s with strong views, constituency interests, or merely acting from motives of party doctrine. Sometimes the very existence of parliamentary pressure can be used by a minister to reinforce his own views against those of a board. It is further exercised by the Treasury, both in its capacity of economic planning department and as commercial banker.

While measures, such as greater security of tenure for board members, might be devised to protect the boards from political spite, it is difficult to believe that any Government could, or should, divest itself of its powers of control over investment or such other matters as are genuinely in the national interest. Criticism of Governments for interfering too much in the investment policies of the boards is directed at the wrong target. What is needed is not less, but more, planning of national investment – including that of the larger private companies. On the other hand, when a minister forces on a board, for whatever reason, a policy which it may feel to be against its commercial judgment, he should do so openly. If the cost of carrying it out is substantial, it should be paid for by the exchequer. This would serve the dual purpose of relieving the industry of unnecessary financial loss or of the need to raise prices against some consumers, and, at the same time, of allowing Parliament to decide whether or not it wishes to provide out of taxation this particular form of subsidy. This right to decide priorities in the use of funds raised by taxation is, after all, one of Parliament's main responsibilities, and it should not be abrogated by forms of executive cross-subsidization, which are covert taxation on particular classes of consumer. If a Government wished to insist on a particular policy against a board's wishes, it would then have to defend it in the House of Commons.

Except for questions on day-to-day administration, on which the rules might well be made more flexible, M.P.s have as many opportunities for inquiry into and criticism of nationalized industries as they have in the case of Government departments. In addition, they can communicate direct with the board chairmen and are always welcome to pay visits to their establishments. The idea that Parliament could in any way investigate the efficiency of operation of these industries is quite unrealistic. Members must use their judgment on these matters, based on such evidence as they receive from the reports and accounts, from the reports of the Select Committee, and from their constituents.

The Select Committee performs the function not of controlling the boards, but of informing Parliament of their policies and problems; of disclosing the degree of ministerial interference and deciding where responsibility for decisions lies; and of ensuring that there is adequate machinery within the boards themselves and within the Government departments for deciding the level and priorities of investment, and for maintaining efficient operation.

None of this will satisfy those who have demanded parliamentary control of the nationalized industries; but this demand was always based on a misunderstanding of what Parliament today does. It is a myth that Parliament in any real sense 'controls' the Government, or even the estimates for expenditure which ministers present. What, in particular, the House of Commons does is to provide from its majority the members of the Executive; to question and criticize them on policy and administration; and to help, by debate, to form future policy where that is not strictly of a doctrinaire character. The idea that Parliament could control in detail the level of investment of the nationalized industries is nonsense. That level cannot be separated from the general level of industrial investment and must always be subject to the economic decisions of the Government of the day, to be supported, as are the departmental estimates, by the full weight of the Government's majority in the House of Commons.

This is not to say that Governments will take no account of the views expressed by M.P.s on the direction and level of industrial investment as a whole, whether these are expressed in general economic debates or in debates on the White Papers on public investment; but the final decisions are those of the Governments, for which they can be criticized, and which can only be reversed by their defeat.

The dilemma with which this chapter opened has clearly been resolved in favour of ministerial control and against the independence of the boards. The question that remains is whether the position of ministers vis-à-vis these industries should not be taken a stage further. The theory that the boards are independent commercial enterprises has been shown not only to be unreal in practice but also undesirable in principle. The pattern now being adopted for the Post Office of a semi-independent board operating commercially outside the normal control of annual estimates and appropriation accounts, with the Postmaster General as its chairman, could be copied. While this would not be a suitable form for industries producing a variety of goods subject to rapid technical and market changes, it is suitable for the basic services, of a largely homogeneous character, provided by the existing nationalized industries. It would still be necessary that a minister should interfere with the operations of an industry as little as possible, leaving its control to a chief executive; and he would always be free, as Mr A. H. Hanson has suggested in his book *Parliament and Public Ownership*, to say in the House of Commons that as there were some matters in which he did not interfere he did not propose to answer questions on them. On the other hand, ministers would no longer be able to refuse to answer on the large number of policy questions, great and small, on which at present they, not the boards, take the final decisions. These suggestions would certainly alter the overt form of the boards of our nationalized industries; but it is likely that the nature of the machinery by which decisions in them are made would be changed remarkably little.

# CHAPTER SIX

# LABOUR RELATIONS[1]

ONE of the benefits expected from nationalization was an immediate and significant improvement in labour relations in the industries concerned, which would serve as an example and a model to the private sector of the economy. That some of these hopes have proved illusory is undeniable, but it is less easy to determine the reasons or apportion blame. Nor is it always easy, in the light of the barrage of hostile Press and other criticism, to compare labour relations fairly as between the public and private sectors.

As we saw in Chapter I, it was never very realistic to expect that the mere act of nationalization would transform labour relations – especially as the achievement of full employment has forced private industry, since the war, to improve its own practices. But this does not fully explain the disappointing record of some – but by no means all – the nationalized industries in this field.

To the general public, 'good' labour relations too often simply means the absence of industrial disputes. According to this criterion, one would expect to find the best labour relations in the armed forces – a conclusion not everybody would find automatically acceptable! In fact, of course, the incidence of strikes is a negative and therefore inadequate criterion of the state of labour relations in a concern. Good labour relations are something much more positive, and can perhaps be described as a mutual desire on the part of labour and management, at all levels, to work together for common objectives. The objectives should be the security, welfare and efficiency of the industry on the one hand, and the improvement of the wages, conditions and well-being of the men in the industry on the other. These objectives should not be regarded by either management or men as contradictory. On the

[1] In the preparation of this Chapter, I have received invaluable assistance from Rex Winsbury – Editor.

contrary, they should be regarded not merely as complementary, but as indivisible. This does not, of course, imply that the interests of labour and management are always identical, but neither are they always opposed.

What is the record of the nationalized industries? If we take as an index (despite its defects) the number of labour disputes, and the number of working days lost through disputes, what do we find? The record varies from industry to industry. Electricity and gas have exceptionally good records. On the other hand, on the railways there have been frequent threats of national strikes which, with one exception, have been averted only at the last moment. The record of the air corporations has been mixed but hardly inspiring. What of the coal-mining industry, probably associated more in the public mind with persistent labour troubles than any other industry? The fact that numerous unofficial strikes have taken place cannot be denied, although their extent can be, and has been, greatly exaggerated. Thus, since nationalization, the time lost through disputes in coal-mining has worked out at less than one day per man per year. More significant is the fact that time lost through disputes is considerably less than it was in the pre-nationalized coal industry. Thus, while the number of unofficial disputes in the industry is certainly disturbing, there has undoubtedly been a substantial improvement since nationalization.

The table on page 115 shows the number of disputes in coal-mining, and the number of working days lost through disputes for the years 1947–61, with the comparable figures for all industry.

It will be seen that the number of disputes in coal-mining is a high proportion of the total number of disputes in British industry – somewhere between two-thirds and three-quarters in most of the post-war years. But if one looks at the number of working days lost by disputes in coal-mining, compared with the total in British industry, a different picture emerges. The proportion here varies very considerably from year to year, reaching about forty per cent at the maximum, and falling to about seven per cent at the minimum. On average, however, the proportion is under twenty-five per cent.

It is clear, in fact, that the characteristic features of strikes in the coal-mining industry are that they are relatively numerous,

## INDUSTRIAL DISPUTES[1]

| | Coal-Mining Industry | | All Industry | |
|---|---|---|---|---|
| | Number of Disputes | Number of Working Days Lost | Number of Disputes | Number of Working Days Lost |
| 1947 | 1,049 | 912,000 | 1,717 | 2,432,000 |
| 1948 | 1,115 | 464,000 | 1,758 | 1,944,000 |
| 1949 | 872 | 754,000 | 1,423 | 1,808,000 |
| 1950 | 863 | 431,000 | 1,339 | 1,389,000 |
| 1951 | 1,058 | 350,000 | 1,719 | 1,692,000 |
| 1952 | 1,225 | 661,000 | 1,718 | 1,793,000 |
| 1953 | 1,312 | 395,000 | 1,746 | 2,169,000 |
| 1954 | 1,468 | 470,000 | 1,994 | 2,470,000 |
| 1955 | 1,793 | 1,113,000 | 2,424 | 3,794,000 |
| 1956 | 2,076 | 502,000 | 2,643 | 2,083,000 |
| 1957 | 2,219 | 515,000 | 2,855 | 8,415,000 |
| 1958 | 1,964 | 450,000 | 2,627 | 3,463,000 |
| 1960 | 1,666 | 494,000 | 2,832 | 3,024,000 |
| 1961 | 1,458 | 737,000 | 2,686 | 3,046,000 |

they involve relatively few workers, and they are of relatively short duration.

In this connection, it is significant that international studies show that in virtually all highly industrialized countries the number of disputes in mining is very much higher than in other industries. This suggests that there is something in the nature of the industry which leads to a propensity to strike – for example, the arduous and dangerous nature of the work, and the fact that the industry is highly localized and the workers tend, in many cases, to live in self-contained and relatively isolated communities. In addition, a most important factor is probably the system of wage payment at the coal-face. The application of a piece-work system to circumstances in which conditions may vary greatly from week to week, and indeed from day to day, provides many more opportunities for dispute than would occur, for example, in a factory.

The factors mentioned above are important, but they provide only a partial explanation of the number of disputes in the coal-mining industry. They do not explain the wide variation in the incidence of disputes between one Coal Board Division and another, and indeed, between one pit and another. There have been

[1] Source: *Ministry of Labour Gazette.*

suggestions that the incidence of disputes, and indeed the whole question of 'morale', varies with the size of pits, but in the last resort one comes down to the question of the relationship between management and men.

The overall record on industrial disputes in nationalized industry is, therefore, somewhat mixed, as indeed it is in private industry. In general, those nationalized industries which had a good record before nationalization have continued along the same vein, while those with a bad record have also continued along the same vein. But this generalization masks the improvement in coal-mining, and it also masks the deterioration on the railways – which springs largely from the relative economic decline in the position of the railways and of the railway worker, intensified by Government interference and in some cases inadequate management.

It is obviously impossible to separate labour relations from wages and earnings, and their negotiation. In some nationalized industries – not only the railways – Government interference on wage claims has damaged labour relations. Unions have tended to be frustrated in their dealings with the nationalized boards, as they felt that real control was being exercised by the Government. There can be little doubt, too, that the unions' belief in impartial arbitration received a blow as a result of Government action in 1957 and again in 1961, and this was also detrimental to good labour relations.

On the more positive side, nationalization has produced a *codification* of labour relations in the industries concerned. All the nationalized industries have comprehensive machinery for both conciliation and consultation. The Nationalization Acts made statutory provision for both types of machinery, and in most cases these have in practice been kept separate. Often, of course, the conciliation machinery existed before nationalization, and, from our point of view, it is the development of the consultative machinery that is of real interest.

This has been most marked in the electricity supply industry, whose labour relations record since vesting date has been exemplary, at least until the Government's 'pay pause' policy led to the threat of an official strike in October 1961. But certainly until then, with the exception of sporadic trouble caused by an unofficial shop stewards' movement, the industry had been totally free of strikes.

More important than this negative criterion, it has developed, under the influence of Lord Citrine, its first chairman and former general secretary of the T.U.C., a system of joint advisory committees that represents one of the most consistent and successful attempts yet made in Britain to bridge the great divide in industry between management and workers. As elsewhere, the consultative (or advisory, in this case) machinery deals with almost any matters not reserved for conciliation (that is, matters other than wages, hours and other things coming under the heading 'terms and conditions of employment').

This reserves for advisory committees such matters as health, welfare, training, suggestion schemes, safety and so on. But in practice these committees have also become forums in which management has reported to, and been cross-questioned by, workers' representatives about finance, investment and future planning. In practice also, these committees, though strictly *advisory* in powers as well as nomenclature, have tended to become *executive* in their functions, at least in the narrower field of welfare and the like.

The structure of the advisory machinery is broadly similar to that of the conciliation machinery. At the top of the pyramid is the National Joint Advisory Council, with full-time union officials making up the employees' side. Then each of the twelve districts has its district advisory committee. At the base of the pyramid, and most important of all, comes a series of about four hundred and seventy local advisory committees, whose nucleus is normally the works committee, with additional elected representatives, from technical, clerical and administrative staffs. Whether this identity of personnel, at least among the workers' representatives, is a good thing or not, is open to question. Probably it is not; but it may be inevitable for the moment. Similar machinery exists for clerical and for engineering staff in the industry.

The main emphasis of the system rests on the local advisory committees. It is important to remember the background against which they started. On vesting day there were five hundred and forty separate distribution undertakings and two hundred and ninety-seven power-stations, with a wide variety of practices in the human relations field – or in many cases a total neglect of the subject. Then, once the advisory system had been set up some months after nationalization, there were numerous subsidiary problems. No one quite knew what the scope of the new committees was. Local managers, who are the chairmen of the local committees, sometimes regarded them as intrusions into management rights, while on the other hand the all-important link between local advisory committee representatives and the general body of employees was neglected. In all these spheres much progress has been made in the last decade, although industry officials are the first to admit that much still remains to be done.

At national level, the acceptance of a large number of recommendations formulated in the advisory machinery had led to the creation of a code of national standards of welfare, safety, health and training. This has now cleared the way for the advisory machinery at all levels to devote more time to questions of the efficient running of the industry. In passing, it is also worth noting that electricity supply has a well-developed education and training programme, which amongst other things provides courses for people active in joint advisory work.

Secondly, it has now become standard practice for the manager of the power-station or the distribution district of an area to present a progress report at every L.A.C. meeting, and this has, on the whole, produced constructive reactions from the workers' representatives. One perennial problem the L.A.C.s have *not* yet solved is the resentment of many foremen and supervisors that the committees are usurping their role as the channel of communication between worker and management.

Thirdly, the problem of communication to the 'shop floor' has been recently tackled. The 1960–1 report of the N.J.A.C. says:

> In several districts there has been a sustained drive to bridge the gap between the L.A.C.s and the individual employee by associating the committees more directly with the small working groups which form naturally on the job. The method most usually adopted has been to encourage informal group meetings ... the principle underlying such meetings is the recognition of the fact that any organization of size must be thought of as a structure of smaller interlocking groups ...

most have been in power-stations ... separate meetings were
held for employees in boiler, turbine, maintenance and
fitting departments. Meetings were held during working
hours ... and it was decided that every effort would be made
to repeat them every two months or so to encourage their
acceptance as a normal feature of station life.

The report concludes:

All who have experience of informal group meetings have
reacted favourably to this method of bridging the gap
between the L.A.C. and employees generally. It is regarded
as a positive attempt to strengthen the industry's effectiveness
by extending communications and improving consultation.
Its outstanding merit is that it gives to every employee a sense
of direct participation in these processes.

It would be idle to claim that all this has produced an immediate revolution in employee attitudes. Indeed, the L.A.C. system
was still sufficiently vulnerable in 1960 for a number of the committees in London and South-East England to be virtually immo-
bilized by attacks from the unofficial shop-stewards' movement
mentioned earlier; the movement regards them as 'efficiency
committees' in disguise. But it does represent a consistent and
worked-out philosophy about the need to associate the rank and
file workers with the management of industry – about the need to
overcome what Marx called 'the alienation of the worker'. This
philosophy is perhaps reflected also in the gradual increase in the
power of the local works committees that has also taken place since
nationalization, though this has not been consciously pursued.

While the other nationalized industries have consultative and
conciliation machinery as elaborate as that in electricity, in most
cases it has been less effective. In the coal industry, for example,
there is a three-tier system of conciliation – operating at pit,
district and national level – with provision for independent arbitration on disputes which cannot be resolved by negotiation. In
1961, over 10,000 issues were referred to pit committees; in all but
500 cases they were settled there without having to be taken
to higher level. Yet the machinery is not fool-proof, as was shown
by the fact that during the year there were over 1,400 stoppages

in the industry. There have been complaints of delays in settling disputes, although the machinery seeks to avoid this by imposing strict time-limits within which issues must either be settled or referred for arbitration. At national level, there have been complaints that arbitration tribunals are liable to be over-influenced by Government policy.

However, the most important factor, in coal-mining and in other nationalized industries, is not the nature of the machinery, but the attitude of the men who operate it on both sides. This applies equally to consultation, where the degree of effectiveness varies not only from industry to industry but between different levels in the same industry – and indeed, in coal-mining for example, from pit to pit.

Nobody would claim that joint consultation has, by itself, transformed labour relations, even in those industries where it has had most success. But it has brought about considerable improvements, and it could bring about many more. With the abandonment by the unions of the traditional concept of 'workers' control', joint consultation has in fact become one of the most important measures for advancing industrial democracy.

Where joint consultation has failed to advance, the blame can be apportioned to both management and unions. In the last analysis, the quality of consultation rests on the calibre and the willingness to make it work of the people who operate it, and not on the formal machinery. This explains the variations in its effectiveness, not only for industry to industry, but in different parts of the same industry. Many managers regard consultation as a chore which has to be complied with, but which should be got through as soon as possible. In this respect, it is necessary for the boards, at top level, not only to set a good example in their own attitude to consultation, but to ensure that adequate training is given to management both on the general question of labour relations, and the importance of joint consultation. Above all, management must not regard consultation merely as a means of informing workpeople of pre-determined decisions. While information is important, and while it is the management's responsibility to take decisions, if the unions feel that they have no chance of affecting these decisions by discussion at consultative meetings, they will soon feel that there is little point in wasting their efforts at such meetings.

Although the unions pay the utmost lip-service to joint consultation, in practice their attitude has often been different. In most cases, far more attention has been given to questions relating to terms and conditions of employment than to matters raised under the consultative machinery. If this situation is to be remedied, there must be a reorientation of attitude on the part of unions. What is required is a deliberate placing of consultative work higher on the list of priorities (and this, of course, is true of management as well). If this were done, many other things would follow. For example, there is an urgent need for unions to provide more training for their local representatives, if the latter are to fulfil their functions properly. While the Electricity Council may be commended for the introduction of training courses for representatives on joint consultative committees, the training of union representatives should, in fact, be the responsibility of the unions. This is not to suggest that the unions have done nothing in this field. The Transport and General Workers Union and the National Union of General and Municipal Workers, both with many members in nationalized industries, have highly-developed educational courses, particularly for local officials. Again, some of the areas of the National Union of Mineworkers run most ambitious day-release schemes in conjunction with the extra-mural departments of near-by universities. Under these day-release schemes, over one hundred men attend courses in economics, industrial relations and so on, for one or two days a week over a period of three years.

It is clear, however, that far more needs to be done on education and training. The unions also need more specialist advice. If they are to discuss intelligently management decisions, which are based in most cases on highly technical data, then the unions must be able to understand this data, and this they will not be able to do satisfactorily unless they make more use of specialist services.

Another positive aspect of labour relations in nationalized industries is the field of 'fringe' benefits, where substantial achievements have been recorded. All the nationalized industries operate sick-pay and pension schemes, and redundancy agreements. Coal-miners also enjoy special supplementary benefits for industrial accidents and diseases, and a special fatal-accident scheme. Great strides have also been made in the provision of medical services, and in safety matters. The provision of housing has also been important, as has the provision of travel and lodging allowances. These 'fringe' benefits could certainly be further improved. There is an indefensibly wide difference between staff benefits, for example regarding retirement pensions and sickness payments, and those of manual workers. Nevertheless, this is a sphere where, to a large extent, the nationalized industries have led the field. The principle of paying such benefits to manual workers has been established, even if the amounts are not yet satisfactory. It is true that similar benefits exist in the best private-enterprise firms, but these are not typical of the whole. It has been estimated that only some 8,000,000 out of the nation's 24,000,000 employees are in industrial pensions schemes, and of these a substantial proportion are in the public sector.

Finally, in the nationalized industries there has been a determined effort to establish proper education, training and apprenticeship schemes. Again, these schemes are far from faultless, but they do make an important contribution to better labour relations, as well as to improving the efficiency of the industries concerned. The knowledge that there is a clear path available from the bottom to the top is in marked distinction to the pre-nationalization position, especially in coal-mining.

Labour relations, however, do not exist in a vacuum. They cannot be divorced from the past history of an industry – particularly unhappy in the case of coal – or from its current economic position. The economic decline of the railways in the post-war period has clearly posed appalling problems. Railwaymen have seen their earnings worsen compared with other industries – and, perhaps more important, compared with their relative position in the industrial league before the war. This, in turn, has adversely affected labour relations. The nationalized industries, in short, are not a homogeneous group. They differ in their histories, their present position and their future prospects – and all these things affect the quality of their labour relations. Moreover, in the last resort industrial relations depend on people – on their relationships, their abilities, their characters. This personal element can transcend in importance the influence of industrial structures or the pattern of ownership. But this all-important factor cannot be legislated for or decreed into existence.

A proper analysis of labour relations must, therefore, go beyond a study of dispute statistics and beyond formal agreements on conciliation and consultative machinery. One crucial test is how labour relations have stood up to change. In all the nationalized industries there have been very considerable technical changes in the past decade – intensive mechanization in the pits, modernization on the railways, concentration and larger units in gas and electricity, and continual technical changes in the air corporations. In addition to technical change, the coal industry had to face a fall in demand of some fifteen per cent in a period of three years, and a corresponding reduction in manpower; and at the time of writing, in 1962, it is apparent that a problem of even bigger dimensions is looming up on the railways.

The nationalized industries' record in response to change has been on the whole a remarkably good one, and there has been comparatively little resistance to mechanization or other technological developments. Undoubtedly, joint consultation has played an important part here, and so have the comprehensive redundancy agreements. In addition, national ownership has made it easier for boards to offer displaced workers alternative work, than it would be in a multi-firm industry. The Coal Board, while reducing its labour force by some 120,000 men in three years, was able to keep the percentage of mineworkers unemployed well below the national average throughout this period. Credit is due both to the union and the board for arranging and facilitating alternative work for men displaced through pit closures, and to the board's policy of stocking coal rather than resorting to large-scale dismissals.

In this case, co-operation between board and union worked remarkably smoothly, but relations have not always been so good. The adjustment of union attitudes to the fact of nationalization has been a patchy affair. On the one hand, the unions have argued – correctly – that their primary duty and responsibility is to maintain and improve the conditions of their members, and that nationalization has not changed this – especially when the public sector remains a comparatively small part of the total economy, and when the economy (particularly the public sector) is under a Conservative administration. The unions are right to insist that in these circumstances they must remain completely independent of the nationalized boards if they are to do their job properly.

On the other hand, one might expect that the unions would try to play a more constructive role in industries once they are nationalized, and to some extent they have done so. The National Union of Mineworkers has stated publicly on a number of occasions that, having demanded nationalization and got it, it has a responsibility for ensuring its success. (Union pressures played a much bigger role in precipitating nationalization in coal-mining than in the other nationalized industries.) But this feeling of responsibility, while shared to some extent by all the unions concerned, varies greatly in its intensity not only from one union to another, but also at different levels in the same union. Moreover, nationalization has so far brought about little change in union structures, and in most nationalized industries there is still a multiplicity of unions. It is, for example, regrettable that the affairs of the railways – difficult as they would have been in any event – have been still further complicated by the mutual jealousies and failure to agree on a common policy of the three railway unions. Here is a clear case where the unions could have done more to make nationalization work.

One interesting development has been the growth of white-collar trade unionism in the nationalized industries. This, in most cases, has reached virtually the highest levels of management, particularly in the Post Office and the electricity industry. This should lead to a greater understanding of labour and union problems by management, and accelerate the trend towards abolishing many of the distinctions between staff and manual workers.

Taking all the factors into account, and making allowance for the very considerable differences from industry to industry, the overall standard of labour relations in nationalized industry compares quite favourably with the average in private industry. All too often public discussion on the private sector pin-points the best and most progressive firms or industries, and these are taken to be typical of the whole. This is clearly not so. There are many important sectors of private industry where labour relations are far from good, where proper consultative machinery is either inadequate or non-existent, and where fringe benefits do not compare in any way with those existing in the nationalized industries.

In this connection, it is interesting to note that some of the official suggestions made for improving labour relations in the motor-car and shipbuilding industries – for example, national consultative machinery and day-release schemes for shop-stewards – have been in operation for over a decade in the nationalized industries.

But is this good enough? No true friend of the nationalized industries would deny that there is still a good deal of room for improvement. First, there is the need to increase industrial democracy – that is to say, to increase the participation of labour in industry. This, in the first instance at least, could be done through the existing machinery. It does require, however, improved communications between management and men at all levels, and improved communications down the line on the management side and on the union side. Also, both sides of industry need improved education and training on problems of labour relations. Above all, there is need for management and men to work consistently at the task of achieving better labour relations. The most perfect machinery for conciliation and consultation will not work satisfactorily unless there is proper understanding on both sides of industry of the true purpose of that machinery, and a sincere desire to make it work.

Secondly, there is an urgent need to reduce, and eventually to abolish, the distinction between 'staff' and 'labour'. Despite the great advances that have been made in fringe benefits, a comparison of staff schemes with those for manual workers reveals an appalling contrast, completely unjustifiable on economic, social or moral grounds. The abolition of this anomaly should, therefore, be a major aim in the future. Its achievement could bring about a substantial improvement in labour relations, for it is not merely a question of increased material benefits, but of transforming the status of labour throughout industry. The nationalized industries could, and should, be in the vanguard of this much-needed revolution.

# CHAPTER SEVEN

# RELATIONS WITH PRIVATE INDUSTRY

*by*

## JOHN HUGHES

ONE of the men responsible for purchasing in a nationalized industry has in his office a statuette of a milch-cow. The aptness of the symbol will not be lost on anyone who has examined the relations between nationalized industries and industry and commerce in the private sector. In general, when nationalized industry has supplied goods and services to private industry it has done so at prices that have not even covered operating and replacement cost. On the other hand, the conditions under which nationalized industries have had to handle their purchases from private industry have been such that the costs they have incurred (both the original cost, and subsequent operating costs) have been higher than they might have been under different rules of the game.

It does not, therefore, involve hyperbole to state that this relationship has been characteristically one involving the economic exploitation of the nationalized industries. This is not, as such, to argue a 'conspiracy' view of their history. For one thing, among the factors that have reinforced each other and combined in the exploitation of the nationalized industries have been organizational deficiencies in purchasing, and 'crash' programmes of investment expenditure. Besides, one has to distinguish between short-run and longer-run effects. Private sector industry and commerce is the main user of nationalized industry products. The economic relations accepted, so far, between the two sectors push up the entire structure of nationalized industry costs, and thus force them to charge higher prices to private industry in the long run. (This in its turn has unpleasant implications for those nationalized industries that are confronted by direct competition from private industries.) The Government, at any rate, has recognized in a number of policy statements and measures in 1960–1, particularly in Cmnd. 1337, 'The Financial and Economic Obligations of the Nationalized Industries', that the previous relationship between nationalized and private industry cannot be continued without serious long-run consequences. Short-run exploitation involves longer-run headaches, both in financing and in cost structure.

Nevertheless, it would be wrong to underestimate either the extent of monopolistic exploitation of the nationalized industries, or the scope of the activities and pressures of industrial lobbies in influencing policies in this field. A perusal, for instance, of the manifold restrictions placed on B.T.C. manufacture by the 1947 Transport Act leaves one extremely conscious of the assiduity of industrial vested interests in securing themselves against competition from the newly created corporations.

The economic relations between the two sectors hinge, in the first place, on sales and purchases. The dissection of pricing policy has already been undertaken, but the income distribution effects and the longer-run consequences for cost structures in the two sectors need some comment here. The process of nationalized industry purchasing, and the factors that have influenced it so far, call for detailed examination, partly because they have received so little attention in writing on the nationalized industries, partly because of the sheer size of the transactions involved. Finally, one comes to the problems involved in handling competition between the two sectors. This aspect links up with the examination of purchasing problems, since here the restraints on nationalized industry competition with suppliers (both statutory and informal) are extremely important. In the mixed economy there is a continual issue of the frontier between public production and private sector production. The question of direct competition between public and private industries appears too, in the context of fuel and transport.

*Nationalized Industry Sales and Services*

So far as can be estimated from national income and other data, only about one-third of the sales by nationalized industries, outside the nationalized industry sector itself, are to individual consumers or to other public users. Thus some two-thirds of these sales are to private industry and commerce. If a yardstick is sought by which to measure desirable revenue against the revenue actually secured, two possible criteria emerge. One is to argue that at least nationalized industries ought to have covered their operating costs and the cost of replacing capital equipment used up. The Government has stated clearly that this was not achieved:

> The total retained income of all these industries taken together has not been sufficient to provide for the replacement of assets used up in the production process, and this is also the case in most of the individual industries concerned.[1]

My own detailed estimation of this short-fall in revenue for the decade 1949–58 (for public corporations as a whole, but the bulk of this was on nationalized industry account) was £1,295,000,000.[2] Moreover, the gap between revenue secured and that required to provide for replacement was widening in the later 1950s as compared with earlier years. Thus nationalized industry revenue has on average failed to meet this minimum requirement by over £100,000,000 per annum; to meet such a requirement nationalized industry revenue from private industry would have needed to be on average some £70,000,000 p.a. higher, rising in the late 1950s to over £100,000,000 p.a. higher, than was actually secured.

The other revenue yardstick that suggests itself is that the nationalized industries should have secured from revenue the same proportion of the cost of gross investment (in fixed assets and stocks) as did large industrial companies. The National Institute study of the finance of quoted companies for 1949–53, some of the data of which was extended by the Central Statistical Office to 1954–5, enables us to assess this fairly accurately.[3] It is worth mentioning that the 'quoted companies' financed less of their investment from their own saving than did the company sector as a whole. On average over the period 1949–55 the quoted com-

[1] Financial and Economic Obligations of the Nationalized Industries, p. 5 (Cmnd. 1337).
[2] See Fabian Tract 328, 'Nationalized Industries in the Mixed Economy', pp. 8–9, where the subject is treated in more detail.
[3] N.I.E.S.R.: Tew and Henderson, 'Studies in Company Finance', pp. 10–11 and table A3, pp. 272–3; also C.S.O.: 'New Contributions to Economic Statistics', p. 12. 'Quoted' companies are those quoted on U.K. stock exchanges; the companies studied exclude in particular finance companies.

panies financed eighty-six per cent of their investment from their own current savings. For the nationalized industries figures are available for 1954–9 which are generally comparable. In these years the nationalized industries financed only twenty-seven per cent of their gross investment from their own saving. In these six years their gross investment was just over £3,500,000,000, and their saving fell over £2,500,000,000 short of that.[1] To have achieved the same proportion of self-financing as did the quoted companies, nationalized industry revenue would have needed to be some £2,100,000,000 higher, or another £350,000,000 a year after tax. On this basis private industry would have found itself paying well over £200,000,000 more for nationalized industry products each year. This is the approximate amount by which nationalized industry prices to private industry fell short of what private industry in its own financial practice would consider appropriate.

While such figures are useful as indicating the order of magnitude involved, care should be taken in drawing conclusions from them. For one thing, although over most of the life of the nationalized industries demand for their products has been highly inelastic, this was least the case for the B.T.C. and is less generally true today. That is, industrial demand for nationalized industry products (and therefore the scale of operation of these industries) would be affected by a major shift towards self-financing in the nationalized industries; this applies obviously to railways and coal, but also to the other fuel and power industries. For instance, supposing the Central Electricity Generating Board through its pricing not merely attempts to cover the capital costs of its plants (its debt here being the consequence of failure to self-finance so far), but also to cover the additional burden of nuclear plants built for non-commercial reasons, *and* to self-finance the bulk of current investment, what is the likely consequence? If electricity prices are thus set well above current generating costs, increased private generation of power by industry is to be expected. In other words, there are evident problems in the way of nationalized industries moving towards self-financing of current investment, while shouldering also the debt and repayment burden (currently a £250,000,000-a-year interest repayment even after the

[1] Cmnd. 1337, table IV.

write-off of railway capital charges) inherited from previous pricing policies.

Secondly, it should not be concluded that increased nationalized industry revenue at the expense of private industry would of itself, in the absence for example of price controls in the company sector, significantly redistribute income as between the two sectors at the expense of company profits. Nothing in the behaviour of our cost-plus economy should lead one to expect that.

Thirdly, if one is thinking of the short-fall in nationalized industry revenue as a redistribution of income in favour of the private industries that are consumers of nationalized industry products, the time scale becomes important. So far the redistribution is clear, but as the whole of nationalized industry net investment and some two-fifths of its capital consumption has had to be financed by borrowing, the burden is transferred to future consumers – including industrial consumers. The economy as a whole has (in the name of anti-inflationary pricing policies) been enjoying a lower level of nationalized industry prices so far at the expense of a higher level of nationalized industry costs in the future.

It is instructive to turn from the overall picture to look briefly and in a specific way at the type of pressure exerted by private industry both to keep nationalized industry charges down and to persuade nationalized industries to undertake investment directly useful to the consuming industry. I take as an example some of the activities mentioned by the British Iron and Steel Federation in its annual reports. Its main concern was with the B.T.C. and the N.C.B. The reader should bear in mind in what follows that accordiᵤg to Cmnd. 1337 during the period 1954–9 – which is the period covered in this illustrative survey – the net income (after depreciation) as a proportion of net assets was for the industries concerned:

Iron and steel    16 per cent
N.C.B.            3 per cent
B.T.C.            Nil (Cmd. 1337, table III)

One of the concerns of the B.I.S.F. was wagon supply and the building in particular of wagons of larger capacity which reduce transport and handling costs per unit. In 1954 it was agreed with the B.T.C. that the building programme (for which, of course, the Commission was paying with borrowed money; no one seems to have suggested that the B.I.S.F. might contribute) should be based on estimated steel production for the following year; in 1955 the B.T.C. agreed to advance its wagon building programme by a year. In the same year, the B.I.S.F. lodged objections with the Transport Tribunal against the B.T.C.'s proposals for maximum freight charges; in September 1956 the Tribunal announced several amendments to the Commission's charges scheme 'favourable to the steel industry and in accordance with the representations made by the Federation'. In 1957 the B.I.S.F. succeeded in 'negotiating important concessions' in the B.T.C.'s scheme to increase the daily demurrage charges for wagons. Interestingly, steel carrying wagons have a much longer turn-round time than other types of wagons – in 1957, eleven-and-a-quarter days;[1] i.e. the steel firms were, in fact, using railway wagons to hold stocks and, therefore, requiring more wagons. They were simultaneously pressing the B.T.C. to build more wagons, while negotiating to reduce the charges falling on them for undue delay in turn-round! In 1957 the B.I.S.F. were pressing the B.T.C. urgently to maintain the wagon building programme despite the restrictions on B.T.C. capital expenditure; in 1958 it reports laconically, 'there were surplus steel-carrying wagons of almost all types during the year'. (And who carried the cost both of the building and of the surplus capacity?) Late in 1958 the B.T.C. increased freight charges on the steel industry's raw materials by seven-and-a-half per cent (these increases should have been imposed earlier, of course, in terms of railway deficits); the B.I.S.F. actually objected, on the grounds that the increases were selective and 'discriminated against the steel industry'. It should be added, though the B.I.S.F. reports do not mention this, that at the same time off-setting *reductions* were made in freight charges for steel products, so that the net addition to steel costs (and railway revenues) was minimal.

Finally, in 1960, the steel industry found itself confronted by the Government's reorganization proposals for the railways under which the railways have freedom to fix freight rates: 'The Federation is supporting objections to the application of this policy to monopoly traffic.' At the same time the federation told the special advisory group on the B.T.C. that 'no attempt should be

[1] Report from Select Committee: British Railways (H.C. 254–1), appendix 44.

made to sustain the railways by restricting the freedom of users to employ road transport'. The B.I.S.F.'s concern with commercial freedom is somewhat selective; so too its apprehension about monopoly. One might mention here that in 1953, prices of colliery arches and pit props were decontrolled, and so were wheels and axles (the latter important in supplies to the railways).

As far as coal was concerned the B.I.S.F.'s main concern has been with adequacy of supplies. Since the N.C.B. was not managing to 'break even', even in terms of nationalized industry accounting, there was no vigorous resistance to price increases till recently. In any case, the B.I.S.F. could use coal price increases to justify before the Iron and Steel Board higher prices for steel. The 1955 report of the B.I.S.F. reports coal supplies as 'adequate but only because large imports were made'; it does not mention that the N.C.B. was required to meet the additional cost of imported supplies, instead of the steel industry (would the steel industry have done the same for the N.C.B.?). However, the steel industry reacted harshly to the increase in coal prices made in September 1960. The tone is interesting; the steel industry intends to

> reduce its vulnerable dependence on British coking coal ... Means to this end – including further reductions in the coke rate, the replacement of coke in the blast furnaces by other fuels, the exploitation of new processes bypassing the blast furnace altogether, and the possibility of importing coking coal – are all under close study.[1]

Subsequently, doubtless as a *quid pro quo*, the federation gave notice that it would terminate an agreement entered into in the previous year to assist outside coking plants (mainly N.C.B.) at times of low demand. It also made representations to the Industrial Coal Consumers' Council arguing that the total increase sought was too high (the N.C.B. in fact made a deficit of £22,000,000 in 1960) and discriminatory.[2] Here again it is neces-

---

[1] B.I.S.F. annual report 1960. The other references occur in the appropriate annual reports from 1954.

[2] The B.I.S.F. rightly argued against the N.C.B. justifying its increased price in terms of labour costs: 'although much was made of the increases following arbitration awards, no account was taken of offsetting increases in labour productivity'. True, but one has not noticed the B.I.S.F. taking their own advice

sary to recall the figures of net income in these industries that were quoted earlier. Throughout the B.I.S.F. has been looking to its own immediate interests; a very one-sided co-operation.

*Purchasing*

Considering the scale of nationalized industry purchases from private industry, it is surprising how little attention has been directed to the study of this aspect of nationalized industry operation. In the decade 1949–58, nationalized industries purchased about £12,000,000,000 of goods and services from the private sector. This was as big an item as the total nationalized industry wages and salaries bill in the same period, yet much more has been heard of the question of wages and costs than of the question of purchases and costs. Some £8,500,000,000 of the total of purchases were on revenue account, and about £3,800,000,000 on capital account.[1] The annual rate of purchases from the private sector is now in the region of £1,500,000,000.

One can hardly say that purchasing and the placing of contracts has operated within generally accepted procedures. Rather, such publicity as has been given to contract procedures has revealed a whole series of arrangements that do not fit commercial practice. It is true that the picture of purchasing arrangements has to be built up from scattered sources since this is a subject that very rarely figures in the annual reports of nationalized industries. The Monopolies Commission Report on the 'Supply of Electrical and Allied Machinery and Plant' throws a light on a major field of purchases, and the Herbert Report in its turn has commented on

in this respect when submitting claims to the Iron and Steel Board for price increases.

(The federation were also on strong ground in condemning the coal price rise as discriminatory. But the criticism should have been directed at the Government, which refused to let the Coal Board raise prices by as much as it wanted on those types of coal on which it made the biggest loss – that is, large coal for domestic households. The board therefore had to recoup by increasing its prices more sharply to those few sections of its industrial market where it had – or thought it had – a technical monopoly. Steel-making came into this category. – Editor.)

[1] Estimates based on tables 30 and 48 of the National Income Blue Book, 1959.

purchasing policy in electricity supply. The Howitt Report ('Purchasing Procedure of the B.T.C.', Cmnd. 262) in 1957, which followed complaints about purchasing procedures by the B.T.C.'s Supplies and Production Adviser, illuminates problems of general interest. Several of the reports of the Select Committee on Nationalized Industries have brought to light detailed material on contracts.

Out of this material emerge a number of interrelated problems that have so far characterized the operation of nationalized industry purchases from the private sector. These are in the first place organizational; nationalization created a *potentiality* of aggregation of purchases, and the economies that flow from large-scale purchasing and the bargaining power it gives are not inconsiderable. But for a number of reasons, these potentialities have only slowly been realized. But bargaining power in purchasing does not depend simply on size. It also depends on the degree of urgency felt by the production departments as to the provision of supplies. The organization of massive investment programmes, in electricity from the beginning of nationalization, and in coal and the railways from the early 1950s, creates a whole series of problems for purchasing departments. The consequences of these in terms both of contract prices and subsequent operating costs are extremely important. In essence, the great programmes of capital investment went through largely without adequate control to hold down unit prices.

This is not all. The purchasing of nationalized industry has been expected to take into account extremely naïve views as to the 'national interest' which may be summed up as 'buy British even if this means surrender to monopoly suppliers'. The argument has been used that placing contracts with British firms was helping to build their export potential. This last argument is found in strange juxtaposition to restraints on nationalized industry manufacture, particularly the direct prohibition of manufacture for export! This brings up a further important influence on purchasing. Not only are nationalized industries over a considerable part of their purchases faced with monopoly suppliers or collusive level tendering. They are prevented in various ways from overcoming such obstacles by vertical integration, that is by the deliberate organization of their own manufacture. It is, therefore, this complex of factors – organization, timing of investment programmes, 'buy-British', monopoly, restraint on self-supply – that creates a situation in which many of the potentialities of securing significant cost reductions remain unrealized.

The obstacles in the way of effective and co-ordinated handling of contract procedures really seem to have been twofold. In the first place, in Sir Harold Howitt's words, on the B.T.C.:

> There were naturally vast problems of control inherent in merging together different organizations with separate traditions and varying procedures ... much remains to be done, particularly in such matters as (a) reasonable unification of procedure as between headquarters, railway regions and divisions, (b) definition of the precise duties and rights of individuals, (c) codes of contract procedure, (d) control and standardization of stores. [Howitt Report, p. 50.]

This statement can stand, with varying emphasis, for other nationalized industries too. In electricity supply prior to nationalization there were a hundred and fifty undertakings responsible for the purchasing of heavy electrical plant. The coal industry had even more separate purchasing units. The second main organizational problem is the relation between purchasing organization and the 'user departments'. In the case of the N.C.B. until 1957 (when purchasing was strengthened following Fleck Report recommendations), all that was established was a supplies branch of production department, clearly indicating the subordinate status given to purchasing procedures. The consequence was that purchasing took place on the initiative of production management in fifty different areas, and that the board failed to secure either the economies from increased standardization of equipment in use, or the full advantage of the board's position as a major buyer. Similarly, in the B.T.C. it was clear (at least until after the Howitt Report) that the production departments were taking the initiative and checking the development of coherent purchasing policies. Sir Harold Howitt's reference to the relation of user departments and supply officers as a 'delicate question' in the B.T.C., and his modest suggestion that the contracts officer 'shall be brought in at an early stage in any negotiations and certainly before any commitment is made or order to proceed issued', is sign enough of the position that existed.

One aspect of this 'delicate question' that should not be omitted is that of the relations between personnel of the boards and would-be suppliers. This involves such matters as treating by sales representatives, and past connections with supplying firms. Sir Harold Howitt, concerned at the suggestion that contracts must 'lead to an element of entertaining, and that personal relationships with old and tried friends must have their influence in the placing of orders', asked the chairman of the B.T.C. if it 'applied to an abnormal extent', only to be 'assured that he does not think so'.[1] But what is 'abnormal', and did the chairman *know*? Clearly, the establishment of a strong purchasing department, ready to centralize purchasing where it is advantageous, and able to employ specialists and formulate firm procedures in contracting, is the real key to limiting the influence of treating and personal contacts.[2] It is, equally clearly, essential if the power of the boards as large-scale purchasers is to be mobilized.

Still, it was not until 1957 that in coal and transport strong purchasing departments were set up, and therefore even more recently that the effects of more coherent organization began to be felt. Even then, there are continuing problems. Production departments have resisted the limits on their power to initiate purchases, and in the B.T.C. the strong emphasis on regional decentralization, and more recently the pending 'disintegration' – as *The Times* called it – of the B.T.C. itself, have limited the scope for co-ordinated and centralized purchasing. In the N.C.B. the emphasis is heavily on purchasing negotiations being carried out at headquarters, and this has evidently been effective in securing price reductions (e.g. in conveyor belting and timber). The N.C.B. managed to hold its 'overall purchase price index' steady from 1957 until late in 1960. Progress in effective purchasing procedure is still uneven, however. For instance, progress chasing and inspection arrangements are still being developed, and more effort is being made to insist on firm contract prices instead of accepting price variation clauses and cost-plus arrangements. The Ministry of Works contract letting procedure has been influential

[1] Howitt Report, p. 7.
[2] This problem is not of course confined to nationalized industries.—Editor.

here, and their initiative from 1957 in insisting on firm price contracts for all building and civil engineering works has been important.[1] Yet elsewhere cost-plus contracts still occur (L.T.E.'s contract with A.E.C. for the production of Routemaster buses is understood to involve cost-plus), and it has not been possible to secure amendment to the price variation clauses of trade associations such as B.E.A.M.A., whose clause more than compensates for increases in labour or raw material costs during completion of the contract. Again, manufacturers resist the insertion of penalty clauses (e.g. for late delivery) and these can only be secured by an effectively organized purchasing department.[2] The ability to secure penalty clauses is extremely important, as in their absence failure to meet delivery dates can be expected. This has certainly added to the problems of the transport authorities (for instance, delays in delivery of steel rails have been notorious).

However, the effectiveness even of properly organized purchasing departments is limited if very large investment programmes are launched under conditions in which either the nationalized industry concerned, or the supply industries, or both, are not geared to handle them. There are a number of aspects of this, often reinforcing each other. Firstly, if production departments are demanding large-scale early deliveries, questions of price and contract procedure (for instance, attempts to secure competitive tendering) are likely to be treated as of less importance, and clearly the bargaining power of the nationalized industry is affected.

[1] How important, may be seen by looking at the contrast between the original estimates and final cost in the case of North of Scotland Hydro-Electric Board constructional contracts. (H.C. 304, 1957, App. II, Annex C.) The four most recent ones listed in the Select Committee Report finally cost £12,000,000; the original estimates were under £6,000,000. This is, of course, far too big an increase to be explained by the operation of price variation clauses alone; there were doubtless other faults in contract procedure too. Cf. Fab. Tract 328, pp. 21–2.

[2] According to the evidence given to the Select Committee (Report on Air Corporations) the B.E.A. always had penalty clauses in their contracts for aircraft. The penalty for late delivery started to operate three months after the contract delivery date. Vickers had to pay penalties for initial delays with the Viscount. On the Elizabethan, penalties were for both late delivery and shortfall in performance. Apparently the penalties were 'very seldom enough to compensate the Corporation', but 'in the case of the manufacturer ... effective' in inducing prompt delivery, (H.C. 213, 1959, qu. 421–3.)

Secondly, the other side of this is that supply industries will become heavily loaded; in the absence of surplus capacity (indeed, with the nationalized industry trying to encourage an expansion of capacity) suppliers are in a strong position. Trade association price-fixing, and purchases from established monopoly suppliers, become more unavoidable. It is just at this stage in the B.T.C.'s railway modernization plan (1955–6) that one-half of headquarter contracts in value were placed with monopoly suppliers or at trade association prices. Sir Harold Howitt stressed the influence of

> the size and phasing of the modernization proposals, the limits of the capacity of the contractors, and the obligation on the Commission to complete its task in a defined and short period ... [and consequently] normal procedure may have to be relaxed.[1]

The same problems had beset electricity at an earlier stage; generating capacity was inadequate, and the load of orders on plant manufacturers had outstripped capacity:

> The Central Authority were concerned to see that plant was installed as quickly as possible ... Against a background of plant shortage and power cuts, the Authority's position as a monopoly buyer was revealed to be less strong than they might have supposed ... also ... they found themselves negotiating with an industry in certain sections of which competition was limited by agreement between firms.[2]

But these problems were further accentuated where the nationalized industry making the purchases did not have the technical personnel to dictate designs and secure standardization of equipment purchased. The success of the electricity authorities in keeping down the costs of power-station construction per kilowatt capacity stems partly from their ability to press for the manufacture of much larger and more technically advanced generating sets, taking the initiative in specifying new standards required. Significantly, the C.E.G.B. since 1957 has been rapidly increasing research expenditure, thereby reinforcing the effectiveness of its

[1] Op. cit., p. 50.
[2] Herbert Report, p. 32.

purchasing procedure.[1] By contrast, the difficulties of the railways have been increased because, as a result of being starved of capital investment for a generation or more, they had not got the design teams and technical personnel to dictate contract specifications. The 'know-how' and the personnel were with the supply industries. Consequently the B.T.C. had (and in many fields still has) to buy equipment designed by the manufacturers; it thereby loses heavily by purchasing a multiplicity of designs instead of being able to standardize. This is, for instance, the case with railway signalling equipment; the railways buy from three firms 'who are themselves not keen to standardize because they are competitors',[2] and the designs they buy are those of the firms. The 'acute shortage' of skilled staff prevented the railways from designing standardized equipment. The railways are saddled with three distinct types of signalling equipment which operate in different ways. I am told that in one of the systems a light goes on when a section of the line is clear, and in another a light goes on when it is not. Whether or not the example is apocryphal, the difficulties arising from failure to standardize are evident enough. They are found, of course, in the case of diesels too. The combination of all these purchasing problems in a period of hectic investment expenditure means simply that much of what might have been achieved by way of reduction of operating cost through installation of new equipment is lost through higher prices for the equipment,[3] and higher operating costs from failure to secure standardization.

[1] In this case the boot is in fact now on the other foot. The C.E.G.B. has exploited the advantages of its monopoly power in a buyer's market to the full – as the financial results of its main suppliers show. But this is the exception that proves the rule. – Editor.

[2] The question of railway signalling equipment was pursued in detailed questioning by the Select Committee; cf. H.C. 254–1, 1960, qu. 1020–33.

[3] It may not be appreciated just how much higher the price may be under these conditions. Some indication is found by mentioning the price reductions offered by monopoly suppliers on finding that there is the risk of a competitive supplier appearing. In one case a price reduction of sixteen per cent compared with the previous order was offered, when in terms of wage and cost increases since the last order the purchasing department were expecting a twenty-eight per cent increase; a competitive supplier had appeared. In the case of vacuum brake cylinders, investigated by Sir Harold Howitt, Westinghouse reduced their price by twenty-four per cent when a competitive supplier appeared.

Apart from the pressures arising from 'crash' investment programmes, a major non-commercial factor in nationalized industry contracting has been the felt obligation to 'buy British'. In the case of the North of Scotland Hydro-Electric Board this policy was narrowed to one of 'buy Scottish'. Water turbine orders were placed with three manufacturers in proportion to their capacity on a non-competitive basis. The manufacturers had been induced to set up plants in Scotland, and this was apparently thought to require the exclusive placing of orders with them.[1] The 'sense of public responsibility' – to use the Select Committee's phrase – which led the B.T.C. to buy British diesels is striking: 'it led them to give British manufacturers the chance of providing the railways' diesels, when they could have gone instead to the more experienced foreign makers.'[2] There were, in fact, a number of complications in foreign purchase; General Motors was the low-cost producer, but major modifications would have been required to make their diesels suitable for British operating conditions.[3] This is not to say that there were commercial grounds for buying British, but the relative merits were less clear than in the case of electric locomotives (which the Select Committee did not look at). Electric locomotives from Alsthom or Oerlikon apparently have considerably better power/weight ratios than British locomotives; however, doubtless in the 'national interest' the railways are having to cope with the 'teething' troubles of inferior British-made locomotives. But what is revealing is the way in which the B.T.C. set about ordering British diesels; it would seem that it felt an obligation to assist a putative export industry regardless of the consequences of multiplicity of types on operating costs and with no attempt to select suppliers on commercial criteria. Here are the actual words of the chairman of the B.T.C.'s Technical Committee:

We have from the very beginning realized that we should give

[1] H.C. 304, 1957, qu. 774–802.
[2] H.C. 254–1, 1960 (p. lxxx).
[3] It is understood, however, that B.T.C. could have had licences from Germany for diesel manufacture; if so, this raises in a particular context the problem of nationalized industry production and the 'frontier' between nationalized and private industry which is dealt with subsequently in this chapter.

our own industry every opportunity of setting up a good home market, and setting their products on to the rails of British Railways before we [he meant 'they'; it is a savage irony that B.T.C. are statutorily prevented from exporting what they manufacture] could hope to sell in large numbers abroad. For that reason, at the beginning of the dieselization programme *we encouraged as many manufacturers as were competent* in the manufacture of diesel locomotives to provide us with their products. Indeed, in the early days we bought a *large number of rather small batches* of locomotives, and the first one hundred and seventy contained quite a large mixture of locomotives, so that there would be in that way *a chance for everybody to get in at the beginning.*[1] (My italics).

All that need be said is that this 'fair shares' approach occurs in other contracts and other nationalized industries;[2] clearly it is an arrangement in which all the advantages are on one side, and all the disadvantages on the other.

The issue of 'buying British' cropped up in its sharpest form in relation to purchases by the Electricity Authority; in three principal fields, turbo-alternators, boilers, and cables, strong trade associations prevented competition between firms. But the Electricity Authority never approached the minister to ascertain Government policy on purchase abroad, as a way of beating the price rings. The Herbert Report argued strongly that the authority should have attempted to purchase abroad:

> If on commercial grounds the boards consider that the invitation of foreign tenders would induce keener trading from home manufacturers, they should invite such tenders unless they have a clear instruction from the Government that such a course must not be taken. The responsibility of the industry is to generate electricity as cheaply as possible. The

---

[1] H.C. 254–1, 1960, qu. 1332A.

[2] For instance, N. of Scotland Hydro-Electric purchased water-wheel alternators on a non-competitive basis. They 'divided it up as fairly as possible taking into account their capacity and how far they do in fact manufacture in Scotland' (H.C. 304, 1957, qu. 803–5). The *Economist* commented sourly on nuclear power-station contracts dealt out 'as if they were a deck of cards' despite a thirty per cent range in tender prices. (*Economist*, June 25th, 1960.)

determination of the national interest is the responsibility of the minister.[1]

Whether or not one believes the problem can be tackled in the rather simplified way the Herbert Report would have it, it should be borne in mind that the economic basis of the 'buy British' slogan was extremely naïve. Shielding firms from competitive tendering at home is not the best way to secure the efficiency that will sustain exports. Nor is the overloading of industrial capacity with home orders necessarily making a contribution to the balance of payments; what is gained on import saving may be lost on exports foregone. This is and was, perhaps, least the case with the purchase of British aircraft by the air corporations; here a more adequate case can be made for buying British. Even here, it must be recognized that the policy has involved the air corporations in higher prices, and therefore higher operating costs. The reason for this is that 'no British manufacturer sets out to produce an aircraft unless he has a requirement from either a British corporation or a foreign company', and therefore the corporations have 'never yet bought an aircraft off the peg ... a much cheaper way of getting them'.[2] Foreign airlines, however, do buy 'off the peg' (for instance K.L.M.) and therefore 'get the advantage', as in their purchase of Viscounts. It is worth bearing in mind when claims are made for licensing independent airlines that the air corporations are expected to face these higher prices for their planes, while the 'independent' can come in once an aircraft has been proved to be effective and purchase on more favourable terms.

The criticisms made by the Herbert Committee of avoiding purchasing from abroad, and the more muted criticism of the Select Committee, may have some effect in making nationalized industry policy more flexible in this field. Another change in the situation is caused by the E.F.T.A. agreement which provides that public buyers should not discriminate against suppliers from other countries in the association.[3] This new factor has already been the subject of high-level discussion, and will certainly strengthen the

[1] Op. cit., p. 115.
[2] H.C. 213, 1959, qu. 360–8.
[3] Similar rules of competition apply in the Common Market.

hands of purchasing departments anxious to secure a bargaining weapon against level tendering by home suppliers (such as cables and lamps).

## Competition and the 'Frontier'

If a purchaser, even a large purchaser, is to bargain effectively with supply industries capable of organizing the restraint of competition, he must, in default of purchase abroad, be prepared to produce for himself, or at least threaten to do so. The extent to which the nationalized industries can attempt to follow such a policy turns partly on their statutory position, and partly, of course, on the extent of resistance or encouragement met from the minister concerned. In one case – the air corporations – the two aspects coincide, since only a ministerial order can give them the power 'to manufacture air-frames or aero-engines or airscrews'.[1] The statutory limits vary widely, and it is curious to discover that the most detailed and the most objectionable restraints on nationalized industry manufacture occur in Labour Government legislation; Conservative legislation simply extends them. What, for instance, is one to think of the wisdom of the framers of the 1947 Electricity Act in giving the Central Electricity Authority power 'to manufacture electrical plant and electrical fittings', but expressly providing that the authority is not thereby empowered to manufacture such plant for export![2] The Gas Act is even more restrictive, for not only does it repeat the prohibition of manufacture for export explicitly, but it also requires Area Gas Boards not to manufacture unless satisfied that facilities for obtaining plant at 'reasonable prices' are inadequate.[3] This is not unimportant, for if, say, the Electricity Authority were contemplating making its own plant requirements it might find such restraints onerous and liable to limit its efficiency of operation. This is apart from the peculiarity of pursuing the national interest by prohibiting export of nationalized industry products, and then buying British on balance of payments grounds! Under the 1957 Act, the Generating Board can manufacture anything it or the Area Boards require

[1] Civil Aviation Act, 1946, section 2(3).
[2] Electricity Act, 1947, section 2(3).
[3] Gas Act, 1948, section 1(2) (e).

'for research or development', but it is prohibited from manufacturing beyond this, i.e. it could not sell outside. Clearly, this seriously limits the possibility of building up large-scale manufacturing capacity as a way of reducing the power of monopoly suppliers. According to the electricity authorities' own figures, the cost of mechanical and electrical engineering materials to them rose between eighty and ninety per cent between 1948 and 1959; in the same period the National Income Blue Book index of the cost of fixed assets rose only fifty per cent – a considerable discrepancy.[1] As the legislation stands, the ability of the electricity authorities to challenge manufacturers by developing their own supply is seriously curtailed.

Much the same may be said of transport. The limits imposed on Transport Commission manufacture under the 1947 Act are extraordinarily detailed. Not only is the commission generally prevented from producing 'anything which is not required for the purposes of their undertaking', which creates the same obstacles to efficient large-scale production already pointed out; it is also prevented even from supplying its own needs in a number of directions. It cannot build ships (only barges); it must not exceed the number of chassis built for road vehicles by its undertakings in previous years; it cannot build road vehicle bodies apart from a small fraction of its own requirements.[2] There are many more restrictions of a similar nature. It is obvious that these manifold restrictions help to explain the decline in the railways' use of their own workshops, since these cannot be used flexibly enough to achieve operating economies. The restrictions on road vehicle construction are even more pernicious. The London Passenger Transport Act (and this provision was carried into the 1947 Transport Act) prevents the L.T.E. from producing more omnibus bodies at Chiswick than were on average manufactured there in

[1] On the operation of price-fixing by the manufacturers in this period, see Monopolies Commission 'Report on Electrical and Allied Machinery and Plant'. Average profit rates on cost on large motors and alternators sold in the home market by members of the ring were over twenty-five per cent in the early 1950s. More recently, however, the emergence of surplus capacity among the manufacturers and the tougher purchasing policies of the C.E.G.B. have led to a considerable squeeze on profit margins.

[2] Transport Act 1947, sections 2(2) and 2(4). The 1962 Transport Act, clause 13, radically extends such restrictions on self-supply.

1926–31. Given this restriction, it does not find it economic to produce its own buses at all. If it were free of these restraints it could reduce the number of vehicle types and organize production as well as flow servicing of buses, with considerable economies of scale. When the L.T.E. tried to place an order for buses with the Eastern Coach Works, Lowestoft, it came up against the same quota restrictions on production, for this firm is a wholly-owned B.T.C. subsidiary.[1] So much for freedom of competition!

Thus, even if one could expect a Conservative minister to contemplate with equanimity the proposal of a nationalized industry to produce for itself what is at present manufactured by a private industry, there are serious statutory limits on most nationalized industries. The N.C.B. is statutorily the least restricted, and yet has shown little initiative either in the field of manufacture, or in the development of retail sales. This may have been politically impossible in any case. What is more surprising is the failure of the N.C.B. to develop highly specialized constructional teams for colliery development. While there were good reasons for the N.C.B. not to have attempted to handle the larger part of the construction that was bunched into the 1950s, more organizational initiative in this field would have provided a valuable check on contract prices.

Similar criticism could be levelled at the other nationalized industries, though again the extent of informal restraint from ministers has been an important if little-known factor. The stress on statutory limits on manufacture, and even on self-supply, should not conceal the fact that corporations have not done all that they could have done within the statutes. Behind this inadequate response to these opportunities may lie more than ministerial resistance. The boards have tended to see themselves as having a single central purpose, which should occupy all their energies, and view such matters as peripheral. For instance the N.C.B.'s approach has been narrowly a 'coal-getting' one; the

[1] While chronicling the L.T.E.'s woes another statutory restraint can be mentioned. Under the 1953 Act the L.T.E. was not allowed to undertake private hire except within its own area and within a radius of ten miles from the boundary. As there is no problem of bus capacity on a Sunday, this involves a direct loss of revenue and makes more difficult the intractable enough problem of financing London bus services. (Cf. Transport Act, 1953, 18(3).)

railways have neglected, until recently, the opportunities of real-estate development of their central urban sites. There is a real organizational problem involved here; a corporation may be operating a heterogeneous range of activities already. To seize the opportunities of organizing large-scale self-supply may require the creation of semi-autonomous executives, and may also involve a co-ordinated action by a number of nationalized industries. As things stand, the power to follow up research and development by manufacture, as well as the obvious opportunities for self-supply, represent a Trojan horse, for all the statutory limits private industrial lobbies have secured. It is the will to use the animal that has been lacking.

But whatever may be ministerial reaction to a nationalized industry proposal to develop competition with the private sector in such fields, there is the even bigger question of ministerial handling of a situation in which the main products or services of nationalized industries are in direct competition with private sector industries. Here the initial ministerial reaction was to laud the virtues of free competition. (This attitude, of course, coexists uneasily with the various restraints on nationalized industry production, not to mention the wide use of subsidies in private industry.) This was, in fact, to lean rather heavily towards the private industries concerned, for the nationalized industries had various commitments imposed on them which the private sector had not. For instance, the coal industry was concerned as to its statutory obligation not to operate unfair discrimination; for some time it hesitated to offer long-term contracts for coal for this reason. The railways not only had their common carrier obligations, but also the procedures by which they could shed the most uneconomic of their services were cumbrous and slow. Both industries had acquired large fixed interest obligations, partly as a result of earlier Government intervention to hold down their prices.

However, the Government have had to pay attention to other aspects of the competition between coal and oil, and railways and private transport. In the case of oil, the balance of payments implications must have had their effect. The import bill for petroleum products reached nearly £500,000,000 in 1960. Although this was only £50,000,000 above the import cost in 1958, oil imports had, in fact, increased by more than a quarter in those two years, and only a ten per cent fall in import prices helped avoid a much larger increase in the value of imports. In the case of railways, working below capacity on most lines, the social costs of more traffic transferring from rail to road are considerable, given the congestion of the road system particularly in urban areas. Nor is the financial problem capable of easy solution; the more the railways seek to recover capital costs by higher tariffs to users, the more transfer of traffic can be expected. Consequently, there has been a shift of emphasis recently and the Government has brought in a number of measures which have been directly helpful to the nationalized industries facing this competition. The Government can, in fact, proceed in either or both of two ways. It can reduce the capital charges to be met out of nationalized industry revenue, or it can increase the taxation borne by the users of the competing product or service. In the case of railways the write-off of £400,000,000 capital charges is more important than the marginal increases in vehicle licence duty in the 1961 budget, but both moves are in the same direction. In the case of coal the 2d. per gallon tax on fuel oil represents a tax on coal's main competitor of over £1 per ton of coal equivalent (and is worth £50,000,000 a year to the exchequer). On this basis the coal industry is likely to be able to stabilize or increase output while making revenue surpluses, but the railways are still not within sight of a financial solution.

*Conclusion*

The development of more effective purchasing departments, the levelling off or decline in investment spending by nationalized industries, and the Government measures and statements of intention in 1960 and 1961 have modified, in some ways, the relations between the two sectors depicted above. Unfortunately, the great programmes of capital spending largely went through under conditions, as described, which prevented the nationalized industries securing the cost advantages that might have been hoped for. A number of problems in the relations between the two sectors are still largely unresolved, however. Nationalized industries are still faced with monopoly suppliers and level tendering in many fields. British entry into Europe may not seriously alter the pressure the industries are under to buy British, even if purchase abroad is one way to beat price rings. The future of the *de facto* and *de jure* restraints on manufacture by nationalized industries, this problem of the frontier between nationalized and private industry, is as much in doubt as the future place in the economy of nationalized industries as such. All these unresolved questions clearly matter a great deal, even in the narrow sense that these constitute the main opportunities for cost reduction open to the nationalized industries.

Nor can there be any guarantee that the statements of intention made by the Government in the White Papers on public investment and on the financial obligations of nationalized industries are more than pious hopes. The Government intends to shift from minimum break-even pricing to some element of self-financing of investment. But it proposes this in the context of an economy characterized by 'cost-push' pressures and beset by comparative cost difficulties. Similarly, it forswears the counter-cyclical fluctuation of public investment programmes which had its impact on purchasing and deliveries and helped to push up costs. But in the absence of effective control over the level, location, and timing of *private sector* investment, how much is this intention worth? However, it should be a comfort to private industries, faced with higher prices for the products they buy from nationalized industries, to recognize that this is no more than the inevitable back-wash from the economic exploitation of nationalized industries in earlier years.

# CHAPTER EIGHT

# COMMERCIAL RELATIONSHIPS
# IN STATE INDUSTRY

THE main nationalized undertakings in the field of fuel and transport have extensive commercial relationships among themselves. They are, to varying degrees, each others' customers. Thus nearly half of the output of the coal industry goes to other publicly-owned services, providing the great bulk of the fuel used by the electricity and gas industries. The coal industry also sells gas to the gas industry and coal to the railways; coal and railways are substantial users of electricity, and the railways carry 150,000,000 tons of coal and coke a year.

This interdependence involves continuous day-to-day contacts among the industries; it also implies a large measure of interdependence in the development of each. Clearly, the rate of expansion that is envisaged by the electricity industry and the sources of fuel required to sustain it are matters of considerable interest to the coal industry; so are the plans for gas. The plans of these industries are of no small importance for the railways. All the major public services are sensitive to changes in the quantity, qualities and prices of coal.

There is also a good deal of competition between the major nationalized industries. Coal, electricity and gas compete both in domestic and industrial markets, and public air services compete with rail. All are, of course, also competing with private industry.

It is often argued that there is far too much competition between these industries, that the nationalized industries are often working against each other's interests. Private enterprise operates through competition: must public industry do the same? Do the nationalized industries co-operate sufficiently? Should they not co-ordinate their activities so as to avoid clashes of interest, whether these emerge as competition between gas and electricity, or the difference of view in the coal and gas industries about methane imports, or competition between public air and rail services?

Moreover, now that the nationalized undertakings are required to show a profit, does this not mean that they are pursuing the same end as private industry – profit within the same framework – competition?

To put such questions in another way, are competition and profit-making consistent with the objectives of nationalized industry? It is only by reference to the objectives of public and private ownership that useful conclusions can be reached about the role of competition and profit. If the purposes of the two forms of ownership, the ends they exist to serve, are different, it is likely that competition and profit will have very different meanings in the two contexts.

### The Objectives of Industry

Any industrial organization, public or private, exercises certain rights and has to meet certain obligations. This interplay of rights and obligations can be conceived of as extending in three directions: first, in relation to the Government, the ultimate power in the community; second, in relation to parallel organizations with which it is engaged as a producer – its labour force, its suppliers, its competitors; thirdly, in relations to the consumer of its products.

For private firms, the obligation is to make profit. That is their raison d'être. They use their rights or powers to attain this objective. Profit is both the objective, and a convenient yardstick of the success with which that objective is being attained. They are given (though this is taken for granted) the right to exist as corporate bodies, and to organize themselves to make profit, by statute law. Their principal obligation, however, is not to the community, but to shareholders. The Companies Act is there mainly to protect the interests of the shareholders. Firms have, of course, certain obligations towards the community imposed on them for purposes of providing communal services (through taxation), or to protect human life (Factories Acts), or to preserve amenities (town planning legislation etc.). Other obligations have been imposed by the countervailing power of trade unions and big buyers. It is true that nowadays some firms take a larger view than formerly of their obligations en route for profit, and no doubt the growth of social consciousness as well as expediency have played a part in this. There remains, however, a wide area in which the private concern exercises its rights to secure its objectives in the way that suits it best. It can and does alter its structure by integration, to enhance profitability. Its aim being to maximize the difference between costs and proceeds, it can and does reduce the scale of its operations – as during a recession – if that enables it to improve profitability. The real wealth created by its activity is treated not as an end in itself, but merely as a means to profitability. Private industry has built up a network of organizations, headed by the Federation of British Industries, to preserve its rights and oppose developments which seem to threaten a greater measure of public responsibility on the part of private industry. (The alacrity with which private industry acts to acquire or regain its rights to profit was amply demonstrated by the commercial television and road haulage campaigns.)

The relationships of public industry in all three spheres – relations with Government, with parallel organizations, and with consumers – are more complex and more extensive. Nationalized industry is of course subject to the social legislation and the countervailing pressures which apply to the private sector. The rights of publicly-owned industry are more narrowly specified – could they diversify, or sell off their main assets? – but the profound difference between the two forms of ownership lies in the matter of objectives. Whereas the objective of private industry is profit, for private appropriation, the objective of public industry is not similarly predetermined.

The real wealth created by economic activity, the real 'value added' by work, is the difference between the value of final output, and the cost of materials and fuel (including wear and tear) consumed in the course of production. It is represented, that is, by the remuneration of labour, and of capital (fixed interest and equity). The fundamental difference between public and private ownership lies in the fact that the aim of private ownership is to appropriate, for the equity holder, as large a share as possible of the real wealth created. Private ownership is not in business to maximize the incomes of labour force or consumers. But from the standpoint of the community, what matters is not the maximization of profit income, but the maximization of the real wealth created. For example, the 'real value added' by a particular activity is, say, £100, of which £70 represents wages and salaries, £10 payment on fixed interest and rent, and £20 payment to equity holders. In terms of real wealth creation, it is immaterial if the division should be altered, to become: £70 to labour, £10 to fixed interest and £20 to the consumer in the form of lower prices.[1] From the standpoint of the profit-maker, the activity would have become worthless. Thus the distinction between the two forms of ownership, private and public, can be clearly drawn if we apply the test of *'cui bono?'* If we look at production through the eyes of the profit-maker, then only activity from which profit can be derived for him is worth while, and naturally the more profitable, the more worth while to him. If then the share of real wealth previously taken as profit were divided between labour and consumer, this manifests itself to him as 'higher costs' and 'lower proceeds'; and he will seek other avenues for his capital. For the community as a whole there is no such simple criterion, and accordingly for a nationalized undertaking, profit – or non-profit – has quite a different significance.[2] The absence of surplus after contractual obligations have been met may mean that some of the contracts – with labour, or suppliers, or for payment of fixed capital charges – are more onerous than in other industries; or that consumers are getting the benefits of lower prices. It cannot be concluded from this that the resources employed in that industry would be better employed elsewhere. Nor does it follow that a high rate of profit in a nationalized concern indicates a more efficient use of resources; Government may have decided to use the industry as a tax-gatherer. In other words, having no built-in compulsion for maximum profit, the nationalized industry can be an instrument of deliberate policy. It can be employed to achieve a variety of economic and social purposes: to show a

[1] The fact that it is immaterial from the standpoint of real wealth creation is quite familiar to national income statisticians: the real national income is not diminished if the share of profits should fall while that of labour rises *pro tanto*. The distribution of incomes may be altered thereby, but that is a different matter.

[2] It is not, and cannot be, denied that profitability is the most efficient guide to the distribution of investment if the primary purpose of work is deemed to be the maximization of private appropriation of wealth.

profit may indeed be one of the objectives which it could be given, but it is not necessarily a very significant one.

In some directions the obligations of nationalized industries have been defined by statute: to consult with the labour force and with consumers, to be accountable to Parliament. But the obligation to pursue the public interest is a general one, and in many respects it has to be defined according to circumstances. There is no simple criterion, such as profit, by which to measure the success with which it is achieved. The public interest is a criterion that must be applied in all its relationships. This gives rise to problems which for private industry simply do not exist.

The profound difference between the objectives of public and private industry suggests that the whole system of relationships through which public industry operates is of a different character from that of the private sector. In this chapter we are concerned primarily with the interrelationships of the main nationalized industries. How in fact have their obligations towards Government, towards their parallel organizations and towards the consumer affected their attitudes towards each other?

Governments have the power to issue general directives on policy to these industries, thus defining for practical purposes where the public interest lies with regard to the social and economic results of their activities. Many of the problems of these industries stem from the fact that the Government has shirked the task of making clear definitions of objectives, and making them publicly.

If we take first the economic objectives of a nationalized industry, there are three objectives which it could be required to attain – to make a predetermined level of profit, or of loss, or to break even. The first would mean that the industry was making a net contribution to the process of capital formation and to Government revenue from taxation; it would mean bringing part of the real wealth created or 'value added' to the surface, as it were, instead of passing it all on to the labour force or to consumers. Breaking even would imply neither net capital formation nor adding to taxation revenue, but that labour would be getting higher wages, or consumers lower prices, than they would be getting if profits were shown. Making losses means a transfer of income from outside the industry to consumers or labour within it. Each of these objectives could represent a deliberate act of economic or social policy decided upon by Government.

In fact, as we have seen, the Government has followed contradictory policies towards the nationalized industries, deploring the inability of coal and transport to break even, and suggesting that the others could be doing much better – and making it harder for them to do so by holding down their prices and encouraging competition from the private sector. Coal and transport have been put under considerable pressure. In both industries it is much easier to start a process of contraction than it is to halt or reverse it. In contraction, their relatively inflexible overhead costs, including interest charges, mean that revenue losses cannot be matched by reductions in cost; yet if they raise their prices, their competitive position is weakened. They are not free, as private firms are free, to alter their structure, diversify or amalgamate in order to maintain revenue or find more profitable outlets for their capital.

## Competition and Co-ordination

The nationalized industries have always treated each other strictly commercially, that is to say they have not discriminated in their dealings, whether as buyers from or sellers to each other, between public industry and the private sector. This competition was endorsed by the Ridley Committee on the use of fuel and power resources, which reported in 1952.[1] The Committee felt that 'the right policy, and the only practicable one, is to leave the pattern of fuel use to be determined by the consumers' own choice between competing services'[2], provided that prices and tariffs for fuel and power corresponded closely to the relevant costs of the particular services provided. Among some forty recommendations, designed to eliminate waste and promote greater efficiency in the industrial and domestic use of fuel, were two which concerned the relationships of the fuel and power industries. The first was that a Tariffs Advisory Committee should be set up to advise the minister – and inform the public – on the price and tariff policies

[1] Report of the Committee on National Policy for the use of Fuel and Power Resources, Cmd. 8647, 1952.
[2] Op. cit., para. 225.

of the nationalized fuel and power industries. This suggestion was not acted upon, presumably because the minister felt that pricing and tariff questions should be discussed directly with the industries concerned; probably, too, because the committee itself, in a separate recommendation, had already indicated where tariffs needed revising, namely by recommending that electricity tariffs should discriminate between 'peak' and 'off-peak' use. The electricity industry subsequently introduced lower tariffs for off-peak use; but as the Herbert Committee suggested in 1959, it is still open to question whether the promotion of all kinds of domestic use of electricity tends to expand off-peak use. In other words, if a substantial part of the domestic use is attributable to peak space-heating, consumers are paying considerably less than the real cost of the electricity they use for that purpose. The introduction of tariffs which discriminate between peak and off-peak use present formidable technical difficulties; however, if consumers were charged prices relevant to peak-load costs, that might well improve the load factor of the electricity supply system – and encourage the use of gas for heating purposes. It must remain an open question whether a Tariffs Advisory Committee, had it been set up, would have accelerated the difficult process of relating tariffs to the relevant costs of production.

The second suggestion made by the Ridley Committee affecting the relationships of the fuel industries was for the establishment of a Joint Fuel and Power Planning Board. Its tasks were to be more modest than its title suggests. The board, it was proposed, should determine which projects should be chosen as possible joint enterprises, and promote co-operation between the industries in carrying them out. No such body was set up. The job it was intended to do has, in fact, been done in a less formal way by the minister's Scientific Advisory Council, which effectively co-ordinates the research activity of the three nationalized fuel and power industries. Special committees have also been set up to investigate and report on possible ways of improving co-operation between them. Thus the Weir Committee of 1959[1] reported on co-operation between Electricity and Gas Boards as regards meter reading and collecting from slot meters; billing and collecting of accounts; service centres and showrooms; advertising, and breaking up of

[1] Co-operation between Electricity and Gas Boards, Cmd. 695, 1959.

streets. The committee found that none of these activities offered scope for more than slight modifications without very considerable dislocation of work. The report described some of the new ideas with which the Boards were experimenting, and suggested that it was along these lines, rather than through co-operative ventures, that the services could best be improved.

The Peech Committee of 1960[1] considered the supply of solid smokeless fuels up to 1965 – a market served by the coal, gas, and iron and steel industries. A third committee – the Wilson Committee of 1960[2] – conducted a detailed investigation into the work done to develop processes of deriving chemicals, gas and oil from coal. Investigations such as these have revealed a high degree of co-ordination and collaboration in the research and development work done in the fuel industries. The recommendations of the expert committees have been for changes of emphasis here and there rather than for major changes in direction. Their reports have done a good deal also to dispel popular misconceptions – such as, for instance, that there are unexploited economies to be gained from joint meter reading by the gas and electricity authorities.

*Collaboration*

Should the public industries collaborate more closely in other ways? The era of close governmental control of prices in the coal and transport industries seems to be passing. Should they exercise their freedom by attempting to sink their differences? It is hard to see why they should attempt to do so. In the first place, acting 'commercially' means for a public industry not going for maximum profit, but for a total revenue that enables it to meet its financial obligations to Government. Secondly, it means doing this in a way that will stand the test of public justification. This is not to say that every detail of its rates and charges should be scrutinized and discussed, but that the principles of its pricing policy must be known, and discrimination between the prices of products or services to different groups of consumers must be capable of rational, public justification. The coal industry, for

[1] Report of the Committee on Solid Smokeless Fuels, Cmd. 999, 1960.
[2] Report of the Committee on Coal Derivatives, Cmd. 1120, 1960.

example, is not in business to maximize profits for a group of shareholders, nor to further the interests of one group of consumers at the expense of another. For the 'public' is indivisible; higher prices charged to, say, the private sector of industry in order to keep down the price to domestic coal consumers would mean that the prices of other goods bought by coal consumers will be higher. An obligation to act in the public interest conflicts with actions taken to further sectional interests unless such actions command general support – which means the support of Government policy. It is, of course, perfectly possible for the nationalized industries to act as agents for transferring income from one sector of the community, or from the community as a whole, to groups within it. That would be implied if they were given the financial objective of making a loss, or specifically requested by Government to give preferential treatment to one sector of their consumers. But in general, the wider obligations of public industry rule out policies which amount to the public industries giving each other preferential treatment, even if the statute permitted it.

In practice, however, there is an appearance more of friction than of collusion. (There is even more evidence of harmonious relations between them, but this passes unnoticed.) It could be argued that the interdependence of the public fuel industries is such that they cannot make proper plans for future development unless they know of each other's intentions. That there is considerable exchange of information between them about their broad future plans there can be no doubt; neither can there be any doubt that their declared intentions do not always suit each other. In some cases this amounts to no more than a relatively minor uncertainty which it would be difficult in any event to clear up. For example, the National Coal Board and the C.E.G.B. work very closely together on the siting of power-stations, coal supplies and so on. The coal industry is aware that on present estimates, ten years from now the power-stations will require almost twice as much coal as they consume today. The fact that they may be consuming a few million tons of oil, and getting a few million tons from nuclear energy, is hardly a source of friction between the two industries. As we saw in Chapter 2, however, co-operation between fuel and transport industries has tended in the past to be a good deal less intimate.

Between the coal and the gas industries there has been considerable disagreement over the gas industry's decision to import methane in significant quantities – up to fifteen per cent of the country's consumption of town gas. This proposal has been resisted by the coal industry, chiefly because its costs would be adversely affected by a large switch from coal to methane. At the same time, the two industries are collaborating on the production of gas by the Lurgi and other processes which could reduce the costs of making town gas by (it seems) roughly the same amount as could be achieved by methane imports. The Gas Council argues, however, that Lurgi gas requires an enricher, and that methane is the most suitable of these (the others being propane or butane), so that Lurgi and Saharan methane should be regarded as complementary rather than as rivals. There is no disputing the gas industry's need to reduce its costs if it is to compete effectively with oil and electricity, and this requires improved methods of gasification as well as improved methods of distribution. The Gas Council's feeling that in the past it has suffered through over-reliance on coal, and that this has hampered it in its efforts to compete, is a very real factor. Its determination to diversify its raw material sources is shown by its increasing use of oil as well as by its plans to import methane. No matter how friendly the relations between the Board and the Council – and they are now a good deal better than in the past – the basic conflict of interests remains.

This disagreement over methane imports raises questions of national importance, of the public interest. It raises questions affecting the balance of payments, industrial location and employment, for instance, as well as the prices of coal and gas. Since neither of the two industries can have an overriding opinion on such questions, it is clearly the sort of question which should be decided at Government level.

The position may be contrasted with that in private industry. How much thought was given to the public interest in, say, the struggle for British Aluminium, the company responsible for the entire ingot output in this country, which took place in 1958–9?[1] The rival bids for its takeover raised many issues of public importance: questions including rates of expansion, balance of pay-

[1] See S. Hatch and M. Fores, 'The Struggle for British Aluminium', *The Political Quarterly*, Oct.-Dec. 1960.

ments, industrial location and employment. So far from being the decisive consideration, such questions were hardly considered even in the public commentaries on the case.

Where the nationalized industries compete in selling to the consumer, their wider obligations again imply behaviour that is different from that of the private sector. It is not easy to make an appraisal of their competitive relationships because there is no important field in which they are competing solely among each other. The fuel and power industries are all competing also with oil, while in transport there is competition from roads and private airlines. The effect is clearly evident in the case of the coal industry, which is unlikely to be greatly perturbed by the changeover from the direct use of coal to its indirect use in the form of gas and electricity. To a large extent the coal industry's advertising campaign can therefore be regarded as a 'holding operation' against the damaging effects upon the industry of a glut of relatively cheap oil, which may or may not prove temporary. Competition between gas and electricity cannot be attributed to oil encroachment; even without oil competition the two industries would be competing.

Here again it is important to apply the yardstick of objectives. The objective of the competing industries is to extend their markets and thereby lower the costs of production; the beneficiaries of lower costs are not a private group of shareholders but the fuel-using public, which means the whole public. From a national standpoint the basic question is: which method of processing primary energy into heat and power represents the most efficient use of the input? And for this purpose, efficiency can be indicated by consumer demand. This implies, of course, that the costs of the two rival fuels to the consumer are not forced up by competitive advertising campaigns! It might be tempting to argue that this is no different from the competitive process in private industry; but is this so? In the first place, competition among the public industries does not result in the private appropriation of wealth. Secondly, the cost of the final product represents the outcome of a process of production at every stage of which – in all relationships – an attempt has been made to secure the public interest. Thirdly, the public industries have the duty of keeping their consumers informed, and of consulting with them. It must be admitted that the machinery of consultation has hardly been an outstanding success, especially for the coal industry, whose contacts with the general public are largely conducted through some 15,000 coal distributors. But at least the attempt is made – which is more than can be said of much of private industry. (There is, of course, one case where competition between nationalized industries may not be *prima facie* in the public interest – namely, where the prices charged reflect extensive cross-subsidization. An example is the competition between B.E.A. and British Railways on the London–Glasgow route, referred to in Chapter 3.[1])

## The new situation

So far we have considered the circumstances in which the public industries found themselves up to 1961. Financially, they were working to a vaguely defined 'break-even' objective largely made unattainable by the Government. For the past few years their position has been made even more uncertain, in terms of the contribution expected of them, owing to the Government's insistence that in the fields of energy and transport increasing competition from the private sector would secure the most desirable results. More recently the public industries have been given a more clearly defined financial objective, that of making a profit. Is this change in objective likely to bring any important changes in the relationships among nationalized industries? Obviously, this implies a major change in the public industries' economic position. For in our society a high rate of tax-financed expenditure by Government, and a high rate of capital accumulation, are taken as imperatives. To have a group of public industries which are substantial investors but contribute little or nothing to taxation or capital accumulation puts these industries in a subservient position. Through the normal process by which investment eventually creates the savings required to finance it, the private sector has become sufficiently profitable both to make a high taxation contribution and the necessary capital accumulation. The White Paper published in April 1961, 'The Financial and Economic Obligations of Nationalized Industries', shows the steadily growing dependence of the nationalized industries on the rest of the economy to finance their investment. Private industry

[1] This subject is further discussed in Chapter 15.

has done most of the forced saving necessary to finance the public industries' investment. This has been a profitable role for private industry.

A profitable public industries sector is therefore strengthened vis-à-vis private industry, a point of no small importance in view of the public attitude towards public ownership and the virulence of attacks made upon it by private industry. For if the public sector contributes to capital accumulation and taxation income, the necessity for high profits in the private sector is diminished.

The profit objective does not directly affect the relations among nationalized industries, but it has important implications for them because of the change in status that it brings. It does not mean that public industries must automatically form themselves in the image of private industries.

Profit means two different things for the two forms of ownership. For private ownership the aim – the sole aim – is to maximize the difference between costs and proceeds, for private appropriation outside the industry. But what can profit mean in a public industry? Merely that part of the 'value added' is brought to the surface, thus becoming available for capital accumulation, instead of being handed back to the consumer as lower prices or to the labour force as higher wages. The decision that public industry should show a profit in fact amounts to saying that in future the public industries should themselves collect from consumers the finances for capital accumulation, instead of leaving the private sector to do it in a more roundabout way, one which unnecessarily swells private profits.

There is another important implication of this decision that the financial obligation of nationalized industries is to show a profit. In the past, under the general 'break-even' rule, it has never been clear whether losses were incurred (or profits reduced) because of market circumstances; or because the industries chose to pursue policies that were not in their own financial interest but were in the public interest; or because they adopted 'non-commercial' policies at Government behest. If profit is to be the final outcome of the industries' operations, then it becomes more evident where the responsibility lies for events which may impede profitability, or create losses. This is not only a matter of substituting openness for secrecy on the part of the Government in dealing with such questions as the level of prices. It will bring clearly into view that irrespective of the financial objective that is given to nationalized industries – whether to make a profit, break even, or make a loss of any given size – there are circumstances in which an industry itself cannot determine its contribution to the economy, as private industry well knows. It will hasten the recognition that there are limits to what can be done without Government intervention to preserve certain activities, to prevent them from shrinking below a desirable size.

What is desirable will involve national considerations of a social as well as an economic character. This recognition has already been extended to agriculture. The social and economic costs of transferring even more traffic from rail to road will force a similar recognition before, it is hoped, any significant part of the mineral traffic is switched to the roads. Is it desirable or indeed feasible, on balance of payments grounds alone, to permit the coal industry to fall below its present annual rate of output of 190,000,000 tons? What size of public air transport covering routes which are profitable does the community wish to have? It would be easy enough to shrink these public industries and they could continue to show a profit (or break even) if the Government were prepared to write off their capital in sufficiently large amounts. The point is that the mere decision that they should show a profit does not alter the market situation imposed by competition. The size of the real contribution to be made by the public industries is a decision for Government which must still be made, irrespective of the financial objectives set for them.

This point is clearly important for the relationship between the public industries. If the earlier argument is accepted, namely, that these industries would be failing in their public duty if they attempted to buttress each other up at the expense of other consumers, and that competition between them is necessary although its purpose and character must be different from that in private industry; then it follows that co-ordination is not something that can be achieved by the industries themselves. The activities of public industry could be better co-ordinated, more closely related to each other, only through a Government policy which assigned, in the case of the fuel industries, a specific task to coal, and created conditions which made that task possible to attain.

The necessity for creating conditions which assign to the coal industry the task of contributing a given amount of coal to carry the 'base load' of the country's energy units is now widely recognized. Economically there are the implications of mounting fuel imports for the balance of payments, and strategic considerations cannot be ignored. There is also a growing recognition of the fact that if collieries with large reserves had to be closed, the nation would be losing irreplaceable assets; and that if industry is forced into attempting rapid changes in supply in order to meet temporary fluctuations in the world oil markets, the cost to the nation could be very heavy indeed because coal supplies, once turned off, cannot be quickly (or cheaply) turned on again.

In the case of transport the effects of running down the public services are less spectacular, less easy to 'quantify' because they include questions of public amenity and convenience and the general quality of life, and these are not taken into account in conventional profit and loss calculations. The necessity for doing more than simply requiring the public transport industry to show a profit may well take longer to percolate.

*Summary and Conclusions*

The relationships between nationalized industries, in short, reflect the objective for which they were created. That objective is to further the public interest, not sectional interests. The public industries are flexible instruments of economic and social policy. They can be given terms of reference which make them show a profit, break even, or show a loss.

The difference in objectives which we have seen to exist between public and private industry, and the different circumstances under which they operate – the one openly, the other secretly – entail a fundamental difference in the meaning of competition and profit as between the two sectors of industry. For private industry, profit can be maintained by contraction, or by 'planned obsolescence'. But the obligations of public industry are much more extensive. The scale of operation of the fuel and transport industries is a matter of considerable public interest, not only because of their size, but also, as was demonstrated by the policy of the National Coal Board during the recession of 1957–9, because they are in a position to act in accordance with national needs. The community recognizes the basic character of the public industries by specifying in the nationalization statutes that they cannot dispose of their assets. And the public interest is further recognized in the elaborate arrangements for public information and consultation built into the organization of these industries.

It is against this background of objectives and how they are pursued that the relations of public industries must be considered.

These industries supply each other, and compete with each other. Both as producers and as competitors they treat each other 'commercially', securing the best bargains possible with each other and with private industry alike, in their attempt to maximize the real value added by their operations. It is not desirable that the public industries should discriminate in favour of each other either as buyers or as sellers, and they have not done so.

As producers they have, of course, many technical interests in common and there is considerable technical collaboration between them, as there is also between each public industry and its suppliers and customers in the private sector. Technical and scientific developments in the fuel industries are co-ordinated by the minister's Scientific Advisory Council, which considers and makes recommendations on the research and development work of the various boards. The relevant fuel industries have worked closely together – with varying degrees of success – on problems such as underground gasification of coal, the development of new processes of carbonization, and on the relationship between the changing pattern of coal qualities and sizes, and the requirements of coal consumers. They are in continuous collaboration on such questions as the siting of power-stations and carbonization plants. Special investigations into problems in which the fuel industries have joint interests have also been undertaken, for example, by the Weir, Wilson and Peech Committees.

As producers, they have from time to time differences of opinion among themselves about their future intentions. Where such disagreements are settled by negotiation between the industries, the policies decided upon become part of the general policies for which they are accountable in the normal course. The question of pit-head power-stations is such an instance. When the disagreements involve national issues, such as questions of methane imports, it is obviously right that the decision should be made by the Government.

Competition between the nationalized industries in the domestic and industrial markets is also conditioned by the higher level of obligations they observe. There is nothing incongruous in competition between the coal, gas and electricity industries if we bear in mind their obligation to maximize the real value of their output. Indeed it would be incongruous if they did not compete, because changes in techniques and costs, both in the production of fuel and in the uses made of it, must find practical expression; which means that the public must be informed about what is available. Hence there is a need for informative advertising.

The public industries also compete through the standard of service which they offer to their consumers. The need here is for more competition to improve the services. In this 'service' competition each of the industries is also competing with the private sector. The National Coal Board unfortunately is at a considerable disadvantage in its contacts with the general public because the board's own retail distributive organization (inherited on nationalization) is a fractional part of the retail coal trade.

If, then, the nationalized industries best meet their obligation by competing as sellers and not discriminating among each other in other respects, does this mean that co-ordination between them is satisfactory from all standpoints? It is important to distinguish two levels of co-ordination; two levels at which their activities can be geared into each other so as to maximize their real contribution to the economy. One is at the technical level. This involves collaboration and commercial interests, and competition between them where they serve the same markets. They are rivals in pursuit of the national interest, and where rivalry reaches disagreement, the disagreement must be settled at national level. In this sense they are properly co-ordinated.

What the nationalized industries cannot decide, individually or collectively, is the size of the contribution that each makes to the economy. This does not affect the principles which guide their actions – in general to act 'commercially' in the public interest – but it nevertheless affects their activities and relationships (the co-ordination between them) to a very large extent. The output of the coal industry, and its costs, will largely determine the fortunes and the behaviour of the other fuel industries and of the railways. If the gas and electricity industries believe that they can lower real costs by importing fuel, it is their duty not to ignore the opportunity. Neither they nor the coal industry can have the decisive word on whether that is in the national interest. The determination of the size of the contribution of the coal and public transport industries is to a very large extent the responsibility of the Government. Until recently, it has been possible for the Government to shirk this responsibility by letting the industries run into heavy losses without making it clear where the responsibility for this policy really lay. Now these industries' terms of reference have been stated more precisely – namely that they must make a certain profit. This will strengthen the public industries' position vis-à-vis the private sector. It also implies that Government must more openly acknowledge and be responsible for the tasks allotted to public industry. The maintenance of profitability may sometimes be possible only by reducing unprofitable services, eliminating unprofitable production, or raising prices to drive customers away.

Yet Government may feel that this is against the public interest and may prefer to relax its requirements of profitability. In that case, as the White Paper suggests, this will be a public acknowledgement that the particular nationalized industry is acting as an agent of Government policy, and that the disappearance or reduction of its profits is not to be taken as a sign of unsatisfactory performance. In other words, the task of deciding how large the contribution of the coal and public transport industries should be will rest more squarely, and openly, on the Government, where it properly belongs.

The question arises, however, whether the Government will accept its responsibilities, or whether it will continue to try to evade them. In the latter case, is there anything more that the nationalized industries could or should try to do themselves to improve the implementation of national policy so far as they are concerned? This is a question which perhaps deserves wider consideration than it has so far received.

# CHAPTER NINE

# STAFFING AND RECRUITMENT

I T has become a truism that Britain's future depends on brains. But manpower budgeting, on which the proper development of resources depends, rarely receives the attention given to financial accounting. This is true of the nationalized industries, as it is of private industry. It is too readily assumed that if the expenditure of $x$ hundred million pounds is authorized, the power-stations, the pits or the marshalling yards will automatically materialize. We have found to our cost that this does not always happen, and that the most serious bottle-neck of all can be the lack of key personnel. But it may well be easier to get £1,000,000 for plant than £10,000 for recruitment, training or staff to do the job.

In mining, it is true, the Reid Report commented before nationalization on the dearth of mining-engineers in Great Britain, and one of the first acts of the N.C.B. was to approve its Ladder Plan and an ambitious university scholarship scheme. The former gave every boy in the industry a chance to learn mining or some other form of engineering, and the latter has brought a thousand graduates into the industry. These steps were followed a little later by a large-scale management training scheme, and they have paid dividends. The other nationalized industries were, however, less quick off the mark.

The Select Committee in 1960 had a sad story to tell about railway modernization and the checks which have been caused by shortage of trained staff, particularly in fields such as signal engineering. The committee concludes, 'the Commission should have taken more steps to increase the numbers of their qualified staff at the time when new methods were being introduced on the railways. The committee are not satisfied that the Commission have treated this with the urgency it deserves and were surprised to find that the B.T.C. keep no records at headquarters of the limited number of their professional staff'. The electricity industry was also criticized by the Herbert Committee for failing to recruit and retain enough graduates. But the training record of this industry is generally good, particularly in the field of consultation. Most of the other nationalized industries too are now active in fields of education and training.

To what extent do major training, as opposed to personnel, problems still exist? It may be useful, in the first instance, to look briefly at how the staffs of nationalized industries were built up. Naturally they derive principally from the men who worked in these industries before nationalization. Managers of collieries, for example, have to be statutorily qualified through an arduous process of experience and examination, and there was no possibility of wholesale importation of outside management on nationalization. Railway and gas engineering are also specialized fields, and inevitably the Electricity Boards are staffed largely with men drawn from the previous electricity undertakings. In the spheres of administration, labour relations and personnel, there was some infusion of new blood. Men like Sir Arthur Street and Lord Citrine created small 'brains trusts' and the adventure of nationalization attracted, on ideological grounds, a certain number of recruits. New labour relations departments drew into the industries numbers of men with a trade union background – sometimes to the detriment of leadership in the unions concerned.

The gigantic shake-up of nationalization had, broadly, three effects. It shed some of the old private enterprise management – sometimes with benefit, but with some loss of talent. It brought in a significant minority of newcomers, and it created a difficult problem of adjustment for existing staff. Some rose rapidly to positions of much greater responsibility than they would have had under the old regime. Others found it difficult to fit into a large organization and suffered a phase of irritation and frustration. This did no good to their industries and helped to blight their 'public image'. By now, the majority have either adjusted themselves or have been replaced by men of the new generation.

Traditions, however, particularly in old-established industries, have very deep roots, and in organizations as large as the N.C.B. and the railways the dissemination and acceptance of new ideas is a major problem. This process is made more difficult by the fact that all the larger industries – railways, coal, gas, electricity and airways – have a predominantly technical or operational management. Neither lay board members, ministers nor civil servants are well equipped to criticize the technical recommendations of their subordinates, and engineers, like doctors, are better trained to deal with their own expertise than with administration and management. Hence higher authority, assisted by a thin and rather suspect cadre of administration, has been engaged in a constant struggle to sell new management techniques to a reluctant hierarchy of technical or operational line managers. The latter, on the other hand, have tended to chafe at the criticism of their plans by men whose competence to do so is sometimes doubted.

The relationship between the administrator and the general manager on the one hand, and the engineer, scientist, etc. on the other is, of course, a problem that affects all large organizations. The dilemma is essentially this: really large organizations are many-sided in their activities and have to take into account obligations and pressures coming from many outside quarters. Moreover, they must not merely react negatively to them like an elephant surrounded by hunters, but must be purposeful and even adventurous. To do so, and to keep their internal and external activities in balance, they need men capable of thinking in general terms, picking out what is relevant from masses of complex detail, and free to formulate ideas which can form the basis of policy. If all this is left to a few men at the top, the strain will either become intolerable – as it has in some cases – or the organization will ossify. At the same time these organizations also need men of highly developed professional, scientific and technological skills, because their activities are extremely technical and cannot be operated or controlled in detail except by those who have been prepared by long years of detailed and specialist training.

It is not yet proved that any organization has wholly solved this problem. The civil service tackled it before the technological age by making the administrator pre-eminent. This system has its critics as well as its admirers, and in any case it would hardly be wise to impose it on highly technical industries such as electricity or coal. It should be noted, however, that in India a common cadre of officials controls both the civil service and the nationalized industries. At worst, in the British civil service, a rigid barrier divides the administrators from the professionals, making the latter frustrated by the amateur control of their activities. At the best, there is the breadth of view which has given the service its renown. The Post Office offers an interesting compromise. Here is a semi-autonomous department with an executive job to do. The Post Office fills some of its administrative and managerial posts from people recruited into the administrative and executive grades and some from engineers and other specialists transferred at various stages of their careers. The system appears to work well, and some unlikely results ensue – such as the appointment of a radio engineer as deputy director of finance.

In the armed services a highly organized system of cross-posting supplemented by staff college courses has stood the test of war, and in the biggest private enterprises there is usually a galaxy of subsidiary companies or a complex divisional organiza-tion – as in I.C.I. – to provide breadth of experience.

Have the nationalized industries similar devices to ensure the flexibility and resource that they need? The answer is: not yet. Their empirical approach is not unreasonable because there are few precedents that fit their circumstances, but none the less the problem is a real one. There are three dangers: first, the present predominance of engineers; second, the existence of separate functional ladders between which it is increasingly difficult to jump; and third, the restricted scope of the general adminis-trator.

Engineers have a vital role to play in all the nationalized indus-tries. Coal and railways are labour-intensive industries whose urgent need is to raise their efficiency and competitive power by replacing men with machines. The need for skilled engineering in electricity and airways is obvious, and gas is now in the throes of a belated technological revolution. But the technological changes needed involve much more than technical expertise. They demand an awareness of economic, financial, social and psychological factors for which the narrow professional training of engineers has too often done little to prepare them. This is a facet of Sir Charles Snow's problem of the 'two cultures'. There are of course excep-tions – engineers who are at the same time first-rate administrators. But the problem is a general one; perhaps especially acute in the nationalized industries because of their inevitable involvement in politics, in the sense of being liable to political dictation, but also by reason of their responsibility for assessing and promoting the 'public interest', which is a social or political imperative. Until, in this country, we give our engineers and scientists a broader and more liberal education at school and at university there will be a need either to put them under the control of administrators, as in the Civil Service, or – the preferable alternative – to take positive steps to broaden their training in the early stages of their career. This can be done academically, by courses such as that leading to the Diploma in Management Studies or parallel courses in universities, by staff college training, and by planned experience.

At the moment, however, planned experience is hard to acquire in the nationalized industries. As technologies develop, functional departments and branches tend to become more and more specialized and, as professional qualifications spread into new fields such as purchasing, etc., even commercial departments are becoming self-contained islands within which no one without a professional passport can go far.

In such a situation the scope for the young 'generalist' will be limited unless the organization takes active steps to push him forward. Traffic apprentices have been recruited by the railways for a good many years, and whilst some have gone far, many have left. The administrative assistant scheme in the N.C.B. has been successful because selection has been stringent, but the intake has been very small in comparison with the size of the industry. There is no similar scheme in gas, and electricity has recently made a very tentative start. Clearly the nationalized industries show little sign of following the civil service lead.

These are serious defects, and it may well be that they are a principal cause of the periodical attacks by the politicians on the structure of nationalized industries. If there is an impression of 'woodenness' or failure to respond to a crisis, there is too much readiness to assume that some fashionable nostrum, such as decentralization, is the answer. Structural changes merely rearrange the pieces on the chess board and do not necessarily add anything to the human assets of the industry concerned. Apart from causing immense labour, surgical operations such as those which followed the Herbert Report and which are now in train on the railways can also do considerable damage to the morale and efficiency of staff – though they may sometimes be unavoidable. The Select Committee, now that it has reported on the major industries, might well turn its attention from structure and finance to an over-all review of the staffing policies of the public sector. In the mean-time, however, the nationalized industries must seek their own salvation, and one of their greatest needs is to acquire and train staff of high quality. What are their chances of success in this field?

The most damaging factor in the quest for skill is undoubtedly the 'public image' of the nationalized industries. Here Tory pro-paganda has done a real disservice to the nation. Old hands can laugh off the jibes of the Press and of their neighbours – though even they have their moments of depression – but, for the young, prestige is vitally important.

The standing of the private enterprise giants has been inflated by Press eulogies and prestige advertising, but an admission that a man works for the railways or the Coal Board is likely to evoke a horse laugh or at least a raised eyebrow.

There is also a more subtle deterrent. Youth has a natural dis-taste for bureaucracy, and the nationalized industries are thought to have the rigidity attributed to the civil service without its respectability and the honours that go with it. Moreover, the civil service offers security and a 'free' pension scheme. The constant threats of reorganization which overhang all nationalized indus-tries inevitably breed some sense of insecurity. Finally, there is the tendentious suggestion that coal and railways are 'dying industries'.

There are few direct incentives to counter these disadvantages. Salary comparisons are unreliable because of the difficulty of equating responsibilities, but it is clear that since the Pay Research Unit (which has no parallel in the nationalized industries) began its work, the pay of civil servants has risen faster than that of nationalized employees earning comparable salaries a few years ago. Local government salaries have broadly kept pace with the civil service, and though the range of private enterprise salaries is probably wider than that in nationalized industry, the average is certainly no lower. Moreover, top salaries in private industry, well known to be incomparably higher than those of nationalized board members, have a glamour appeal that is telling. Nor do these salaries, as happens in nationalized industries, keep the whole concertina so squeezed that proper differentials are hard to maintain.

The £24,000 salary paid to Dr Beeching on his appointment as chairman of the B.T.C. focused public attention on the disparity between normal board salaries and the rewards of private enterprise, and more recently the chairman of the West Midlands Division of the N.C.B. joined the board of a private company at a salary which Lord Robens said that his board could not match. Does the Beeching precedent imply a change of policy, and would this be a good thing? There is a tradition in this country that 'public service' brings fewer material rewards than work in private enterprise. This tradition would be worth keeping if other rewards, such as respect and prestige, were forthcoming. But as we have seen, in the nationalized industries they normally are not. Inevitably, therefore, one falls back on cash incentives. Higher salaries for the key people in nationalized industries are indeed needed if they are to attract and retain their fair share of the available talent.

At present there is little doubt that, for comparable responsibilities, able staff in nationalized industries are underpaid in relation to managers in private industry. The ratio between senior staff and employees in coal and railways is low compared with industry as a whole, and pressure of work is heavy. The ratio between staff and capital employed is also low in electricity, gas and probably in the Post Office.

Finally, there is the question of conditions and perquisites. No one in nationalized industries gets the generous holidays of civil servants, but they share with them their rather shabby standards of office accommodation and strict rules about perquisites and gifts. Concessionary coal (to most but not all employees) and travel concessions in transport are minor advantages, but they are strictly controlled and are well known to the Inland Revenue. There is no scope in these industries for the tax-free 'company car', the 'business lunch' or the 'educational endowment scheme' of private enterprise. Moreover, the gap between the salaries of staff and supervisors and those of manual workers is tending to narrow. This tendency might have merit if it led to the abolition of outmoded distinctions between 'staff' and manual workers, but it can go too far if it robs real responsibility of its rewards.

This situation is dangerous. Most of the nationalized industries make the annual pilgrimage to the universities in search of graduates, but their harvest – except for a small number of arts graduates – has not been encouraging. Scholarship schemes have attracted some good men; whether they will stay, however, depends on the attraction of their job and its prospects. It says a good deal for the management training schemes of the industries concerned, and for the class of work provided, that wastage has not been high. The Herbert Committee commented on the loss of graduates from electricity, and the trials of the coal industry have in recent years led to the disappearance of some much-needed talent. But by and large, wastage, except on the railways, has been less than might have been expected.

Graduates, however, form only a small proportion of the technical staffs of the nationalized industries. These industries traditionally draw recruits from the families of their employees, and this talent has been systematically developed. Day release to technical colleges is granted to those who can benefit from it, and the youngster who combines practical experience with a higher national certificate or diploma is widely regarded as a more serviceable young official than the raw graduate who does not always find it easy to integrate himself fully in the industry. Much the same pattern obtains in the administrative and commercial fields – though here educational opportunities have hitherto been less generous.

Such a system, however, invites parochialism. The long grind of part-time education produces homespun virtues and technical competence, but it does not give a broad view of the world. Existing standards and traditions, both good and bad, are accepted uncritically, and since promotion is often affected by the opinion of a man's immediate boss, there is a great temptation to conformity. This is a different conformity from the self-conscious 'all-roundness' of the 'organization man', but it perpetuates bad habits and slows up change. Possibly this also causes the undoubted prejudice against the promotion of women to senior posts! In this respect the nationalized industries compare very badly with the civil service.

Conformity might be lessened if there were some objective system of evaluation. Annual reports, however, are not general in nationalized industries – though they exist to some extent – and although much depends upon promotion interviews, they are not always skilfully conducted. Local candidates frequently have an advantage, and hence mobility is not easy to achieve. Moreover, there is nothing comparable to the civil service system of posting. Union agreements and the tradition derived in some industries from local government make it essential to advertise all posts. Something can be done to encourage promising men by inviting them to apply for jobs and by recommending them to selection panels; but this is not done on a comprehensive scale.

Finally, staff planning is still in some cases rudimentary. Reference has already been made to the absence of such machinery on the railways, and in electricity there is no department with an overall responsibility in this field. It was the Fleck Report which created such a department in coal. Until that time posts were filled on a hand-to-mouth basis in divisions, and estimates of the numbers of youngsters needed at the bottom of the pipeline were largely guesses. In recent years departmental staff reviews have been undertaken with valuable results, and similar exercises are badly needed elsewhere.

All this shows that if nationalized industries are to flourish a good many nettles will have to be grasped. But there is also a brighter side. In the first place, it is necessary to compare like with like. It is not reasonable to contrast nationalized industries with the few bright spots in private industry. Rosemary Stewart's *Management Succession* shows that even our larger firms are staffed, at top level, largely from men who have risen from the ranks and who, in many cases, have not even had a grammar school education. 'Graduate' qualities are probably of particular importance in large organizations, but it would be wrong to suppose that nationalized industries are behind industry as a whole.

Moreover, they have a good many assets, both tangible and intangible. The first is the advantage of size and the possession of large resources. It is possible to develop expertise in almost every field. Research, though possibly still inadequate, has bounded ahead since nationalization. Great advances have been made in safety and in medical care. Training has had to contend with economy drives but, by and large, few firms, even the wealthiest, have systems of training as comprehensive and as solid as those of the nationalized industries. If decisions have been made to use advanced techniques, such as electronic data processing, major developments can be quickly effected. Engineering changes can take place on a scale reminiscent of war-time, to speed up the building of power-stations or the mechanization of pits. Purchasing can be rationalized and many millions saved by bulk buying.

All these activities present challenges to which the staff have, on the whole, responded vigorously. The complexity and magnitude of the problems which face these industries are exciting, and breed absorbed devotion to the job. Electrical, mechanical, mining and railway engineers have more varied opportunities in nationalized undertakings to practise their professional skills than they are likely to get elsewhere. Moreover, pride in working for a public service is not absent. Staff in nationalized industries at least feel that they are providing basic services or commodities which are essential to the nation. Moreover, there is little secrecy. Information is pooled and co-operation is encouraged. There is no reason why morale, which glows intermittently at present, could not be fanned into a flame of enthusiasm if these industries entered a period in which their achievements were recognized and their tasks more clearly defined.

Nationalized industries are now doing a good deal to develop the skills they need. Their staff colleges are as good as any, miners and power-station foremen go to schools at Oxford and Cambridge, and there is a multitude of courses in managerial techniques of all kinds. The problem of communications is increasingly recognized, and in the electrical industry, in particular, consultation is a real force.

What, in the light of this account, are the improvements necessary? Probably the greatest need is a drive to create the conditions in which an imaginative, purposeful and humane cadre of higher managers can develop. It is unrealistic to suppose that, in the short run, the nationalized industries can capture a big proportion of the nation's high flyers. They must, however, secure the essential minimum and also make the maximum use of the talent they already possess. To do this there must be some sacrifice of expediency to long-term ends. To allow the nationalized industries to become self-contained empires full of locked doors is to guarantee sterility. What is to prevent a systematic interchange of staff between the nationalized industries themselves, and between them and the civil service? And should there not be more cross-fertilization with private enterprise and with the academic world? Given the will, obstacles such as conditions of service, superannuation, etc., could be overcome, and the main problem would be to sell the idea to the unions and the staff themselves. Here again, strong leadership should be quite sufficient. The Post Office system of transfers between administrative and technical or semi-technical posts should be copied, and more openings must be made for arts graduates. Some technical posts may be beyond their reach, but it is a great pity that experiments such as the creation of posts like assistant area general manager in the N.C.B., which were designed to provide experience for non-technical men, are not being pursued with greater vigour. Finally, commercial education – both at junior and senior levels – must be developed with speed to provide a field from which really promising young administrators can be drawn.

This plea for mobility does not, of course, mean wholesale transfer of staff. Management development is a subtle and complex process and, whilst the aim must be to provide interest and variety of experience for all the staff, its refinements can only be applied to a minority. But this minority is vital, and for them experience needs to be supplemented by internal courses and by staff college training. This latter is still, throughout industry, inadequate in scale and in depth. The management courses run by the railways and by the coal and electricity industries are broadly at one level, and Henley, though highly selective, follows much the same pattern by providing a single once-for-all course in general management.

The practice in the Services is very different. After Sandhurst and its equivalents comes Camberley, followed by the Joint-Services Staff College, with the Imperial Defence College at the top of the pyramid. The problems of the nationalized industries are no less complex than those of the Services, and their activities are just as interrelated. Moreover, the nationalized industries operate on a bigger scale. Service personnel total 485,000. Nationalized industry employees, including the Post Office, number nearly 2,500,000. At present, only a proportion of the eligible men in nationalized industries ever get to a staff college, and then only once in a lifetime. The absence of any progressive development is particularly serious.

There are two ways in which this situation might be improved. There is only one Henley, and this provides a mere handful of places annually for the whole of British industry. The establishment of a Nationalized Industry Staff College would not only create new training capacity at a high level, but also form a unique focus for the discussion of the problems of large organizations. Students from private 'leviathans' and from overseas might also be admitted.

Such a college could, in addition, form the base for another form of research which might have an important bearing on the problem of accountability. The Select Committee have tried unsuccessfully to obtain technical and economic assistance, but, even without it, their probes have uncovered defects and successes which would otherwise be unknown to Parliament and the public. This work would be enormously assisted if they could have access to objective reports which ranged over the whole of the industries with which they are concerned. This should not be too difficult to achieve. All the nationalized industries have work-study teams, O. and M. branches, and, in some cases, operational research units. These, however, only operate 'domestically', and there is no machinery to compare and contrast their results. A college with an independent principal of the highest status could recruit a group of operational research teams which could examine, in turn, the various departments in all the nationalized industries. Their reports could be discussed at the college and then, with appropriate safeguards, be either published or made available to the Select Committee. Whilst such investigations might provoke initial resistance from the boards, the resulting gains in efficiency would probably be so striking as to disarm criticism. Moreover, each industry has its new and valuable developments, and there is no reason to think that the reports would be all brickbats and no bouquets.

Each team would have to be led by a permanent or semi-permanent expert, but he could employ, on a temporary basis, selected members of the staff of all the industries within his parish. These could include engineers, scientists, administrators and others. The exceptional opportunities such men would enjoy for

broadening their experience might soon form them into a new
*élite* who, if they proved themselves on return to their own industries, could look forward to rapid promotion.

There is a democratic tradition in the nationalized industries,
and the creation of any kind of *élite* is not likely to escape criticism. Experience, however, seems to suggest that some sort of *élite*
is essential to the health of any large organization, and the
nationalized industries are in a good position to avoid the common abuses. They take great pains to cultivate the talents of their
manual workers, they provide scholarships to all who show
academic ability and there is an almost complete absence of the
cruder forms of nepotism. The main bar at present to promotion
by merit is the inadequacy of current personnel techniques. If
these were improved, there would be little jealousy of high flyers
who emerged, as a result of native ability, from every social
stratum.

There is, however, one caveat which affects all large organizations – the need to prevent the 'establishment' (used here to mean
those in authority) from rejecting or disillusioning the non-
conformist. The nationalized industries have one advantage over
the civil service in that their employees are not barred from
political activities. These, properly, have to be pursued tactfully;
to be overtly political (especially on the Left) is not likely to help
a man's career. This, however, is a special problem. More important is to ensure that nationalized industries do not become a
'yes man's' paradise. The man who conforms, who never rebels,
who sticks by tradition, is often the man who makes progress
since he seldom questions the authority of those above him. Such
men are the comforters of inefficient, unimaginative management.

Large organizations (whether they be privately or publicly
owned) tend to breed and nurture such men. The more management is departmentalized, the easier it is for the conformist to
establish himself and prosper.

Those who rebel against established practice (often because
they have the imagination to see better ways of doing things) are
usually frowned on. Organizations, and the men who run them,
tend to ossify unless they and the assumptions they rely on are
constantly challenged. Too often, boldness is regarded with
distaste; a reputation for unorthodoxy weighs more heavily in the

balance than the achievement of success. The maxim, 'He who never makes a mistake never makes anything' should be engraved on the hearts of all those who manage and administer our affairs.

To maintain morale throughout the industries, an imaginative approach is also needed for those who have character and capacity without great intellectual distinction. These are the men who make good power-station superintendents or colliery managers; in the present situation they are tempted to enter the general race for promotion and feel frustrated if they fail. Often, indeed, in conditions of shortage they are successful, and there are some instances of men who have been promoted to higher management although their abilities would have been far more valuable at a lower executive level. There is, in fact, no man more useful to the coal industry, for instance, than a first-rate colliery manager, and unless such a man has a marked administrative flair he should regard the successful leadership of his pit as an honourable summit to his career. If he is to do so, however, the prestige of his office should be enhanced, and his salary, if his work is good, should be substantial. Some public recognition of outstanding work would also help. Would, for example, a travel bursary for a successful manager and his wife be amiss? Other devices might be developed.

But even if the brilliant and the good are adequately catered for, there will be some who fail or flag; the result of even reasonable security is the occasional 'lame duck' or misfit. To deal with these, more flexibility is needed in retirement policy. As the Fleck Report remarked, money paid to retire the ineffective is money well spent, and superannuation funds would not be wrecked if retirement after fifty were allowed as a result of agreement between the board and the employee. Misfits can often be useful to society in another context, and nothing is more corrosive of morale than promotion blocks caused by the occupation of middle management posts by the lazy or the cynical.

How can all this be summarized? It is clear that the first aim of personnel policy should be to recruit enough first-class and broadly trained talent to provide an adequate field of selection for the higher management of the future. The next must be to develop to the maximum the sound but limited men and women who will fill the majority of posts. To attract and retain enough high flyers, the glamour of nationalized industries must be increased. This depends very much on their 'public image' and on salaries, but much can be done by other means. Management development must be improved, and there would be many advantages in encouraging able men to move from one industry to another, both via the operational research teams advocated above and by transferring suitable men to appropriate jobs in sister industries. The grant of sabbatical leave, at first in selected cases, and later perhaps more generally, would also provide an invaluable shot in the arm to men in their forties and fifties. Training must continue to expand, particularly in the managerial, commercial and supervisory fields, and more attention should be given to internal public relations and to consultation.

In relation to capital expenditure and labour costs, salaries form a small proportion of expenditure, and it is false economy to stint money on increasing staff who will foster efficiency, or to pay less than the market rate. Parkinson's Law does not operate at present under nationalization. The reverse indeed is true: namely that technological change is held back through lack of staff to promote it. It is the Shell and the Vickers buildings that dominate London, not the humbler offices of the nationalized industries. The danger is rather that, in their desire to avoid criticism for lavish spending, the nationalized industries should allow themselves to be dominated by ideals of false economy, and should come to accept subconsciously the public impression that they are the 'poor relations' of private enterprise. Too much scrimping and saving eats into the soul of a man and of an organization. A little less humility and a little more panache – even a touch of ostentation here and there – might work wonders for recruitment, for the public 'image', and for efficiency. Fortunately, at least one nationalized board chairman – Lord Robens of the Coal Board – has fully grasped this point; and the transformation he has been able to achieve in the morale and the image of his industry is one of the most heartening features of the entire public sector in recent years.

CHAPTER TEN

# THE BACKGROUND TO ORGANIZATION

*by*

ARTHUR PALMER

I F, WHEN passing into law nationalization bills, Parliament had been content simply to decree the fact of nationalization, and give a minister the power to appoint a governing body and arrange the terms of compensation; and if this approach had been applied impartially to all the industries involved, then a decade later a natural diversity would be expected in managerial structure and organizational forms. One board, looking at its inheritance and liking it, would have preferred to keep change to a minimum; another would have concluded that only a decisive break with the past would suffice in their case to achieve the tasks delegated by the Acts. Between these extremes would be several varieties of approach, using objective circumstances both to justify and excuse them.

Even if Parliament had planted seeds all apparently of the same kind, the grown plants would inevitably still have shown variations. But Parliament did not sow standard seeds. From 1946 until the extinction of the great Labour majority in 1951, an indefatigable House of Commons was extruding nationalization Bills – starting with coal and ending with steel; each, it is true, embodying the same public corporation principle, but dissimilar in the degree to which the structure of the industry to be nationalized was determined by the contents of the legislation.

The Coal Act did not go beyond appointing a National Coal Board, leaving it to this body to arrange its own internal organization as it thought fit. The gas and electricity industries were, by contrast, nationalized in far greater detail; Parliament in each case going so far as to determine the geographical boundaries of the regional organization in a schedule to the Act. But while with gas the sixteen area boards were made self-contained production and distribution units, with electricity the area boards were restricted solely to distribution functions. They were forbidden by the Act of 1947 to make their commodity, being compelled to buy all electricity from a central generating authority which had, in addition, supervisory responsibilities for the whole industry. As a result, for the ten years that passed between the coming into effect of the 1947 Act and the vesting date of the second Electricity Act of 1957, the independently appointed area electricity boards were virtually prisoners of the C.E.A. – a situation brought about, although certainly not intended, by the Act itself. When eventually the outcome was noticed at Westminster the clumsy remedy of an outside investigation (by Sir Edwin Herbert's committee) and a new Bill was resorted to – a manoeuvre which, after occupying many months of parliamentary time, resulted in the creation of the excellent Central Electricity Generating Board, but at the same time fastened on the industry the incomprehensible Electricity Council, apparently at the whim of a politically short-lived minister who said such an arrangement had 'worked well for gas'. This optimistic view of the organization of the gas industry was not sustained by the subsequent report of the Select Committee on Nationalized Industries, which pointed out the weakness of a confederal body when it comes to effective executive action. It drew attention to the failure of an 'advisory' council to make decisions quickly on important technical questions such as large-scale national production of gas, and the continued neglect of fundamental research by the industry.

The appointment of Dr Beeching as chairman of the British Transport Commission in 1961 was a reminder of the vicissitudes that the organization of nationalized transport has gone through since the Nationalization Act in 1947. Then the original commission supervised a second tier of 'executive' corporations for railways, road haulage, road passenger transport, hotels and docks, with a special executive to inherit the already publicly owned London transport system. The return of the Conservatives to power at Westminster and the consequent new Act of 1953 broke up a tidy arrangement which had proved lifeless in practice, and introduced instead a more diversified system, bringing some aspects of the working of the railways closer to the commission, while leaving others for more local control by area boards.

Atomic energy, broadcasting, civil aviation likewise all show their own special variations on the basic theme of the public corporation in practice. Iron and steel, now returned to very much modified private enterprise, enjoyed the distinction (in the opinion of the writer but yet to be proved) of being perhaps the most promising model for future nationalization schemes. Here, a central holding corporation compulsorily acquired the share-holdings in nearly a hundred iron and steel companies, and in this way in one stroke did four things: (1) established full public ownership, (2) gave power of general organization and direction to a central body, (3) left the everyday life of the separate concerns unmolested, (4) kept open opportunity for future adaptation and evolution. Iron and steel was the last and perhaps the most realistic Labour incursion into the immensely difficult business of nationalizing industry and kindred services under a constitutional parliamentary regime. Mr Emmanuel Shinwell, who had much experience as a nationalizing minister, said in a moment of candour when out of office that Labour had given attention to the principles of nationalization but had neglected plans for carrying it into effect. Judged by the immense nationalization statutes, the party, or at any rate ministers and the departments, had far too many and differing plans which by their very detail have sometimes stood in the way, under changing circumstances, of achieving the object of the exercise: to establish the public sector as a model of progressive, benevolent and efficient industrial administration.

The trouble may have been that those responsible for drafting the Bills were more concerned with getting over the initial problems of the change than with laying a foundation which would give the chance of assured future growth. Hence they committed the usual error of those in a hurry: they did too much, because there was no time left to them in which to exercise restraint. They should be excused, for they were children of their time – of the heady victory years of 1945–50. All too often in socialist thinking peeps through the assumption that nationalization is the full flower of parliamentary wisdom, imposing final order on chaotic nature. A more sensible approach is to see nationalization as only another *step* in the process of modern industrial growth from smaller to larger scale organization, carried through under a political direction which, because of its ideals, has imposed new social and community obligations, and it is this direction which should be the primary concern of the politicians – the setting down of clear social responsibilities and plain economic goals.

It is hard then to find in the nationalized industries standard forms or consistent organizational structures. Statutory detail or lack of detail, post-nationalization interference and advice by committees and commissions, varying interpretations by the boards of the powers given, have all had their influence on the way things are now done. But because to generalize is to attempt the near impossible, this is not to say that there are no common issues of right or wrong organization. Some arise indeed from the fact of public ownership and the legitimate expectations of the public and the workers from the new system. For instance, a change involving the movement and transfer perhaps of a number of employees from one area to another cannot be dealt with in a nationalized industry by simple managerial decision, and then *afterwards* waiting for possible trade union repercussions. The statutory obligations and assumptions of joint consultation mean that nationalized management must discuss *in advance* the proposed changes with the unions. Such discussions, if they are to win confidence and retain sense, must allow for objections. Objections may compel modifications of the original plan. All this will be irritating to the go-ahead board member if he is addicted to large-scale private enterprise thinking, but nothing has been so damping to the morale of those who work in nationalized industry as the cool assumption on the part of ministers, Tory M.P.s, and some outside inquirers, that all would be well if efficiency and service reaches the standard of that normally found in privately-owned industry. No declared socialist should accept the implied snub: nor should a manager at any level in a nationalized industry, who is a practising socialist – even if he votes Conservative – sit back confined by such limitations. His aim must be to study organization and its problems in a new light altogether: against a pitiless scrutiny by political authority and public opinion, and with, in addition, an accountability to employees that no privately-owned industry could possibly carry.

It is worth recalling how the mishap to a reactor at Windscale a few years back resulted in parliamentary questions and statements, intense activity by local authorities and finally a special inquiry which enforced changes in the structure of the Atomic Energy Authority. More recently Sir Christopher Hinton, after a major electricity breakdown, felt obliged to discuss on television and at Press conferences the departmental arrangements of the C.E.G.B., an obligation which to his great credit he accepted as perfectly right and proper. Nationalized industries cannot draw the curtains – they must dress and undress in public.

A question which has been magnified out of all sensible proportion until it has become a violently contested doctrinal dispute is 'centralization' or 'decentralization'. Let it be said at once that in the eyes of most people nationalization classically means centralization. It is public ownership under state direction. The political powers and boundaries of the nation embrace the industry nationalized: neither more nor less. Whatever the theoretical autonomy of the public corporation, this is undoubtedly the view the British public take of their contemporary nationalized industries. And unless a method can be devised for appointing the boards from below or internally it is not easy to say the public are wrong. Hence it is natural that the public as consumers and customers should show a decided preference in their everyday attitudes for nationwide prices and standards. The varying price of coal – and electricity and gas as fuels derived from coal – in different parts of the country always brings questions and criticism from the public, as letters in local newspapers reveal. It is all very well for a particular region of British Railways to think that its autonomy gives it a right not to provide some service found in another region, but any aggrieved traveller will be quick to point out the anomaly with the gibe, 'I thought you were *nationalized.*'

Another factor leading the public to expect centralized dealings and policies on the part of nationalized industry is the simplicity and straightforwardness which the House of Commons still has as an institution in the eyes of the average citizen. Although he or she may not have exhausted progress through the recognized local channels, district and regional offices, consultative councils and the like over a grievance, it seems natural enough to approach an M.P. about the action of a body over which John or Jill Citizen knows Parliament has or has had a big say. And democratic politics being as they are, few M.P.s would either be so complacent or so hardy as to turn such inquirers back to the point from which they may have started. A letter will go either to the minister or to the responsible chairman of the appropriate national body – be it board, authority or commission – and the facts of the case will be probed from above, however far down the source of the trouble.

Again, with trade unions organized nationally, union leaders and officials prefer to keep negotiations under their own control, and this becomes virtually impossible if these are conducted locally without reference to a national pattern. It is true, of course, that in general the nationalization statutes compel initial national arrangements in any case for wages, salaries and conditions, but even if this were not so, in order to present a united front to union strength, the separate components of a nationalized industry would prefer to act together as one body, and this in turn has a powerful influence on organization.

Altogether, then, it is no good saying – as some observers do – that nationalization is compatible with overall decentralization, because life will not allow it. A nationalized industry may be over-centralized or under-centralized at a particular time and give rise to legitimate criticism, but centralized in part it must be. In a model, hypothetical nationalized industry a single central authority, board or holding company, with powers defined and limited either by statute or straight managerial decision, would take responsibility for matters of national concern whether falling in the political, technical, financial or psychological sphere – using the last unsatisfactory adjective to cover issues where the public as consumers or customers, however irrationally or inconveniently, demand standardization or a single consistent policy operated on a country-wide basis. Normally, therefore, relations with the minister, Parliament and unions; research and forward planning; capital raising or receiving and capital allocation; publicity and public explanations, should be reserved federally. Outside the reserved federal powers, the regional operative organizations, whether subordinate boards, regional executives, controlled companies, or management units with a span of authority dictated by changing technical conditions, should be free to run their own affairs subject to effective checks on performance by the federal authority.

# CHAPTER ELEVEN

# STRUCTURES AND THEIR ADAPTATION

*by*

JOHN HUGHES

SINCE long before there were nationalized industries, and as long as there have been, the subject of structure has been controversial. This is hardly surprising in view of the needs such structures are called upon to meet. To evaluate a structure it must be examined in its relation to the achievement of:

(a) Operational Efficiency. This is not only a matter of controlling and minimizing costs of production, though these at once involve a wide enough range of activities, including the handling of wages and purchasing, as well as technical control of operations. There is a time-scale involved here; it is not only a matter of costs *now*, but also of costs, and indeed of products, in the future. The structure has to provide for, and cope with, the development of new techniques and products – and these in turn may require a changed structure to handle them.[1]

(b) Consumer Needs. This may be thought of in terms of quantity (e.g. frequency of rail service), quality, and range of choice. Within limits, the price mechanism may provide nationalized industries with a guide as to how far and in what way to meet consumer demands. But it may not be possible to price a particular good or service to a particular customer so that it is directly related to the costs involved. In any case, it is a familiar enough point that there may be social costs (or benefits) attached to sales

---

[1] As an illustration, in the dispute within the N.C.B. in the 1950s as to how far and how fast the N.C.B. should develop coal utilization (new types of processing, smokeless fuels, by-products, etc.), those who resisted such developments were known as 'little N.C.B.ers' (as they saw the function of the structure solely as coal-*getting*), and those who wanted rapid expansion of activities in this new direction were the 'big N.C.B.ers'. Some among them thought a new authority – a coal carbonization one – was needed, just as currently the case is argued for a separate coal marketing authority.

of particular goods and services which do not figure in accounting costs, and make these an unreliable guide to action. But apart from that, the authority must decide whether it is providing goods or services at times or in ways that meet consumer needs, and to decide that it must involve itself in finding out what consumers want, but do not have (not to mention whether they want or like what they do have). The structure has to be responsive to consumer needs. There is, moreover, the question of how far aggressive marketing of a product should be taken, since this involves costs that a consumer must finally bear. This is perhaps a less difficult decision for a nationalized industry facing aggressive selling from a competing private industry. But whether it is the best way of meeting consumer needs when rival nationalized industries engage in it is another question.

(c) General Economic Planning. It is generally understood that nationalized industries are to be capable of working within an overall national plan of resource allocation, and, one might add, of income distribution. This not only imposes certain pressures upon the structure, but also requires a structure that can be in various ways related to the needs of ministerial control and, more widely, of social accountability. In this field both the planning objectives, and the ways in which the structures have been made to fit into them, have been subjects of controversy. Even the Conservative Government's partial retreat from this relationship between national economic direction and the functioning of the nationalized industries merely creates new structural problems for old. The formula 'let competition prevail' is in any case heavily qualified (e.g. by Treasury control of investment expenditure). To take a different point, if the Labour Party were to develop its views as to the need for extension of ownership and control of the 'commanding heights' of industry, this question of the relation of structure to centralized planning controls would need to be looked at afresh.

(d) Morale and Participation. Much socialist thinking about nationalization starts out from a critique of decision-taking and order-giving within the capitalist firm, a critique too of the commodity status of labour. The long-drawn-out dispute within the Labour movement in the inter-war years about structure and control hinged on this question. It was, and is, a dispute not only about the degree of emphasis to be given to participation and to democratization of managerial procedures, but also of the methods by which these goals are to be achieved. One can associate this question (especially as management too becomes unionized) with the problem of alienation that develops within large managerial structures and about which operational management has also voiced its discontent with 'anonymous bureaucracy'.[1] The need for the structure to meet demands for participation and to overcome the alienation felt by its personnel is therefore wider than manual worker participation (and far wider than the formal structures of consultation provide for). To a greater or lesser extent a necessary function of the structure is the creation of a meaningful association between its personnel and its organizational ends and techniques.

Evidently, it is not an easy task to develop a structure that will reconcile all these major functional requirements at the same time. In the analysis that follows, the attempt is made to survey some of the most important problems of nationalized industry structures that have developed, while keeping these functional requirements in mind. But there is really an additional dimension to all the needs that have been listed which structures such as these must fulfil: that is, their ability to handle *change*. For the enterprise must be able not only to adjust to change, but also to comprehend early enough what changes are going to take place. The structure needed is one that can operate efficiently in the new and developing technical and market conditions that are emerging; and this may not be identical with the structure that suited the *old* organizational, product, or technical base. The struggle to adjust to change was particularly in evidence in the early years; for nationalization created an entirely novel situation, in that a revolutionary change in scale of operation occurred virtually overnight. But this should not be thought of as a once-for-all situation; the characteristic of the technological and market environment of these industries is rapid, uneven, and often unexpected change. The structures, then, must be judged also in terms of their ability to cope with the need for large-scale adaptation.

Given all these factors, it is little wonder that the great debate on

[1] One revealing phrase used was, 'It's like working for a ghost'.

structure goes on, and little wonder that it is so confused. There are disagreements about which objectives of the structures should be accorded priority. There is also the fact that the action taken in changing nationalized industry structures stems from different, indeed in some cases diametrically opposed, views of *how* to manage very large-scale firms. For instance, the Fleck Committee (on coal) and the Herbert Committee (on electricity supply) looked at industries which followed similar principles so far as formal management structures were concerned. Both committees had similar views as to the 'commercial' nature of these corporations. But the Fleck Report accepted the general principles of the structure it found (although it was highly critical of the level of management achievement within that structure[1]); the Herbert Report, by contrast, was highly critical of the principles and assumptions upon which the management structure was based. These reports therefore led in markedly different directions (which are examined in more detail subsequently); indeed, it has been a source of wonder and interest since to ask what would have happened if Fleck had investigated electricity supply, and Herbert coal. What should be noticed, though, is that the Government, presented with highly contrasted reports, accepted and implemented both, while the Labour Party begged the whole question of which was the better approach.[2]

There is on this subject a mass of material, a long bibliography of disputation, but very little sure ground. But before attempting to guide the reader through the labyrinth by analysing the main permanent, or at least persistent, structural problems of the nationalized industries, it is necessary to review the legacy they inherited – their point of departure as nationalized industries.

In fact, as we have seen, there is little uniformity in the initial legacy of these industries. There is a world of difference between the freedom the Coal Board was given to decide the management structure of its industry, and the detailed structure of the electricity supply industry and the Transport Commission, which inherited

[1] Cf. the scathing criticism in Section VIII of the Fleck Report, 'Making the Organization Work'.

[2] 'Public Enterprise', the policy statement, avoided the question of structure by saying, 'it calls for inquiries on the lines of the Fleck and Herbert Reports' (p. 24), without any further comment on either.

perhaps the most unfortunate legacy of all. Although a unitary structure for transport was adopted, in the shape of the commission, the organization of separate executives for road and rail and other transport services was laid down. It would seem a strange way to pursue the declared objective of an integrated transport system, to create separate management structures particularly for road and rail, linked only at the level of the commission itself. The L.T.E. was left as a lonely example of the pursuit of at least partial integration within a distinct transport region. This heritage was doubly unfortunate, as it meant that integration of services had hardly begun, let alone been consolidated, before the resurrection of the dogma of competition by the Conservatives.

The other legacy that varied was the capacity to handle large-scale management, and the need to centralize and create co-ordination and uniform procedures. It is roughly true to say that where the need for strong centralizing and integrating authority was at its greatest, the dearth of personnel able to deal with large-scale management was also at its greatest. This contradiction applied most to the industries where a very large number of small units were taken over, without a sufficient admixture of hitherto large units to leaven the lump, e.g. coal and road haulage.[1] Under these conditions, the attempt to centralize, together with an orthodox approach to the span of control, created in the consequent multi-tier structure of management above operational level serious stresses felt over a long period. Road haulage had perhaps some advantage from war-time experience of integrating a large long-distance fleet of vehicles. The stresses were most obvious in the case of the N.C.B. Even eight years later few managers understood 'the purpose and function of National Headquarters', and 'the ramifications of the coal industry'.[2] The higher echelons were staffed up, after a fashion, although the Fleck Report concluded that to pay reasonable compensation 'for retiring many ineffective people who are kept in the industry' would be 'money

---

[1] Road haulage involved the acquisition of some 4,000 undertakings, owning roughly 40,000 vehicles.

[2] The Fleck Report said these things of 'some area general managers', and added 'they had no idea how National Headquarters fitted into the board's organization' (p. 59). If even some A.G.M.s did not understand these matters, we can hardly expect other managerial personnel to do so.

well spent'.[1] Operational management was denuded and starved of both really capable managers and any adequate system of a specialized team of managers in the larger pits. Only very recently has the N.C.B. begun experimenting seriously with the provision of an adequate management team, organized on functional lines, in the biggest pits.

This problem was a unique one, in the sense that the large managerial aggregates in private industry emerged from a much more protracted process of growth-cum-merger; but here for the first time the whole time-scale of growth was abruptly fore-shortened. In other nationalized industries this problem was less acute, as a basis for larger scale organization existed (in the four railway systems, the Central Electricity Board, and a few large gas and electricity supply undertakings), but it was still by no means negligible. The problem was inherent in a programme of nationalization of industries other than the monopolistic and highly concentrated 'commanding heights'.

The long-term problems and opportunities connected with nationalized industry structure are substantially different from these early dilemmas. The protracted argument between the centralizers and the decentralizers, which has dominated the literature on the subject, does little either to clarify the issues, or even illuminate the actual trends that have emerged. This is partly because a number of analytically distinct questions are telescoped into what is taken to be a single argument. Partly also it stems from the obvious difficulty of generalizing as to the best location of different managerial functions and the decision-taking attached to them; for instance, the case for centralized buying is palpably stronger than the argument for centralized selling. Partly it arises because decentralization in one industry could have quite different economic implications from those in another, e.g. in coal this could involve competition between different coalfields in ways which simply would not occur in rail transport or electricity or gas.

The main issues involved in the development of these structures, apart from the initial problems stressed above, appear to fall under five main headings. In some of these we are concerned with developments and disputes which affect nationalized industries simply in their capacity as large-scale firms; others are more

[1] Fleck Report, p. 60.

particularly connected with their role as publicly-owned firms. But all seem directly relevant to unravelling post-nationalization developments and the future course of change.

## Integration or Dis-integration

The question of how far to push integration in the field of fuel and power, and in the field of transport, together with the problem of the best *form* such integration should take, is one of the most important unresolved issues of nationalization. It is clearly one on which political alignments influence views, in the sense that the general drift of Conservative policy has been towards dis-integration, justified in terms of competition; this has sometimes seemed little more than a rationalization to cover the absence of coherent policies. On the other hand, the Labour Party is committed to integration and co-ordination of operating and investment decisions in both main fields; although the shape of such relationships and the co-ordinated policies envisaged are far from clear.

In the field of fuel and power, the issue of integration has affected relations between coal, gas and electricity, and it therefore raises the question of relations between nationalized industries pursued elsewhere. The rival statistical appendices to the Ridley Report[1] demonstrated that where the boards were in direct competition, in the field of space heating, there was vehement partisanship and no disposition to concentrate on a rationalization of their activities in the interests of fuel economy in a period of shortage. Similarly, in the field of appliance selling (as the vanguard of domestic supply) there has been no disposition to substitute a comprehensive public service for the rivalry of competitive salesmanship. No one even seems to have contemplated a localized experiment in combined showrooms, or an integrated local service. When my house is connected to the gas and electricity supply, the lane is still dug up twice over on different days by teams of public servants working in rivalry. On the other hand, close co-operation is emerging as the result of the economic gains from building very large power-stations and Lurgi plants in the closest proximity to the necessary supplies of low-cost coal. Technique at this level

[1] 'National Policy for the Use of Fuel and Power Resources', Cmd. 8647.

imposes an *ad hoc* integration which is sadly lacking elsewhere, most of all in distribution and sales.

In transport, the British Transport Commission has, so far, pointed to an acceptance of integration which never went very far in practice; the potentiality remained a largely unrealized one, now deliberately reversed. The 1962 Transport Act involves the ending of the B.T.C. and with it of any overall *executive* authority in public transport. The railways, London Transport, Inland Waterways, British Transport Docks, appear as separate boards, and British Road Services and the various bus groups, hotels, and other holdings as separate companies under the limited supervision of a holding company. It may be that this structure is designed, *inter alia*, to make easier the return of various sections to private ownership. In any case, the complete reliance on competition between separate authorities – doubtless under the slogan of consumer choice – is dictated by the existence of a large and growing private sector in road transport. Any counting of *social* costs and *social* benefits, rather than basing prices on commercial accounting which does not have to measure these items, would swing policy not only heavily towards integration but also heavily in favour of the railway network and public passenger transport. The lobbies associated with private transport and vehicle production may gain from disintegration and 'competition', but the operation of a structure and pricing system that counts only some of the costs and neglects the direct gains from integration can only be to the community's loss.

The unrealized potentiality in transport is the regional integration of transport services. Except for the partial integration achieved by London Transport, this does not emerge. The 1947 Transport Act created a structural apparatus that separated transport services under distinct and centralized management precisely at the operational level. No major investment on the part of the railways to make road-rail integration a reality by rationalizing handling and trans-shipping of freight was undertaken until the mid-1950s. Both the structure adopted, and the failure to win a share in the investment programme from the Labour Government, meant that integration, far from being consolidated, was stillborn. After 1953 it looked, paradoxically, as if extended road-rail integration might be won out of the chaos and confusion involved in breaking up the best of the B.R.S. road fleet. The boards established to exercise control over the railway *regions* were called *area* boards, a semantic point not without significance. Sir Brian Robertson, giving evidence to the Select Committee on railways, said in a reply to a question on this from Mr Albu :

> We have always wished to make provision for the possibility that these boards should take care of matters other than railways. We are a Transport Commission and we at least wish to provide the possibility that some of our other activities should owe an allegiance to the board and provision is made in the Act for that to happen with the minister's consent ... we have already told the boards we would like them to watch the transport picture as a whole.[1]

Here, then, was another 'possibility'; that it did not materialize may be connected not only with the fact of dependence on the consent of the minister, but also on the felt separateness of identity as between road and rail which the 1947 Act's structure had done little to dispel. It is ironic to think that a useful approach for a future Labour Government trying to create a transport system that can meet the community's needs would be (in repealing the 1962 Transport Act) to revert to this unrealized potentiality in the 1953 Act, a gradual – instead of overnight – integration of transport services on a regional basis. As an example, a Scottish Area Transport Board might enable a more adequate system to emerge than is likely to be achieved by the proposed operation in Scotland of a regional railway board, a docks board, an inland waterways authority, B.R.S., the hotels, Scottish Omnibuses, *et al.*, all operating as separate undertakings, and linked only by a Transport Advisory Council of (at present) unspecified functions meeting infrequently in London. This, apart from the increasing need in the future to integrate air services more closely with land transport.

*Unitary or Federal Structures*

What is, and what should be, the relation between centre and regions? Instead of the confused categories of centralization/

[1] H.C. 254–1, 1960, qu. 315.

decentralization, it is helpful to import a distinction familiar enough in political constitutions, that between unitary and federal government. A unitary authority may delegate wide powers to subordinate formations, but the decision is in its hands, and the residual authority is centralized. A federal structure may be no more than a loose confederation of largely autonomous regions or companies delegating only very limited functions to a central authority, or it may involve a more formal separation of powers as between regions and centre, and more comprehensive centralized services. But in either case, some or all of the residual power rests with the constituent units. For all this variation within the two categories, the distinction between federal and unitary structures remains real.

The general tendency is evidently in the direction of replacing unitary structures by federal ones. The major industries that have so far remained unchanged in this respect are coal, which has always been unitary, and gas, which has always been federal (if anything, a confederation). The railways have edged slightly towards a federal structure, though the nature of railway operation imposes limits, and what emerges is a division of powers still heavily weighted towards the centre.[1] For publicly-owned transport undertakings as a whole, the 'Nationalized Transport Advisory Council' would seem to provide no more than vestigial traces even of a federal approach. The electricity supply industry, under the aegis of Citrine, was operating very much as a unitary system until 1957, even if the nationalization statute appeared to give some semblance of federation. The 1957 Act has created area autonomy on the distributive side, but left the generating side still unitary in structure (this is, of course, dictated by the needs of technology). The Electricity Council as the federal body therefore groups together structurally dissimilar authorities.

An interesting situation, by contrast, has arisen in the gas

[1] The wording of the 1962 Transport Act suggests a conflict between advocates of federal and of unitary organization. The earlier intention (Cmnd. 1248) to represent each railway region on the Railways Board is not pursued (cf. clause 1(3)). Clause 2(4) states that Regional Boards' functions are 'delegated to them by the Railways Board', but the latter is not a free agent on this and must 'act on lines settled with the approval of the Minister'. Elsewhere the Regional Boards are said to 'share between them responsibility for all parts of the railway system' (clause 2(1)).

industry. Here potentialities of economies of very large-scale operation in production and distribution, greater than can be handled by an area board, have emerged in recent years. To quote the Select Committee 'Report on the Gas Industry', the emphasis of the 1948 Gas Act 'was on the independence of area boards; technologically, the emphasis today is on their inter-dependence. To make gas more cheaply, to store it and transmit it more cheaply, require collective action of some kind.'[1] In this situation the Gas Council has suggested a plan under which it would be given powers to manufacture and supply gas, and this has 'the unanimous support of the area board chairmen, although it would lead eventually to a derogation of their powers'.[2] That such an initiative should command the support of area boards is some token of the flexibility and capacity for adaptation of such a federal structure.

It is difficult to pronounce a final judgment in this field. Initially, a unitary structure enables standardization and co-ordinated policies to be achieved more quickly and over a wider field than if they had to wait upon the recognition of mutual interest by largely autonomous bodies. But after that, it does not seem unreasonable to argue that it is beneficial to have final executive authority situated near the operating units. There remain obvious cases where technical factors require a national authority, as with airline operation, some aspects of railway operation, the electricity grid, and the development of a gas grid. That coal is not yet pushed in the direction of a federal structure is due to a number of factors. The most important is the very unequal economic position of the different coalfields (varying in 1960 from a deficit of 14s. 3d. a ton in one coalfield to a surplus of 7s. 10½d. in another). In this situation, to allow autonomous regions to compete with

[1] Select Committee on Nationalized Industries, 'Report on The Gas Industry', H.C. 280, 1961, para. 452. The implications of this for the structure of the gas industry are dealt with at length in the report, paras. 445–75.

[2] Op. cit., para. 471. The solution which the Select Committee themselves preferred mirrors the present structure of electricity supply: 'a thirteenth board ... to undertake all new gas generation on a large scale, and to control ... a national grid, and underground storage'. (Para. 472). It is the ministry, apparently, who are the structural conservatives. In face of the transformation in the scale of the technical optimum, they would prefer to leave the structure unchanged. (See para. 470.)

one another for coal markets would be a ruinous and retrograde step as compared with a planned development (which by no means ignores production costs) handled nationally. It is this, and their bitter experience of district wage systems in the inter-war years, that explains the hostility of the miners to any attempt to move in the direction of a federal structure.

Clearly, the federal bodies emerging in the nationalized industries will concentrate largely on research and development, and on the co-ordination of investment and financial policies. Critics argue that the importance of large-scale research may be neglected under these conditions; the low expenditure on research and the lag in development of the gas grid and of Lurgi plants by the Gas Council is taken as a case in point. But inadequate research expenditure has been a general feature of nationalized industries until very recently, whether unitary or federal in structure. The rapid increase of research expenditure by the C.E.G.B. in recent years shows what can be achieved, but it does not demonstrate that federal bodies will necessarily lag in such directions. It should not be forgotten that ministers have powers to issue general directives in either case, and there is therefore an authority which can intervene if federal action is failing to develop in the directions needed.

Before leaving this subject, the extremely interesting case of steel nationalization is worth a comment. A federal structure was inherited, as the steel companies had since 1934 built up a powerful co-ordinator and central service agency in the shape of the British Iron and Steel Federation. The nationalization statute, curiously, neglected completely the existence of this institution, which was the main seat of power in the industry on a number of the most important questions (such as cost and profit pooling through the Industry Fund). The corporation that was set up was a unitary structure, but limited largely to the functions of a holding company. In the longer run, the corporation would doubtless have been able to make major changes in company structures, for instance, to secure some of the neglected benefits of integrated operations between neighbouring plants in different companies. Thus the Act did not prejudge the final structure of the industry. But what it did do, by neglecting the existence of a federal power in the industry, was to prevent the corporation – in the time available, which was what mattered – from exercising any control over the operation of the federation (whose most important members were nationalized). In this case a powerful and entrenched federal authority beat the fledgling unitary authority, and the people who directed the federation were the leading directors of the nationalized companies. It is to be hoped that next time any nationalization statute will not 'forget' the federation.[1]

## Methods of Control

What should be the 'span of control' within a structure of higher management, i.e. how many subordinate formations should a manager have reporting to him, how many should he be responsible for? If the emphasis is placed on personal control of lower levels of management, the orthodox answer would seem to be that, to be effective, the span of control should be narrow. There are some who attach mystic significance in this connection to the number five. But what does this involve in a unitary nationalized industry made up of hundreds of operating units? What has emerged has been a multi-tier structure above the operating unit. Must this necessarily be accepted? Is it the best solution? May it not lead to a situation where authority becomes anonymous, responsibility diffused, decisions referred up?

The Fleck and Herbert Reports provide an instructive contrast; the Fleck Committee believed in a narrow span of control as an article of faith; the Herbert Report challenged the concept directly. Both committees, in examining area organization in the respective industries, found the same tendency had developed, that an intermediate tier of management (group, or sub-area) had been developing between the area authority and the operating units. The Fleck Committee thought that this should be investigated by the N.C.B. and recommended that 'the line of command should pass from the divisional board through the area general manager and the agent to the colliery manager', that is that the intermediate level should be systematized. This was in fact done, using the nomenclature 'groups' rather than 'agents';

---

[1] If there is to be a next time – Editor.

some two hundred groups emerged. Needless to say, these, rather than the pit manager, became the first level of real managerial authority. The structure of management above the operating unit is therefore: group, area, division, and national board.

The Herbert Committee, confronting the same situation in electricity distribution, set down their analysis in considerable detail,[1] and concluded that where sub-areas had developed they had become the effective level of management and had subordinated the districts, so that there was 'no real chance of securing managerial experience below the level of sub-area manager'. Consequently area boards contained only 'five or six truly managerial posts'. They concluded that there should instead be only one management level below the board headquarters, and that the number of 'genuine management districts should be increased to perhaps fifteen or twenty in each area'. In other words they advocated a deliberate widening of the span of control at this point so as to ensure 'genuine managerial experience' at operational level. The contrast could hardly be more extreme.[2]

If the need for a narrow span of control is thus called in question, particularly with the objective of creating posts of considerable managerial responsibility near or at operational level in such industries, there would at least seem to be a case for controlled experiment at area level with alternative control structures. This looks the more promising when it is considered that the 'narrow span of control' approach may have set up something of a vicious circle. It can be argued that concentration on strengthening the staffing of higher management levels has both pulled talented

[1] Report, p. 76–8.

[2] Another instructive contrast is in their respective attitudes to structure at area board level, and the degree of autonomy of such area boards in arranging their own structure. The Herbert Report thought the Central Electricity Authority's insistence that area boards should not make important changes in their organizational structure was 'interference which the area boards ... resent' (p. 64). The Fleck Report reached the opposite conclusion, that the N.C.B. 'should lay down a pattern of organization ... which should be adopted by each area' (p. 42). What is more, they suggested in Appendix C what form the pattern might take, and this 'suggestion' was subsequently rigidly imposed. This is the more striking as they had 'not gone deeply' (p. 53) into colliery organization, and still less into the effects of colliery development.

management away from operational level, and led to relative neglect of management needs at that level. The consequent weaknesses in operational management would then seem to require and justify close personal control by higher formations. The lack of a sense of personal responsibility and initiative, and the inadequacy of operational management, would thereby be perpetuated. Such an effect would seem to have some application in the coal industry, and the Herbert Report stressed the aspect of decline in initiative and sense of personal responsibility in electricity supply.

Two factors are at work that may make possible and even more desirable a wider span of control, thereby reducing the levels of management needed. One is the process of concentration of operating units referred to below. The other is the development of standard yardsticks of performance, which enables standard costing and measures of comparative performance to replace with their statistical checks some of the close personal supervision otherwise required. Nationalized industries have been moving unevenly in this direction; it is interesting to note that serious attempts at costing of traffic as between railway areas have only recently begun to be undertaken. In large-scale concerns such as these there are great potentialities in such developments, and in the associated technical developments in processing information. Yardsticks for measuring performance at operational level are being developed and made more accurate: this development alone could revolutionize the control functions required from higher management.

### Departmental Co-ordination

The other general problem facing large-scale organizations has also been much in evidence in the nationalized industries. The main problem appears to have been in the stress on departmental, or functional, management at the expense of the chain of command of general management. On the railways, the structure was modelled on the highly departmentalized organization of the L.M.S.; the crucial weakness here was the lack of provision for co-ordination with the power of decision-taking and the settlement of differences except at a high level. The structure of railway management has now undergone a major change, with a new emphasis on general management at district level, in what appears to be a bold attempt to overcome this problem.[1] 'Emphasizing the management chain of command rather than the functional, and reducing the risk of conflict between them', was one of the reasons the Herbert Report gave for giving the district manager in electricity distribution real managerial authority.

In the coal industry the problem is twofold. Firstly, the full range of functional departments exists at national, divisional, and area level (with minor exceptions), but operational management has been starved of functional specialists. Secondly, despite the emphatic recommendation to this effect on the part of the Fleck Committee, a strong staff department has not yet emerged. The staff department has, it is true, been created, but it has not had the backing from the board that would enable the development of selection procedures, and systematic planning of movement of staff between departments. In the absence of this planned selection, and training and interdepartmental movement of *higher* management, the problems of departmental rigidity and narrowness remain. The Fleck Committee argued:

> We would expect the setting up of a staff department to help to resolve one of the problems which is always met in large organizations, and is very evident in the coal industry, namely, how to reconcile the desire of the man on the spot to have the last word in the appointment of his own staff, with the need to ensure that responsible posts are filled in accordance with the needs of the industry at large. The Staff Department must also deal with the problem of the excessive turnover in some posts.[2]

The staff department is there, but so too is the power of the separate departments on appointment, so too is the game of musical chairs ('excessive turnover'). Behind this the problem of departmental co-ordination is perpetuated.

[1] 'In five regions the new organization, representing a revolution in railway management, is now functioning.' B.T.C. report 1959, para. 62.

[2] Report, p. 27. On *this* question the Fleck and Herbert Reports were in agreement. The Herbert Committee found the same situation prevailing in electricity supply, and were 'seriously disturbed about this whole matter to which we attach the greatest importance'. Their recommendation of 'deliberate selection ... of potential leaders' is similar to the Fleck Committee's aim. See Herbert Report, paras. 325–8.

## Concentration of Operational Units

A most important factor which is beginning to have, and must increasingly have, major effects on the structure of the nationalized industries, is the rapid process of concentration that is going on within them. When the Fleck Committee examined the N.C.B. in 1955 there were nearly nine hundred collieries; there are now under seven hundred. In 1960 alone forty-four collieries were closed or merged (only six of these mainly for economic reasons), while three new ones came into operation. The same process proceeds apace on the railways, with modernization and rationalization both contributing. Parcel traffic is concentrated into zonal centres, accounts are concentrated; one new marshalling yard is typically replacing eight existing yards; Eastern Region's freight sundries traffic is brought into twenty-two centres instead of one hundred. In gas and electricity, power-stations and gas plant of very large size and connected by grid with consuming areas are transforming the industries. The gas industry had only four hundred and twenty-eight producing plants in 1960, compared with one thousand and fifty at vesting date, but of the four hundred and twenty-eight plants the seventy-one largest produced seventy-one per cent of the gas made.

Two rather obvious points need to be made about this evident process of concentration of operating units. On the one hand, it forces a strengthening of operational management; the general management posts in these larger units carry more responsibility, and call for more functional assistance; it is this that has led the N.C.B. to experiment with a greatly strengthened management team with more functional specialization for the larger pits. Secondly, so far as the control and co-ordination carried out by higher management is concerned, the effect is to simplify these tasks, and this again facilitates the strengthening of operational management. It would not be far wrong to say, for instance, that the management levels of the N.C.B., and the concentration of functional management within these higher management formations, are being rendered obsolescent by the changed character of the operational units as a result of a decade of heavy spending on major colliery development. The balance between functional experts in higher management formations and functional management at plant level is changing, alongside the strengthening of the calibre and responsibility of operational management in the new and larger units. It is the familiar question of 'base and superstructure'; what is needed above all is a recognition of the direction of change, and early adaptation of structures to meet it.

Clearly, some of the factors analysed separately above reinforce one another. To take advantage of the new potentialities, structural change appears necessary, particularly at the level of significant operational responsibility and at the level above that. The major change in railway management systems is perhaps a harbinger. Overcoming weakness in co-ordination between departments by general management authority at district level connects with the concentration of operations and the need for stronger 'line' control (i.e. general management) of such large units.

Even without venturing towards policy conclusions, the trends that are in evidence have interesting implications for structure viewed in its relation to participation and accountability. The process of consultation and worker participation, especially at plant level, has been affected by the problems of operational management, such as their limited area of responsibility and initiative, and high rates of staff turnover. The changes taking place open up the potentiality of a wider and more meaningful area of participation, while the development of standard yardsticks of performance makes managerial authority less arbitrary.

The other major accountability problem arising from the structure has been the blurring of the area of responsibility of corporation and ministry respectively, not least on prices, wages, and development. At the same time, there is what might be termed, using the nomenclature of the analysis above, a disintegration of accountability at national level, split up as it is between parliamentary accountability (including the Select Committee), employee consultative, and consumer consultative arrangements. This dis-integration occurs despite the obvious overlap and interconnections of the subject matter.

On the first of these problems, the development of federal structures in place of unitary boards may limit the overlap of functions between ministry and nationalized industry. It may also make the minister more forthcoming about, or less able to avoid, the use of open directives, in place of the informal pressures that evade parliamentary scrutiny. Not that one should be too optimistic about ministers being bold enough to give a clear policy lead in this way. The possible integration of accountability at national level looks more remote. At first sight, the Herbert Committee's recommendation (which was not adopted) of 'a central organization relieved of the Central Electricity Authority's present executive responsibilities for generation and transmission, but with certain clearly-defined supervisory functions', appears relevant. But the Herbert approach was a non-starter for obvious reasons. It envisaged the intended 'supervisory' authority as handling functions which would otherwise have developed federally, i.e. it restricted the natural development of the area distribution boards and generating board. It sought also to give the 'supervisory' authority the power of issuing formal directions, thereby increasing the extent of overlap with ministerial functions. Finally, it did not look to a representative element on the 'super-visory' authority, and was therefore unrelated to the various forms of consultation with and accountability to representative bodies at national level. Thus it was clearly not the model for a possible integrated 'scrutiny' committee at national level.

In conclusion, the management structures of the nationalized industries are in process of further development and change. These changes point particularly to a strengthening of management at operational level, and (with some exceptions) to a federal structure. What is far more controversial, and therefore uncertain, as it depends on political factors, is whether there will be an extension of integration (e.g. of transport regionally, of fuel and power investment, distribution, and sales) or of dis-integration. These structural changes in turn may affect both the extent and the forms of worker participation and of accountability to repre-sentative bodies.

# CHAPTER TWELVE

# STATE INDUSTRY AND THE PUBLIC

*by*

## MARK ABRAMS

ONE of the incidental advantages of general elections is that they produce a great many sample surveys concerned with measuring the electorate's attitudes on a wide range of political issues.

By the time the 1959 election came round, it was clear from several dependable opinion polls that most people were not only opposed to any extension of nationalization, but were also convinced that the general performance of the already nationalized industries compared unfavourably with that of private industry. Undoubtedly part of this disapproval of nationalization was either created or crystallized by the extensive and costly campaigns carried out against nationalization by industrialists during 1958 and 1959. But it would be unwise to conclude that but for these campaigns the electorate would have looked favourably upon the nationalized industries. During the late 1940s Research Services carried out a series of sample surveys on political attitudes. A typical inquiry in April 1949 asked: 'Are you in favour of Labour's proposals for the nationalization of further industries such as sugar, cement, and so on?' The answers showed that already slightly over half the electorate was opposed to any extension, and little more than one-quarter favoured any further nationalization. Even among Labour Party supporters two out of every five were not in favour of any more nationalization. At the same time, very few voters attached much importance to the efforts made by the Labour Government to nationalize various industries. Indeed only five per cent of Labour supporters thought that nationalization had been the chief accomplishment of the Labour Government.

Over the next decade, at least as far as the general public was concerned, nationalization as a decisive political policy interested fewer and fewer voters, and by the summer of 1959 the Gallup Poll reported that only six per cent of people interviewed were mentioning nationalization as a major issue.

It is probable that the main effect of the 1958–9 anti-nationalization campaign was to establish the word as a convenient shorthand for many people who had once voted Labour and now wished either to transfer their support to other parties or else to abstain. But obviously it was only possible for it to establish this position because, in fact, some of the nationalized industries had failed to demonstrate that they were efficient parts of the economy.

It was because of this 'stereotype' character of the word 'nationalization' that *Socialist Commentary*, when it carried out its post-election survey at the beginning of 1960, both avoided using the word and also concerned itself with each of the nationalized industries separately. It was hoped in this way to arrive at more considered views. People were asked about 'publicly-owned industries' and invited to give their views separately on coal, electricity, airlines, atomic energy, and railways. Half the respondents were prepared to say that the public ownership of electricity had been a success; one-third felt the same about atomic energy, the airlines and gas; but clear-cut majorities asserted that coal and the railways had been failures. In commenting on each of these industries there were appreciable minorities who said they knew too little about them to be able to judge, and this criticism came from Labour supporters as well as from Conservatives.

*Views on publicly-owned industries*

| Industry | Success | Failure | No difference | Don't know | = 100% |
|---|---|---|---|---|---|
| | % | % | % | % | |
| Electricity | 50 | 16 | 19 | 15 | ,, |
| Atomic energy | 39 | 5 | 5 | 51 | ,, |
| Airlines | 35 | 9 | 6 | 50 | ,, |
| Gas | 33 | 22 | 20 | 25 | ,, |
| Coal | 25 | 52 | 12 | 11 | ,, |
| Railways | 16 | 62 | 10 | 12 | ,, |
| Average | 33 | 28 | 12 | 27 | |

These findings – showing wide differences of response for the various nationalized industries – suggest that the campaign to turn 'nationalization' into a general smear word had failed. The public was still able to discriminate between the performances of nationalized electricity and that of the nationalized railways (between successful nationalization and unsuccessful nationalization). But even after it had made this discrimination, when the sample was asked if any more industries should be publicly owned it voted almost seven to one against any extensions; even Labour supporters opposed them by nearly three to one.

This massive unwillingness to contemplate any further public ownership was expressed even by those who recognized the success of the electricity industry and of the airlines, and this suggests that the nationalized industries have so far failed to cope effectively with their public relations – to make the public fully aware of their achievements, to admit their shortcomings, and to convince the electorate that adequate and energetic efforts would be made to remedy these defects. Indeed, the past (and in some cases, present) neglect of public relations by the nationalized industries has been obvious for many years, and yet this is the one function of management where failure can be least justified. Most large organizations in private industry deal successfully with their public relations, and in the public services there is a long tradition of intelligent and informed discussion of the problem.

Almost thirty years ago Sir Stephen Tallents put forward, in a paper read to the Institute of Public Administration, the case for the use of publicity in the public service.[1] Sir Stephen defined the scope of 'public service' widely so that it embraced not only Government departments staffed by civil servants (Agriculture, Education, Post Office, etc.), but also various newer undertakings whose activities in fact, if not constitutionally, represented a mixture of public and private interest; two of his examples of these were the London Underground Railways and the Empire Marketing Board. At the same time Sir Stephen's account of what he meant by publicity was sufficiently broad to cover not only advertising but also what would now be recognized as public relations. In short, well before the appearance of nationalized industries an

[1] 'Salesmanship in The Public Service', Summer Conference, Oxford, July 1933.

O

experienced authority had described the essential part to be played
by public relations in such industries and had set out the necessary
scope and appropriate techniques for this work. Since his account
is still valid, and since there is no evidence that those responsible
for setting up the nationalized industries had ever read and
absorbed his paper, it is worth quoting here some of the main
points. Sir Stephen started by offering his audience a list of the
legitimate purposes of publicity in the public services. They were
(and are):

(1) To interest the public in work done in their name, and
to create an intelligent criticism of the public services ...

(2) To justify to the public action based on considerations
too technical, too complicated ... to be fully compre-
hended by the public.

(3) To encourage the public to take the most economic
advantage of the facilities which they have caused to be
provided for themselves ... It is as important to explain
to the public truthfully what it will gain by acquiring a
particular commodity, as it is to produce that commodity.

(4) To make known to the public concerned .the results of
scientific research ...

(5) To carry out by modern publicity media special functions of public administration ...

(6) To create *esprit de corps* between the different branches of
a widely-scattered or multifarious public service, and a
proper pride of service within a large organization ...

Before going on to describe the methods which should be
adopted to pursue these ends Sir Stephen discussed some of the
developments which by 1933 had made systematic publicity
along these lines essential for the efficient operation of public
services. He pointed first to the general transfer of interest,
throughout the economy, from the problems of production to
those of distribution – a transfer which has been greatly accelerated since he spoke. Secondly, he argued that, whereas in the
past Parliament had been able to carry out more or less effectively
the task of interpreting the actions of the state to the public, the
new organizations and departments were often engaged in

activities too complicated to be interpreted either to Parliament by the new bodies, or to the public by Parliament.

Sir Stephen's paper continued with a discussion of the publicity methods which should be adopted by public authorities.

The first essential is that their publicity should be based on sound knowledge ... The second essential is that it should be founded on sincerity and truth ... Third ... our publicity should be a job for professionals and not for amateurs ... It is no use relegating the preparation of publicity material to an officer on the ground that he can produce good official memoranda, still less on the ground that his other duties do not fully absorb his energies ... Publicity should be recognized as a professional job demanding special training and special capacities. [And, in conclusion] Our first need is that our governors should recognize publicity as a positive and useful function instead of as a timidly defensive operation.

In 1962 it would still be hard to improve on this 1933 account of the legitimate and fruitful part to be played by public relations in the organization of the nationalized industries in a democratic society. But that Sir Stephen Tallents' analysis and advice was and is still ignored by some of these industries will hardly be disputed. Within a few years of the post-war nationalization legislation, Parliament itself was complaining strenuously that it knew too little of how the nationalized industries conducted themselves, and in November 1952 a Select Committee was appointed 'to consider the methods by which the House of Commons is informed of the affairs of the nationalized industries'.

The committee's report in July, 1953, properly enough, did not go outside its terms of reference, but in the course of his evidence the then chairman of Unilever pointed out that the nationalized industries had not yet had time to settle down as integrated bodies, and that 'in due course they, like Unilever, and other great commercial undertakings, would develop their own ... adequate relationships with the outside public'. In fact, over the next few years most of the nationalized industries failed 'to settle down as integrated bodies'; in most of them the work of public relations was neglected.

While the Select Committee was considering this one aspect of the public relations of the nationalized industries – accountability to and through Parliament – the Acton Society Trust was preparing its study of nationalized industry's relations with the public at large. The report[1] was thorough, objective, depressing and apparently without any effect on the nationalized industries.

It concluded that the industries had made no systematic attempts to discover through consumer surveys the attitudes of the public towards the services provided, and that, by and large, they had limited their attempts at communications with the outside world to the 'duties imposed by the nationalizing Acts in respect of their relations to Parliament and the consumer councils'. Some of the industries had produced publications intended to inform the public, but 'the publications of all the boards display a tendency to caution, and avoid mention of the industry's more controversial problems ... Some board members seem to have formed a limited conception of their responsibilities ... In general, board members seem confident that they know what the public wants ... This attitude appears to reflect the composition of the boards, whose members ... were chosen for their expertise in technical and administrative affairs.' Most of the boards considered that the work of a public relations officer encompassed nothing more than the issuing of routine Press releases and the collecting of Press clippings, that this work certainly did not call for men of special ability and training, and that, in any case, in the opinion of some people, public relations was a waste of money.

With one or two exceptions this remained until the end of the decade a fair, and indeed generous, account of the attitudes of the boards towards public relations and of most of the reasons that led to these attitudes. One further and important explanation, however, should be added. Almost certainly, much of the neglect of public relations by the nationalized industries sprang from extravagant expectations that the consumer councils would provide an effective two-way traffic of information and stimulus between the boards and the general public. In fact, they have failed to provide this link. The reasons are by now obvious: the members of the councils are largely laymen nominated haphazardly and lacking the support of adequate full-time 'civil servants'. From the begin-

[1] Acton Society Trust, *Nationalized Industry: Relations With The Public*, London, 1953.

ning they concentrated on the negative task of receiving complaints from consumers and year after year they found the flow of complaints slight in volume and often trivial in content.

It is hard to see how this can be avoided under the present arrangements. A drastic reorganization of the local consumer councils would seem to be necessary, broadly along the following lines:

(1)  There should be approximately twelve councils to cover the whole of Great Britain.

(2)  Each regional council should concern itself with the work of all the nationalized industries within its boundaries.

(3)  The members of each regional council should be drawn from the elected local government representatives within the region.

(4)  Each regional council should have at its disposal sufficient funds to publicise its work effectively and to employ its own full-time 'civil servants'.

(5)  The central board of each nationalized industry should develop its central public relations activities at least in part through the regional councils.

(6)  The regional councils, either separately or co-operatively, should have and use the necessary funds to carry out consumer sample surveys covering all the nationalized industries, and should, through local facilities, publicize the findings of these surveys.

But the reconstruction of the consumer councils will not by itself be sufficient to cope with the total public relations functions of the nationalized industries. This can only be achieved when every one of the national boards handles public relations with the seriousness it has long received in many large private corporations – and is beginning to receive in one or two of the nationalized industries. This means that the top management of each board builds its public relations department on a full recognition of the nature of public relations. The International Public Relations Association defines public relations as:

a management function, of a continuing and planned character, through which ... institutions seek to win and retain the understanding, sympathy and support of those with whom they are or may be concerned – by evaluating public opinion about themselves in order to correlate their own policies and procedures and to achieve, by planned and widespread information, more productive co-operation and more efficient fulfilment of their common interests.

In the case of the nationalized industries these basic 'common interests' are obvious enough in economic terms – that the man-power and capital they absorb should be employed efficiently and that they should not draw from the economy manpower and capital that could be used more efficiently elsewhere. 'Common interests' which necessitate the wasteful use of economic resources may emerge, but their definition must come directly and con-sciously from the public and not one-sidedly from the boards.

For effective public relations the implications of the above definition are several for each nationalized industry.

(1)  It is concerned with gaining the understanding and sup-port of several publics – its employees, the consumers of its goods and services, the local communities within which its productive units operate, the rest of industry, tax-payers and voters. The neglect of any one of these publics will inevitably harm the total effort.

(2)  Responsibility for public relations must be a manage-ment function under the direction of someone equiva-lent to a management director at board level, taking part in management decisions and making clear to his peers the public relations aspects of their decisions.

(3)  This work must be of a continuous character and not an occasional panic operation only undertaken to meet a crisis or an obviously deteriorating position.

(4)  It must be of a planned character, and this means, in military terms, that it must be based on the systematic accumulation of 'intelligence', on the setting up of a long-term 'directive', and that anyone carrying any responsibility in the work of the department must be 'briefed' on the intelligence, the objectives and the directives. It goes almost without saying, that in all its aspects this is a full-time job and not a spare-time chore

for the advertising manager, the sales manager, the board's secretariat, the librarian or the press officer.

There are signs that those nationalized industries which have most neglected public relations in the past are now, with something of a rush, showing a new enthusiasm for refurbishing their 'public image'. Their unsophisticated enthusiasm contains new dangers for the public relations of the nationalized industries. There is first the danger that the board deceives itself about the industry's real weaknesses by believing that the only thing wrong is a bad 'public image'. There is nothing to be gained and much to be lost by projecting an image of efficiency, progress, service etc., if, in fact, these do not exist. A second danger is that the public relations of the converts allows itself to be guided excessively by the desire to gain public approval – public relations officers, like politicians, gain in stature and effectiveness by leading rather than following, and by facing their defects and mistakes rather than by hoping to smother them under popular slogans.

A third danger is that with their new stature and wider activities the new enthusiasts automatically come to resent criticism from those with whom they must deal in their everyday work – the mass media, the journals of opinion, their competitors and even their political opponents. The public image of the nationalized industries will flourish best in a climate of free and informed public debate.

PART TWO

# LOOKING AHEAD

# CHAPTER THIRTEEN

# 'ISLANDS OF SOCIALISM'

C<small>AN</small> one draw up a balance sheet of the success or failure of nationalization in Britain so far? The question bristles with difficulties. Many of the problems which beset the industries now nationalized when they were still in private hands have been solved. Major programmes of reconstruction and expansion have been carried out – on the whole, with a considerable degree of success. There have, of course, been some mistakes of investment programming and misallocation of resources. The railway modernization programme in particular has hardly been an outstanding success, and the nation has had to pay heavily for the investment in nuclear power. But, given the 'crash programme' nature of much of this public sector investment, and the shortage of key personnel with experience of directing such work, the mistakes on the whole have been remarkably few. Moreover, concentration into single ownership has enabled a good deal of rationalization to take place. The country has been able to enjoy the products of public enterprise at remarkably low prices over most of the post-war period. Nationalized industries have also made significant advances in the field of labour relations, in codifying procedures of industrial democracy which are only now starting to become at all general in private industry.

On the other hand, nationalization has failed to provide a new dynamic for the British economy, or to convince the British people of the advantages of public enterprise. So far from being the advance guard of socialism, as many of their founders and original advocates hoped, the nationalized industries have remained isolated, and in many ways unhappy, enclaves in the surrounding ocean of private industry. Inevitably, perhaps, they have tended to take their tone from private industry. They have not been very successful in pioneering new forms of managerial control or techniques, or in creating a public enterprise *esprit de corps*. Their freedom of manœuvre in such things as wage and price policies has been strictly limited. Relations with the consumer – and there-fore the general public – have been less happy than they could have been.

But it is impossible to apply any single generalization to the whole variegated field of public enterprise. By almost any standard of performance that one chooses, some industries come out much better than others. Not surprisingly, it is in the labour-intensive industries of coal and the railways, where the problems inherited from private enterprise were most daunting, that the biggest obstacles to making nationalization work have been encountered.

In one particular respect, of course, nationalization has meant a very considerable advance in our handling of the national economy. It has greatly enlarged the area of public accountability in the most vital sector of industry. However much people may grumble at the 'remote bureaucracies' of the public boards, in fact these boards pay far more attention to the public interest and public opinion, and provide far more information on their plans and operations, than all but a very small minority of private firms. Indeed, the average citizen can usually find out a lot more about any of the nationalized industries than the average shareholder can about the firm of which he is, in theory at least, a part-owner. This lack of secrecy surrounding the operations of nationalized indus-tries is indeed a serious handicap when it comes to competition with private firms. And it is at least arguable that the leaders of the nationalized industries would in fact serve the public interest better if they stopped bothering about it quite so much, and con-centrated on looking after the interests of their own industries rather more. A little more enlightened self-interest in the public sector and a little less universal benevolence would probably be no bad thing at the present juncture!

For the top management of nationalized industry has through-out been hampered by the absence of any precise definition of its responsibilities and duties. Private industry, by and large, devotes itself to the maximization of profits. No such easy moral imperative faces nationalized industry. So long as these industries operated as natural monopolies in a seller's market, it could be argued that their responsibility was simply to expand capacity up to the level of demand, and for the Government to determine their price ceilings and therefore the level of profitability. But, as we have seen, the situation has become rather more complicated than that.

This built-in indecision at the top has shown itself in all sorts of ways. John Hughes shows in his chapter on relations with private industry, Chapter 7, how public enterprise has offered concealed subsidies to private industry by buying dear and selling cheap. How far has this sprung from weak purchasing departments, how far from a vague feeling that nationalized industry should 'support British industry'? (It must be admitted straight away that chauvinistic buying policies are characteristic of most public enterprises in most countries; this does not necessarily prove them to be right ones.) In the case of the North of Scotland Hydro-Electric Board, a deliberate attempt has been made over a number of years to ensure that orders go wherever possible to Scottish firms. As a result, the board's customers in the Highlands have tended to get their electricity later and less cheaply than they could have done; here would appear to be a clear example of misplaced benevolence defeating its own object.

No organization can work to its fullest effectiveness where top management is unclear about its ultimate objectives. This has unfortunately been characteristic of much of nationalized industry so far. There is also little doubt that the spirit of enterprise in the public sector has been subdued by fear of incurring ministerial displeasure or becoming the target for hostile parliamentary questions or newspaper articles. There has been a natural tendency to 'play safe', to 'go by the book', not to stray too far from the text of the nationalization Acts. The mixture of civil service and industrial attitudes has not always been very healthy, and caution at the top has inhibited enterprise and damaged morale below. The hostile political climate in which the nationalized industries have had to operate has intensified this problem.

This is in many ways the central problem facing the nationalized industries. It is a problem which it is really up to Government to solve. Broadly speaking, there are two possible ways in which nationalized industries can be run. The first alternative is to integrate them into a planned economy, where the crucial policy decisions are taken by the Government or by some central planning body, while the nationalized industries themselves are responsible for their execution. This is the route which France is following, and towards which the Conservative Government now seems to be gingerly moving. In the British context this must eventually involve a national energy policy and a national transport policy – and it would presumably be necessary to integrate the oil industry into the one and road haulage into the other.

The second alternative is to treat the separate nationalized industries as sovereign industrial concerns and encourage them to behave as such, the minister remaining in the background to intervene only when he felt the public interest was being damaged by the operations of the public boards in his bailiwick. Such intervention should, as the Select Committee on Nationalized Industries points out, take the form of public directives which can be debated in Parliament. In this case, one might expect in time to see the emergence in Britain of that typical Continental post-war figure, the 'public enterprise buccaneer', whose most conspicuous representative has been Signor Mattei of E.N.I. in Italy. (To show that public ownership and planning are not synonymous, Italy probably has more of the former and less of the latter than any other large country in Continental Western Europe.) The nearest approach to 'Mattei-type tycoonery' in British nationalized industry is Dr Beeching's single-minded ruthlessness on the railways.

Either of these alternatives would be preferable to the situation hitherto in Britain, where we have had neither planning nor unfettered enterprise in the public sector. The Government has neither given leadership to the public boards, nor allowed them to exercise it themselves. Instead we have had a succession of more or less inefficient ministerial 'back seat drivers', whose interventions have been in too many cases capricious, negative and politically motivated. Moreover, while the boards have been publicly accountable for their actions, their ministerial masters have not.

If one has to choose between the two alternatives, there is no doubt which would be preferable to socialists. Austen Albu has made it clear in Chapter 5, and Ernest Davies makes it clear in the next chapter, that the responsibility for defining the public interest and for seeing that the nationalized industries conform to it is the minister's. For those who believe in planning there can be no other solution. What is at issue is not the attempt to exercise control by Government, but the nature of the control which has been exercised so far. It is not that ministers have intervened, but that they have tended to intervene in the wrong way, at the wrong time, for the wrong motives.

In particular, nationalized industries have suffered from the fact that Governments have tried to use them as a substitute for a fully-planned economy. Whenever the Government has been worried about cost inflation, it has tried to make up for its total lack of control over the wage and price policies of private industry by excessive control over the wage and price policies of nationalized concerns. The greater the concern over inflation, the tighter the screw has been turned – though not always effectively. In 1961 and 1962 the attempt to impose wage restraint on private industry via the public sector assumed enormous importance in ministerial minds. The Guillebaud doctrine of comparability with private industry was rejected in favour of an attempt to tie wage settlements in the public sector to movements in *national* productivity – not because this was felt to meet the needs of the nationalized industries, but because it was hoped that it would set an example which private employers would follow. In short, Guillebaud was to be stood on his head. Instead of the public sector following the private, the Government hoped to make the private sector follow the public.

At the time of writing, early in 1962, it is becoming plain that this policy will not succeed. It is already clear that it does not meet the needs of the nationalized industries. The N.C.B. and British Railways, after all, have to compete for labour with private industry, and if they cannot get workers they cannot do their job. The doctrine of wage comparability is not just a lawyer's formula; it reflects the facts of demand and supply in the labour market.

This illustrates the fundamental problem, that controls cannot be placed on one sector of industry alone without seriously distorting the economy. Where resources are in short supply – as labour is in modern Britain – they will flow to where the reward is greatest. If part of the economy is 'frozen', and the rest is not, they will move from the 'frozen' part to the 'free'. The moral is obvious, and it does not only concern wages. Abraham Lincoln's dictum applies. An economy cannot be 'half slave, half free'. The same rules of planning must apply to the private as to the public sector; if there is to be discrimination against the public sector in one respect, sooner or later this will have to be offset by subsidy or protection to right the balance.

But is there in fact a conflict between the demands of planning and the need for more freedom in public enterprise? Would it not be both possible and desirable to combine the two – to encourage the leaders of nationalized industry to show more enterprise in managerial matters, within the framework of a comprehensive national plan which assigned to the public sector of industry clearly-defined tasks? Is this not in fact the answer to the problem?

Again, the point can best be made by taking a single example. Until recently the B.T.C. did virtually nothing to exploit one of its best potential assets – namely, the considerable real estate in London and other big cities. At a time when property values in city areas have been soaring, the railways made little or no attempt to cash in on the boom. Only now is this attitude changing. Again, there is little doubt that many of the nationalized industries could strengthen their financial position considerably by diversifying or rationalizing their activities, by adjusting the frontiers they inherited on nationalization in the light of a changing market and technological situation. The existing frontier between the public and the private sector is after all little more than a historical accident; it is unlikely that it represents the best possible division of resources in our economy. If nationalized industries were permitted, and indeed encouraged, to adopt a more flexible and adventurous attitude to their responsibilities, this would increase their efficiency without in any way impinging on the sphere of national planning.

This crucial question of what the role of the nationalized industries should be in the present situation is discussed at greater length in the next three chapters, and a fourth chapter in this second part of the book analyses the lessons that can be drawn from foreign experience. It is unfortunately typical of attitudes in this country that the experience of public ownership abroad should be so little documented. Anybody would think the 1945–51 Labour Government invented nationalization!

But there are also pressing internal problems in the public corporations, which have tended to inhibit progress. Mark Abrams draws attention in his chapter to the poor record of almost all the nationalized industries on public relations – taking the term both in its narrow and in its broader sense. This cannot be ascribed entirely to political hostility, or to the discouragement of publicity by ministers in the past (including, particularly, Labour ministers who disapproved of advertising on ideological grounds!).

It is surely rather a product of the fact, discussed in Chapter 9, that the nationalized industries happen to be ones traditionally dominated by technologists. They are in many ways technocrats' paradises. This is a product not of nationalization, but of the type of industry which the Labour Government decided to nationalize first. But nationalization has intensified the curiously inbred, conservative, rather parochial character of the bulk of management in the public sector. In the first place, both their structure and their circumstances have hitherto made the nationalized industries unrewarding places for people with a bent for salesmanship. This is now proving, in the new era of cut-throat competition, a serious liability. Second, the frontier between public and private industry has not been an easy one for management to cross. There have been prejudices and suspicion to overcome; and, more particularly, the salaries and conditions in nationalized industry have not been such as to attract really able men from private industry.

The significance of Dr Beeching's appointment as chairman of the B.T.C. in 1961, at a salary some two-and-a-half times as high as those of his opposite numbers in other nationalized boards, was that it revealed how far the under-payment of top men in the public sector had gone, and the sort of salary needed to attract men from private industry. On balance it seems highly desirable that there should be a free flow of technical and managerial talent between public and private enterprise – a two-way flow – and there is therefore a strong prima facie case for raising salaries at the top of the public service by substantial amounts. The Guillebaud principle of comparability makes sense at all levels of the ladder! It is also not unimportant, given the record of the last decade, that Dr Beeching is in a much stronger position to say 'no' to the Minister of Transport on an issue of policy than the average nationalized industry chairman has been in the past.

A greater effort needs to be made by the nationalized industries to improve the calibre and range of management, and to tackle the problems of morale, of co-ordination and communications which arise in every large bureaucracy, but which can be particularly intractable in the public corporation. They need to regain their lost sense of direction, to establish themselves not only as islands of socialism but as growing-points of public enterprise. As Mark Abrams has pointed out, the public is no longer in a mood to decide for or against public ownership on ideological grounds. It judges by performance. The nationalized industries have in many cases a better record of performance than the public recognizes or than could reasonably have been expected given their peculiar difficulties. But it is still nothing like good enough to convince a majority of the people of Great Britain that more nationalization would be a good thing in itself. The remedy lies in large measure with the nationalized industries themselves. If the public attitude is to change, they must show that they know where they want to go, and have the skill and energy to get there.

# CHAPTER FOURTEEN

# WHO DECIDES THE PUBLIC INTEREST?

*by*

ERNEST DAVIES

'PUBLICLY-OWNED industry can serve the public interest better than private enterprise based on the profit motive.' This belief has always been among the main reasons for the inclusion of nationalization in the programme of the Labour movement. It has generally predominated over the theory that public ownership constituted a transfer of economic power necessary for the achievement of the egalitarian society. This ideological opposition to the profit motive as the main economic incentive with its anti-social implications predominated in the early years of the movement. The public interest may never have been defined, but by and large, it was considered to include a better deal for consumers and workers alike, and it was assumed that this, as well as more efficient and economic production, greater security and better conditions of employment, would follow from the nationalization of industry. After the minority Labour Government of 1929–31, public ownership was seen to be essential for effective economic planning, and it became clear that its duties and responsibilities would consequently include an obligation to assist in the implementation of Government economic policy.

The model for the structure of nationalized concerns had already been evolved before the war, and was accepted irrespective of whether it was suited to this concept of the subordination of nationalized industry to the public interest. Chief responsibility for this rests with Herbert Morrison, who was the architect of the public corporation, the chosen vehicle for nationalized industry.

The public corporation, as he conceived it, preserved the corporate structure of private industry, with private industry's requirement that it pay its way, including the earning of interest on its capital. At the same time, public service obligations were

imposed upon it by statute. This organizational structure constituted a complete break-away from nationalization as an adjunct
of Government – its departmental operation – since nationalized
industries were to be free both from Treasury control and political
influences. Chairmen and members of the boards were to be
appointed by the responsible minister, but they were to have
managerial independence; they were to be experts concerned with
commercial success, and not civil servants responsible for carrying
out the public interest as interpreted by Government policy. In this
way the public corporation combined financial and managerial
autonomy with public service obligations.

This dual role inevitably posed certain difficulties. In theory,
rationalization resulting from consolidation, and the corporation's
ability to fix charges according to costs – including those arising
from serving the public interest – should enable it to pay its way;
in practice, it was to prove difficult to do so. If serving the national
interest raised costs and therefore forced an increase in charges,
consumers might go elsewhere, and the corporations would then
be unable to maintain their competitive position. Conflict could
develop between the public and commercial interest, and decision
become necessary as to the extent to which the public interest
should be served. It was therefore desirable that the public interest
should be defined. But, if the public corporation were to succeed,
obviously it would have to be confined within the limits required
by commercial and financial practicalities. The two could well be
irreconcilable. In fact, many of the difficulties that have confronted the post-war nationalized industries can be traced to this
conflict between their operation as public services in the national
interest and as commercial concerns, and to failure to draw a clear
demarcation line between the two, or to determine in whom the
responsibility was vested for defining the extent to which the
public interest should be made a first priority. Failure to resolve
this conflict has led to a great deal of confusion, and to increasing
encroachment by the responsible ministers on the managerial and
financial prerogatives of the corporations. The minister is the
victim of the conflict because, while he is under pressure to protect
the consumer against high prices and to secure provision of
services, he is expected as well to ensure that statutory requirements are met, including the financial solvency of the industry. A

vicious circle results, because the minister is driven to back the community against the corporation's commercial judgment, and to intervene to prevent this judgment being exercised; this may lead to greater financial difficulties, which in their turn result in more ministerial interference. At the same time, Parliament demands greater control because of the industries' difficulties and their dependence on the state for finance. In the process, the original basis of the public corporation, as a financially viable entity free from managerial interference, is undermined.

Such has been the result of failure to resolve the conflict between the public interest and commercial obligations. The corporations are expected to achieve the impossible: they must accept the minister's interference and yield to his demands to serve the public interest even when contrary to their commercial requirements, as the reports of the Select Committee on Nationalized Industries have pointed out. Consequently, the corporations are blamed on the one hand for failing to provide the services required, and, on the other, for failing to fulfil their commercial obligations or to finance adequately their capital investment out of surplus.

Only in the 1961 White Paper on the financial and economic obligations of the nationalized industries[1] was it accepted that the problem existed. The White Paper failed, however, to resolve it because it went no further than to accept that the nationalized industries were 'neither straightforward commercial concerns nor social services, but a combination of both'. Although it stated that 'while it is legitimate to look for the same rate of return in a publicly-owned enterprise which is fully commercial in its nature and is engaged in the same type of business as private enterprise, the main nationalized industries are not in this position', the nationalized industries were still required to pay their way over a five-year period. Accepting that costs may be affected by commercially unprofitable activities, the White Paper conceded that these could be taken into account in fixing the financial requirements; but, where subsequently such obligations were imposed, the corporations would be entitled to ask for an adjustment. At the same time, it concluded that the nationalized industries could not be regarded only as commercial concerns judged by commercial results, and that they had wider obligations than com-

[1] Cmd. 1337, 1961.

mercial concerns in the private sector. The object of these proposals was declared to be, 'to find for each industry or board a reasonable balance between these two concepts'. The Government thus merely squares the circle: it requires financial probity at the same time as service of the public interest, but makes no contribution to reconciling the two. The position, in effect, is that ministerial intervention has been accepted as inevitable, and that the minister on occasion can decide on policies that must be followed if the public interest is to be served, but as to how the cost is to be met the White Paper is very vague. No definite provision is made to compensate the corporations for any additional cost of carrying out such policies, since they are still required to pay their way over a period, although adjustment of the financial targets is conceded as being necessary. This could mean higher charges, or subsidies, or both.

The question therefore arises whether this compromise is in the best interest of the nationalized boards and the community they serve, or whether there is an alternative which will enable the industries the better to fulfil their obligations. Before deciding this, it is necessary to examine briefly in what way the nationalized boards have been required by statute to serve the public interest, how far they have succeeded, and to what extent the imposition of Government policy has prevented their doing so.

\* \* \*

The duties and responsibilities defined in the constituting statutes embrace far more than managerial, financial or commercial functions. The National Coal Board, for instance, was required to make supplies of coal available, 'of such qualities and sizes and at such prices, as may seem to them best calculated to further the public interest in all respects, including the avoidance of any undue or unreasonable preference'.[1] It will be noted that although the board's function of coal production was linked with public responsibility in regard to quality, size and price, it was left to it to interpret what was the public interest. In practice, interpretation was largely taken out of its hands by successive Governments, particularly as regards price, and the inevitable conflict developed. Further, the Government, in time of shortage, favoured

[1] Coal Industry Nationalization Act, 1946, section 1 (1).

production at almost any price, and on occasion was not unin-
fluenced by political considerations.

The British Transport Commission had its duties defined more
comprehensively than any other corporation under the Transport
Act, 1947. Its general duty was described as 'to provide, or secure
or promote the provision of an efficient, adequate, economical and
properly integrated system of public inland transport and port
facilities within Great Britain for passengers and goods with due
regard to safety of operation; and for that purpose it shall be the
duty of the commission to take such steps as they consider necessary for extending and improving the transport and port facilities
within Great Britain in such manner as to provide most efficiently
and conveniently for the needs of the public, agriculture, commerce and industry'.[1] The commission was also required to
preserve freedom of choice of transport to the extent that alternatives were provided; that is, the Act prevented it from directing
passengers or consignors to any particular mode of transport.[2]

The different attitude of the Conservative Government was
revealed in the changes made when it enacted its transport policy
through the Transport Acts of 1953 and 1962. The general duties
of the commission under the 1947 Act were considerably watered
down by the 1953 Act and limited to the provision of railway
services and such other transport as seemed to the commission 'to
be expedient',[3] subject, of course, to the limitations imposed by
the Act. The commission was still required, however, to have
regard to the needs of the public, agriculture and industry. Even
this last survival was dropped from the 1962 Act. The Railways
Board's duty was limited to the provision of railway services, and,
in connection with them, other services and facilities as appeared
expedient with due regard to efficiency, economy, and safety of
operation.[4] London Transport, however, presumably because of
its monopoly of passenger transport in the London Passenger
Transport area, was still required by both the 1953 and 1962
Acts to provide an adequate and properly co-ordinated system of
passenger transport.[5]

[1] Transport Act, 1947, section 3(1).
[2] Ibid., section 3(2).
[3] Transport Act, 1953, section 25(1).
[4] Transport Act, 1962, section 3(1).
[5] Ibid., section 7(1).

There were obviously considerable possibilities of a clash between the commission's all-embracing obligation to provide the transport system it deemed necessary to meet public needs and the requirement that it pay its way, so much so that ministerial interference has probably been more extensive here, and financial difficulties greater, than in any of the other corporations, with the possible exception of civil aviation.

The Electricity Act, 1947, also imposed duties which could be inconsistent with commercial success, because it required the area boards to distribute electricity supplies to those 'who require them' and also to develop and extend rural electrification and to cheapen the supplies 'so far as practicable'.[1] Here also interpretation was left to the boards. Possibly because electricity was an expanding industry, probably less difficulty was experienced in regard to the fulfilment of these requirements than in any other nationalized industry.

The Hydro-Electric Development (Scotland) Acts, 1943–54, imposed very definite public service functions upon the North of Scotland Hydro-Electricity Board, not only in regard to the provision of electricity to meet the demand of ordinary consumers and to meet the needs of large power users in the district, but also in regard to development of the area. The board was thus required both to give priority to demands of consumers over all other demands for the electricity generated by them, and to 'collaborate in the carrying out of any measures for the economic development and social improvement of the North of Scotland district' as far as its powers and duties permitted.[2]

The Gas Act, 1948, modified somewhat the electricity requirement because, although the area boards were required to develop a co-ordinated and economical system of gas supplies, they were only obliged to meet demands to the extent that they were 'reasonable' and so far as it was 'economic to do so'.[3]

The Iron and Steel Corporation had somewhat similar responsibilities vested in it with regard to the production of steel as the National Coal Board had for coal. The Iron and Steel Act, 1949, required that the products of steel companies acquired were

[1] Electricity Act, 1947, section 25(6).
[2] Hydro-Electric Development (Scotland) Act, 1943, section 3.
[3] Gas Act, 1948, section 1(1).

'available in such quantities, and are of such types, qualities and sizes, and are available at such prices, as may seem to the corporation best calculated to satisfy the reasonable demands of the persons who use those products for manufacturing purposes and to further the public interest in all respects'.[1] The reference to the 'public interest' is therefore precisely the same as in the case of coal. Reversion to this form of words could easily have resulted from the political controversy that surrounded the nationalization of steel.

Civil aviation comes under a somewhat different category than the other industries because the development of British airlines was a matter of policy. Consequently, from the outset, provision was made for its subsidization. The Civil Aviation Act, 1946, required the civil aviation corporations to develop 'to the best advantage' the services they provided and to provide them 'at reasonable charges'.[2]

In addition to the specific duties appropriate to the particular industries referred to, there were a number of general matters common to all. These included the efficient and economical development of the industries; avoidance of any undue or unreasonable preference or advantage to any person to whom their products or services were supplied; the carrying out of research; the training and education of the staff; promotion of the welfare, health and safety of persons in their employment, and provision for consultation with them.

It will be seen that the functions of all the corporations were extended beyond those of production or provision of services according to commercial standards to include public needs. Interpretation was left, in the first instance, to the boards themselves, but ultimately it rested with the responsible minister, through the overriding powers vested in him to give directions to the boards when required in the national interest. Although such directions must be 'of a general character as to the exercise and performance' of the boards' functions, the power could clearly be interpreted to cover any failure on the board's part to fulfil its statutory obligations as laid down by statute. As pointed out in Chapter 5, this power has been rarely used, but it assists the

[1] Iron and Steel Act, 1949, section 3(1).
[2] Civil Aviation Act, 1946, section 2(1).

minister considerably in influencing the board, and unquestionably the knowledge that in the last resort it can be employed has enabled him to 'persuade' many a board to carry out policies against its commercial judgment. The minister's interpretation of national interest might, of course, be very different from the board's, or from that of the public; and can on occasion be a euphemism for party political interest. That this is so, can be read into much of the evidence given before the Select Committee on Nationalized Industries.

The commercial operations of both the National Coal Board and the British Transport Commission have, in particular, been affected by their statutory duties. In its report on the former[1] the Select Committee pointed out that these had led the board to give absolute priority to the quantity of coal production so that uneconomic pits had consequently been kept open, and that the priority the board had been required to give the home market had prevented it from taking advantage of export opportunities at favourable prices and had involved it in costly coal imports, the loss on which it had to bear. Since the board's duties were clearly defined, there appeared to be no dispute over these matters, although in regard to imports there were differences of opinion as to whether the board or the state should bear the loss. The committee reported: 'As a result, the board have found themselves in a "kind of half world" in which they are neither wholly a public service nor wholly a commercial undertaking.' It also referred to the board as 'part-business and part-public service', and stated that it would be unjust to criticize it for not always behaving like a commercial firm.

Although the committee did not criticize the British Transport Commission, it appeared to consider that it was over-influenced by its public service duties, and took many decisions which were unjustified on economic grounds to the considerable detriment of its finances. It concluded that 'It is easy to understand how public-spirited motives, and indeed earlier railway practice, have led the commission to take this view of their duty. But your committee consider that this confusion in judging between what is economically right and what is socially desirable has played an important

[1] Report from the Select Committee on Nationalized Industries (Reports and Accounts), H.C. 187, 1958.

part in leading to the situation in which the commission now find themselves.'[1]

In a somewhat different context, the air corporations' fares were found also to have been affected by this conflict. If the provision of public or social services results in losses, and if a corporation's statutory obligations are also to be fulfilled, higher charges must be imposed on other of its services or made for its products; there must be cross-subsidization if it is to pay its way. On the loss-making services to the Scottish Highlands and Islands provided by B.E.A. for social reasons, the committee questioned whether 'B.E.A. should on their own initiative provide un-economic services which could not be made profitable or which did not offer some other commercial advantage such as "feeder traffic".' It asked, 'Is there any reason why travellers carried by B.E.A. between two foreign cities should subsidize those from the Scottish mainland to the islands?'[2] By contrast, it is interesting that in its first report it rejected the suggestion that the North of Scotland Hydro-Electric Board's fulfilment of its obligations to proceed with rural electrification was imposing an unfair financial burden on urban consumers because a common tariff was applied throughout the board's area. It justified the board's policy on the grounds that tariffs throughout the board's area were not unduly high, much of the board's income was derived from sales to the south of Scotland, so if anyone was subsidizing rural electrification it was consumers there, and if the large towns produced their own electricity, charges would be higher in the towns.[3] By and large, the committee, like the boards themselves, found it impossible to take a consistent view as to the extent to which the carrying out of statutory duties of a public service character should be financed by cross-subsidization. In effect, it appeared to consider it a matter of degree, and compromised by hoping a balance would be struck between commercial considerations and social service obligations.

These cases have been referred to because they illustrate the pull between the two and are relevant to the question as to where

[1] Report from the Select Committee on Nationalized Industries (British Railways), H.C. 254, 1960.

[2] Report from the Select Committee on Nationalized Industries (The Air Corporations). H.C. 213, 1959.

[3] Report from the Select Committee. H.C. 304, 1957.

responsibility should rest for determining the public interest. As stated, there was apparently no confusion about their interpretations of their general duties by the Coal Board or the North of Scotland Hydro-Electric Board, but the committee considered that the boards of B.E.A. were taking too much upon themselves and that Government directions and assistance were preferable. Decision as to services and facilities as a rule has been left to the public corporations, which have endeavoured to strike a balance between commercial and public service requirements. In general, they have done no more than carry out the general duties assigned to them, but their fulfilment could not always be complete without commercial results being affected. They have tended to sacrifice the latter to the former, and more so as on occasions they have been denied flexibility to adjust prices to meet the consequential higher costs.

It is in regard to prices that the minister's interpretation of the public interest has probably had its greatest impact, certainly on current operations and results. In this connection it is sometimes difficult to distinguish between the minister's duty to implement Government policy and his responsibility for ensuring that the corporations carry out their statutory duties; it is difficult to see which affects the interpretation of his duties more, the public interest or party political policy. The minister's responsibility for ensuring that Government policy as a whole is carried out by the corporations, to the extent that it is relevant, affects the policies of the nationalized industries for which he is responsible. This is most likely to apply to economic policy and authorization of capital investment programmes. If such programmes are cut back, however adversely corporations may be affected, while the policy may be wrong, the minister's action in seeing it is carried out is not – provided the requirements of overall capital investment planning and Treasury financing necessitate giving ministers this statutory power. In the long term, it may affect corporations' earning power – and certainly has done so – but there is no denying that national interest as interpreted by Government policy should predominate.

Statutorily ministers have no direct responsibility in regard to prices, but as the Select Committee has shown, all Governments have exercised considerable influence over charges, particularly in the cases of the National Coal Board under the 'gentlemen's agreement', and the British Transport Commission – despite the advice of a statutorily responsible tribunal. The Select Committee did not criticize the Government's decisions on coal prices; indeed it favoured its consultation with the board because it considered this provided 'a useful check on any definition of the "public interest" which the board might otherwise be tempted to make.'[1] Thereby the committee, perhaps inadvertently, implied that the board rather than the minister was liable to be at fault in its interpretation of the public interest. Not all members of the committee, however, felt this, and there was some sharp questioning over the price application submitted by the N.C.B. before the 1955 election, which was not approved by the Government until the election was safely won.

There is even more convincing evidence that political considerations influenced Government action in regard to transport charges. The committee reported on two cases of direct ministerial intervention:[2] in 1952 when the minister issued a direction forbidding an increase in charges authorized by the Transport Tribunal, and in 1956 when he halved the requested increase in freight charges, although, after being consulted by the minister, the tribunal had recommended the full increase. At the same time, on his request, the commission delayed any action on passenger fares which it was seeking to increase. In Parliament it was suggested that the minister's 1952 directive was influenced by the set-back the Government had met at the London County Council election and that it was aimed to influence the remaining municipal elections not yet held.[3] Certainly, it would be difficult to justify withholding the increase at that time on grounds of national interest; general economic policy did not appear to be affected by the comparatively small increase nor could it be greatly affected by the six months' delay to which, in the event, the period was limited. Suspicion was also raised in 1959 when, following discussions with the minister, the commission agreed to postpone until after the holiday season increases authorized by the tribunal. It is difficult to believe that, any more than in the case

[1] H.C. 187, 1958.
[2] H.C. 254, 1960.
[3] H.C. Debates, vol. 499, April 28th, 1952.

of coal prices in 1955, this delay was not influenced by the imminence of a general election. Unquestionably, since 1951, ministerial influence has been considerable in determining transport charges, even though most of the time it has been neither by direct intervention nor direction but through informal discussions, during which the commission was no doubt continuously conscious of the directional cane its master was holding behind his back. In Parliament the minister may deny his influence and announce, as he did, that the commission's agreement was voluntary, but whatever form of words is used in public explanation, the fact is that the minister is in a position to ensure that in dealing with a nationalized board his wishes will always prevail. As the committee states: 'Private discussions between minister and chairman are not in evidence; but in view of the overriding power which the minister has, it would seem unlikely that as a result of these informal discussions, the commission's formal proposals about fares should vary in any great degree from what the minister thought best.'[1] In these circumstances, the minister is always in a position to act in the public interest, but equally to impose political decisions.

Clearly, therefore, the aim of managerial freedom from capricious ministerial interference has not been fully achieved in the nationalized industries.

The Select Committee has generally been careful to refrain from commenting on Government policies as such and has confined itself to revealing the impact the minister's decisions have had on the corporations. Throughout its reports it goes no further than to imply that ministers may well have gone beyond their statutory powers – though in the case of civil aviation it was more than an implication – and to recommend that where statutory powers are lacking they should be provided, and where imposed on an unwilling corporation they should be by directive and published. Further, that where specific losses arise from ministerial action, they should be met by specific subsidy. The committee therefore leaves unresolved the main issue: who should be responsible for deciding what is the public interest and how to ensure its objective interpretation? The committee places on the minister the burden of decision when there is disagreement and, by implication, leaves to him the final interpretation of the public interest.

[1] H.C. 254, 1960.

But it makes no attempt to restrict his powers nor to suggest there should be any distinction as between his rights in regard to managerial and to policy decisions. All it is concerned with is that the minister's intervention shall be statutorily defined, in order that it shall be known where responsibility lies should his intervention affect the commercial results of the corporations.

Nor does the committee suggest there should be any different approach to intervention in the management of the corporations for reasons of national policy, or for political purposes. Thus, when in examining the civil aviation corporations, it found that Government policy in regard to the independent airlines, which the corporations opposed, had affected B.E.A. on its Cyprus route, and B.O.A.C. on its West and East African routes, the committee did not question the minister's right to do so. It made its usual recommendation that the minister's powers should be made statutory, but it could not desist from expressing its own opinion that the effects should be considered by the minister when these policies were reviewed.[1] However, in drawing attention to the Government's request that B.O.A.C. should invest in a subsidiary, Kuwait Airlines, despite the corporation's opinion that it was not economical to do so, the committee merely commented that 'if a nationalized airline, which is statutorily required to pay its way, is to be used as an instrument of foreign policy, it should not be required to bear substantial losses as a result'.[2]

A further matter arising from the committee's reports, which has a bearing on the way in which decisions concerning the public interest are made, is that of the relationship between the chairman, the board, and the minister. All board members are appointed by the minister and responsible to him, but their responsibilities are clearly defined by statute. If the minister goes beyond the letter of his statutory duties or the spirit of the constituting legislation, their authority is lessened and the managerial autonomy of the public corporation is further undermined. They are then in a weaker position to hold the balance, which the committee considered desirable, between the commercial and public interest. The committee felt strongly on this, and after listing those matters on which the minister had appeared to exercise unofficial powers

[1] H.C. 213, 1959.
[2] Ibid.

in his relations with the civil aviation corporations in influencing them in a manner detrimental to their commercial operations, stated: 'But, faced with the total extent of the minister's non-statutory powers, they are bound to ask if these do not add up to a degree of control far in excess of that envisaged by the statute under which B.O.A.C. and B.E.A. were created and so lead to an undesirable diminution in the authority of the chairman and boards, and in their feeling of responsibility.'[1] When on grounds of national interest the minister overrides the commercial judgment of a chairman, the only way out they suggested was a ministerial directive. It is doubtful whether this would be enough.

Clearly, the stronger the position of a chairman vis-à-vis a minister, the more likelihood there is that due weight will be given to the corporation's statutory duties, including its commercial obligations. Of course, much depends on the personalities of the minister and the chairman; some succumb more readily to persuasion than others. The fact remains, however, that if the chairman's dependence on the minister for his job were less, or his security of tenure were greater, he would be in a stronger position, and better able both to resist the minister's encroachment upon his authority and to make the corporation's case better known. This relationship clearly needs review.

Apart from the minister and Parliament, the consumer councils established under the constituting statutes can, in a rather indefinite and indirect way, act as guardian of the public interest. Their function is, of course, to safeguard the consumer who has the right to make representations to them, but in practice they have been concerned with comparatively minor matters, except in the case of transport and civil aviation. They have probably acted more as buffers between the consumer and the boards than anything else. Potentially, they could play a more important role, especially since both ministers and boards can refer matters to them. The most important instances of ministerial references were those of the Minister of Transport in 1952, when an increase in London Transport fares in relation to fare stages was referred to the Central Transport Consultative Committee. Shortly afterwards he also referred to it the use made by the commission of its discretion in fixing railway fares within the maximum laid down

[1] Ibid.

by the tribunal. Where the minister is in doubt as to whether a corporation is acting in the public interest, he can, therefore, seek a consultative committee's advice and, once having received it, he can direct the corporation to act on the council's recommendations. He can also do this where recommendations have been made following representations by consumers but have not been accepted by the corporation. There is no record, however, that this power has ever been used. Consequent on this, the minister can give directives in regard to charges, services, or facilities, which might normally be considered the responsibility of management and outside his general directive power. In such cases, the consumers' interest can be interpreted as the public interest, with the minister as arbiter.

The most important role assigned to these committees – and one not specially provided for – has been as consultants on proposals for closure of sections of railway lines. Following protestations at certain branch line closures the commission agreed with the minister that no line would be closed to passenger or freight services without reference first to the appropriate regional Transport Users' Consultative Committee. Although public inquiries have been held, they have never assumed the form of quasi-judicial hearings, but have been confined to consideration of the commission's case and of objections from consumers directly affected. The briefing of counsel by objectors has not been permitted. In some cases the committee's decisions have been entirely based on acceptance or rejection of the commission's evidence as to whether closure was justified on economic grounds. Only to the extent that the committee has considered whether alternative services were available has the public interest been considered. Even here, the committee has no power to require the provision of such services by other transport operators, nor to ensure that once the undertaking has been given they will be provided indefinitely. In some instances, the commission has subsidized such services, but ceased to do so after a period and they have been withdrawn. In others, when assurance had been given that alternative road services would operate, they have ceased to run after they have been found to be unremunerative. In such cases, it seems reasonable to conclude that the consultative councils have failed to protect the public interest.

R

Under the Transport Act, 1962, the powers of the consultative committees and of the minister in regard to closures are given statutory definition. Where it is proposed that passenger services on any line are to be discontinued, notice must be given and, on receipt of objections, the committee must consider any hardship that might result and report to the minister, recommending provision of alternative services if it wishes. Meanwhile, no closure can take place. The minister can then direct the board. In such cases, therefore, the responsibility is clearly placed on the committees for recommending where the public interest lies, and on the minister for requiring that it be met.

The Air Transport Advisory Council was assigned an additional role to its function of receiving representations from consumers, namely to consider and make recommendations to the minister on applications by airlines for licences to operate specified services. This was possible because the minister could refer to the council questions concerning facilities for transport by air in any part of the world and questions requiring consideration in connection with the improvement of air transport services. Since the council functions within terms of reference framed in conformity with Government policy, it was acting as an instrument of Government policy rather than a judge of the public interest. The minister was not bound to act on the council's recommendations and on occasion has not done so. The Civil Aviation Act, 1961, established an Air Transport Licensing Board which superseded the council, and to it were transferred its functions of dealing with consumer representation. The minister has, however, continued to reject its findings when he chooses.

It can be concluded, therefore, that only indirectly and by accident rather than design has the machinery for consumer representation been used to decide where the public interest lay, except where it coincided with the consumer interest as interpreted by the councils. The final decision has remained with the minister, because he has the power to require the corporations to enforce their recommendations and to decide on those made on matters he has referred to them. In effect, the consumer councils have not encroached upon the minister's role as a final arbiter of the public interest.

Who then *should* define the public interest? Clearly, given the socialist doctrine that the transfer of economic power to the community is a prerequisite for comprehensive and successful planning for the welfare state, economic expansion, and full employment, then the first requirement is that the nationalized industries be operated in conformity with national economic policy as determined by the Government of the day. This applies equally to their capital investment programmes, development and expansion, and levels of production. Secondly, if the nationalized industries are to live up to the general expectation that the services they provide and the goods they produce will serve the community as a whole, they must put their provision before commercial considerations. Fulfilment of the ideological objectives of nationalization, interpreted in terms of production, distribution and service, must have priority. If it be accepted that these should be the objectives, the question arises whether the present concept of the public corporation is a suitable administrative structure for their achievement, having regard to its strict commercial requirements.

The obvious alternatives before us are the present ill-defined situation with its tug of war between minister and board, between the public interest and commercial success, on the one hand, and abandonment of the public corporation and reversion to departmental operation under a minister on the other. The present system is untenable because it has resulted in confusion over responsibility, irresolution about the public interest and, in some cases, public dissatisfaction and failure to achieve commercial success. By and large, the public corporation has failed to meet its obligations as judged by the consumer in prices and services – or at any rate to live up to expectations in these respects – and at the same time its losses have had to be met by the community, because ultimately they fall on the state. It cannot be said that a satisfactory compromise between the two irreconcilables has been reached. Rather, because of the failure to resolve the conflict, the public corporation has just muddled through in typical British fashion.

On the other hand, the abandonment of public corporation for Government department would not solve the basic problem. It would fix responsibility on the minister for determining the nature of the service and defining the public interest, but the importance to be given the commercial yardstick would remain undecided. It would merely transfer the difficulty of reconciling the two from the boards to the minister; and it is interesting to note that of late the trend has been for Government trading services, such as the Post Office, to have more stringent financial obligations imposed upon them and for them to be operated more on commercial lines. The principles governing the public corporation – freedom from detailed Treasury control, no ministerial interference in management, and financial autonomy – have theoretical advantages which may have been experienced in far lesser degree than anticipated by its advocates, but they are inherent. That they have not been achieved so far, does not necessarily mean that the public corporation should be written off as a failure, nor that it cannot yet fulfil its purpose if there were a clearer definition of its objectives and demarcation of its duties and responsibilities, and if less rigid commercial obligations were imposed. Drawing of lines of demarcation between policy and management, and public and commercial services, is extremely difficult, since the two overlap and one frequently dovetails into the other. But, with the lessons of the post-war experience to draw upon, particularly as exposed by the Select Committee on Nationalized Industries, it is in this direction that the solution to the conflict must be sought.

It must be understood that the boards have a responsibility to act in accordance with the national economic policy for which the Government is responsible, and which the appropriate minister is responsible for conveying to the boards and for ensuring that it is carried out. Already, much of this policy is effected through the capital investment programme for which he has some statutory responsibility. But equally, prices, working conditions, including wage levels, and the level of production are all related to it. It is in this area that responsibilities have been least defined, the conflict consequently greatest and inconsistency most rife. In effect, production requirements are laid down in the definition of the functions of the boards, but their fulfilment has clashed with commercial obligations. Except in transport, there was no statutory provision for price fixing, but in practice ministerial influence has been exercised frequently to the full, and the same applies in part to wage levels. It would appear reasonable, failing a national wages policy, that when the Government's economic policy requires action on wages and prices, then any obligations resulting from it should be imposed upon public and private industry alike; no case can be made out for discriminating against nationalized industry, for example, on wage and price restraint as has on occasion been done. If the principle were accepted that in imposing an economic policy all industry, irrespective of owner-ship, be treated equally, new statutory provisions would only be necessary where it was decided that ministerial powers should be permanently extended and used. In sum, responsibility must rest with the minister for ensuring that the nationalized industries serve the general public interest by acting in accordance with the national economic plan, and he must have the requisite statutory power to enable him to exercise his authority in this respect. In this area, therefore, the minister should define the public interest in the light of Government policy and it should be the duty of the boards to meet it. Equally, the minister must be finally responsible for co-ordinating policies as between corporations operating within the same industry, e.g. fuel.

Ministerial intervention, therefore, is not necessarily a bad thing – in fact it can often be desirable in the wider interest of the community. The minister is both the guardian of the public interest and the vehicle through which Government policy is implemented. He may have to intervene to fulfil these responsi-bilities adequately, and would be failing in his duty if he did not do so when it was clearly necessary. Statutorily the boards are required to carry out duties and responsibilities, but these are defined in very general terms, and it would be reasonable to assume that they were expected to interpret them so that their fulfilment did not conflict with their commercial obligations. Since the two have proved irreconcilable, it is necessary to be more precise as to the type of public service the boards should provide. The Select Committee's recommendation was comparatively simple, but only goes part way to solve the difficulty. It placed responsibility on the minister for deciding the public interest in specific cases, and for seeing that it is met by direction where there is conflict with the board.

The Government goes a little further than the committee by stating in the White Paper that in fixing the financial standards required by the boards, costs affected by unprofitable activities, so far as practicable, will be taken into account, and that if additional ones are subsequently imposed the boards would be entitled to ask for an adjustment of their financial obligations; but, like the Select Committee, it leaves the basic issue unresolved. While it makes provision for contributing towards the cost of unremunerative services, no attempt is made to define what public services the nationalized industries should provide, and who shall decide their nature and extent. Further, the White Paper is inconsistent because, while it makes these proposals, it still requires the boards to reach financial equilibrium over a five-year period without presumably making provision for permanent subsidization of unremunerative services, though it may be that the White Paper is intentionally vague on this.

Here, then, is the crux of the problem: the determination of responsibility for deciding the public interest element in the activities of the corporations, and whether over a period costs should be adequate to pay for them; in other words, whether prices should also include social benefit costs. Unfortunately it is not easy – nor always possible – to divide the operations of an undertaking into those which are essential to the running of its normal business, that is to the satisfactory fulfilment of its functions, and those which would not be undertaken but for social factors. It is not enough to decide that all uneconomic services should be eliminated – as the present management of British Railways plans to do – nor, for that matter, is it always easy to distinguish between the economic and uneconomic. If all the latter are dropped the former may well be affected. In most businesses there is an element of both service to the public and of uneconomic production which is met by cross-subsidization. Frequently its extent is not known because there are so many variables and so much sharing of common services and costs. Where such activities appear to a public corporation to be necessary to its normal operation it must be left free to use its own discretion as to whether to undertake them, and to meet the cost in the normal way by cross-subsidization. The greater flexibility on pricing, the easier it is for prices in such cases to be adjusted to costs. There are generally also a number of border-line cases where, if commercial standards were strictly applied, the corporation might drop the service or cease production, but which it nevertheless considers, in the general interest of its successful operation, to be worth continuing for goodwill or other reasons. Here again it seems reasonable to leave the decision to the corporation. There are cases, however, where there is a definite conflict between commercial judgment and the public interest, where to initiate or continue activities would result in losses, and if the decision were left to the boards they would not undertake them. In such cases there should be consultation with the minister and if the conflict were unresolved, the final decision would have to be his. If he decided that these activities were required in the national interest, then he should give a directive and, in accordance with the provisions of the White Paper, adjust the board's financial targets. Similarly, the minister could take the initiative, and if, for commercial or other reasons, the board opposed his wishes, a directive should be issued.

Unfortunately there can be no simple, precise answers to this problem of defining the public interest, because of the impossibility of drawing clear lines of demarcation: there is so much dovetailing, so much interrelation between the normal business activities and service to the public in any large undertaking, and an element of cross-subsidization of an unknown extent in most. Where the activities are clearly managerial, the board must be responsible, and where they are obviously matters of public policy the minister should be. Between the two there is, however, a vast no man's land in which there must be much give and take.

# CHAPTER FIFTEEN

# NATIONALIZED INDUSTRIES AND ECONOMIC POLICY

*by*

## J. R. SARGENT

'SINCE God has given us the Papacy,' Alexander VI is said to have remarked, 'let us enjoy it.' Perhaps not the sentiments, but at least the optimism and the gusto one would welcome hearing from the pontiffs of the nationalized industries as they survey their inheritance. Yet it is a defensive and dispirited way in which they shoulder their vast bag of assets. In this they reflect the altered mood of the faithful. To some of the latter, of course, the bringing of industries into public ownership is self-justifying; the enlargement of the public sector is a good thing in itself. Those who get no comfort from this rather mystical view get little either nowadays from the suggestion that the role of public ownership is to improve industrial relations and set them on a new footing of dignity and respect. While nationalized industries should obviously do all they can to this end, it is now clear that it is not their existence but that of sustained full employment which is responsible for such progress as has been made. It is also doubtful whether there is any system of large-scale production which will engender a natural harmony of interest among its participants. Whoever owns the assets, the division of the product can always be changed so that more goes to some and less to others. Even under complete control by the workers themselves, there would be those who identified themselves predominantly with the success of the enterprise, and those who were most concerned with hours and conditions.

Another role which was frequently assigned to the nationalized sector in the years before it existed was that of being an agent of economic planning. In its most limited sense this was understood to mean that the net revenues and the investment programmes of nationalized industries should be so manipulated as to moderate inflationary and deflationary pressures. The carrying-out of such a policy has been confused by differences of opinion among economists, politicians and the public, whether incipient inflation, for example, requires the enforcement or the prevention of increases in prices in the industries. It has also been realized that their investment programmes are too inflexible, as well as too important in themselves, to be good anti-cyclical stabilizers.

This is a pale kind of planning in any case. Most socialists would ask for more. But what is meant by planning? The word is ambiguous enough to make the question worth asking. To some it means a system under which production decisions, defined more or less closely in quantitative terms, are made and carried out by some public authority. In such a system public ownership must play not merely a positive but a dominant role. If it did not, there would be difficulties about carrying into effect the production decisions specified in the plan. One could spend a good deal of time debating the merits of such a system, its efficiency, and the extent to which it is compatible with democratic liberties. But it would be premature to do this now, because as it stands this conception of planning is extremely unhelpful; it tells us nothing about what the planners are to do. No social purpose can be served by a set of empty boxes. To set up an organization for arriving at a set of production decisions may be a satisfying exercise, but the important question is that of the criteria by which the decisions themselves are arrived at. (Ask any Eastern European economist.) If planning is to have any real meaning, any operational content, it must involve the application of criteria for production decisions which differ from the ordinary commercial criteria of a private enterprise economy. Thus socialists would not be satisfied if, having set up a State Planning Commission, they found that it reproduced identically the production decisions of the previously existing private enterprise system. The question of what things to produce, in what proportions and where, is common to all societies, and all have some kind of system for answering it. What planning must be understood to involve is a decision-making *procedure* which yields more of this and less of that than would be provided by entrepreneurs asking themselves the question, 'will it pay?'[1]

[1] Since I am assuming that the minimum objective of planning will always be

Planning means bringing about a pattern of output, a collection of goods and services, which differs from what would have emerged from unplanned private enterprise. This does not mean that *any* pattern of output different from that of unplanned private enterprise is evidence of planning, let alone of planning for socialist ends. For one thing, planners in a democratic society will find themselves conditioned by powerful forces which differ little from those which condition private entrepreneurs. They will have to work to a highly complex and variable structure of individual wants, and submit to being judged by the success with which they adapt their plans to meet them. They will soon come to realize how facile is the distinction between 'production for profit' and 'production for use', and how difficult it is to apply the latter criterion without constant reference to the former. There is no room in our society for a planner who regards the shifting flux of market demand as a tiresome intrusion on his privacy, and is prepared to use any amount of manipulation of prices and taxes to cram it into his pre-ordained pattern. This does not contradict the principle that planning seeks to achieve some pattern of output other than what would be elicited from profit-seeking entrepreneurs by the uninhibited operation of monetary demand. It draws attention to the fact that there are limits within which democratic planning has to work. The consumer is not sovereign; neither is he a serf.

There are two distinct ways, however, in which planning should aim to improve upon the pattern of output which emerges from the workings of private enterprise. One of these is that the quantities in which the various goods and services are produced should be determined by a balancing of social benefits against social costs, rather than of the revenue accruing to the producer against the costs which he himself has to meet. The other way expresses the feeling that some people and some purposes should enjoy more of the national product than they would be granted even by the most scrupulous balancing of social benefit and social cost. The changes that will be made in the private enterprise pattern of output as a result of the application of each of these principles of planning will be sometimes in the same direction, sometimes in the opposite

the maintenance of full employment of labour and capacity, more of one good must involve less of another.

direction to each other. We will consider them, and the relevance of public enterprise to their application, in turn.

Consideration of the first principle of planning must begin with the recognition that, as long as there is full employment, the great bulk of private costs – that is, those costs which the enterprise must meet – are also social costs. The fact that an employer must pay a certain sum for his labour (or any other factor of production) indicates that other employers are willing to pay just about as much and are therefore confident that the labour will produce for them an output for which the consumers are prepared to pay that sum. The private cost to the industry which actually employs the labour thus has undeniable social relevance. It gives us a first approximation to the value of (say) the carpets that society cannot have because of the cars that it does have. It is this information which, in a competitive economy, is transmitted to the consumer through the price system, so that he chooses between alternatives on the basis of a true representation of the relative cost to society of providing them. But this private cost is the first approximation only to the total social cost, and there are important cases where for society as a whole the cost of production of something adds up to more than has to be met by the producer.[1] Two of the commonest examples of such a situation concern the public sector of the economy. There is the cost of smoke pollution which society has to meet after it has paid for mining the coal which causes it; and there are the costs of urban congestion, felt particularly in the form of a reduced speed of flow of traffic, which mount with each new drift to the cities, but are borne by many people other than the newcomers who are the cause of their doing so.

Since these (and other) social costs exist, planning should see that they are felt where they occur. What is the role of public enterprise in this? It may be argued that what is needed can be done through the fiscal system by taxes and subsidies. Smoke pollution, for example, is not all caused by coal as such, but mainly by the antique devices which are widely used for burning it, so that the appropriate remedy is not the fixing of higher prices by the National Coal Board, but a subsidy to the makers of efficient

---

[1] Sometimes it can add up to less, e.g. the social cost of the National Health Service may be less than what it costs to maintain, in so far as its preventive success lowers industrial costs due to illness.

burners. Similarly urban developments can be taxed for the social costs which they create in the form of congested traffic or the ancillary expenditure on public amenities which falls on the local authority. It may be that fiscal devices are often less cumbersome means of exacting the social costs than handing over the activity where they arise to a public corporation with instructions to recover them through its pricing policy. But it would be absurd to pretend that this is always so. Where subsidies are in question, it should be a matter of principle that public funds are not paid to industries which are not publicly accountable in the fullest sense. Given this principle, the relevance of public enterprise to planning policy – or at least of public participation in private enterprise – stands out in much sharper relief.

Apart from principle, however, there will be practical arguments for recovering social costs through public enterprise rather than through taxation. For example, in the case of land use, the social costs caused by office development may be much higher in one part of a city than in another. In such a case, taxes discriminating against the former would be justifiable; but they might not seem to be so, especially if other types of development showed no significant difference of social costs to merit similarly discriminating treatment. It is important that, however onerous taxation may seem, it should also seem to be fair. A public enterprise for the city's development would be in a stronger position to adjust its rents according to social costs, although the experience of the railways with 'undue preference' in the past reminds us that it would not be an impregnable one. Again, the social costs of traffic congestion are what they are because the motorist is not generally made to bear the cost of his parking space, and because the traffic congregates in morning and evening peaks. To reduce these costs, charges for parking must not only become the general rule but must also be made to vary according to the time of day; that is, charges must be higher for cars entering and leaving the parking spaces during morning and evening peaks. Such varying charges would be best enforced through a public enterprise having a monopoly of parking facilities, both on and off the streets.

The recovery of social costs is likely to involve new forms of public enterprise as well as of taxation. The history of public enterprise hitherto, however, reveals little attention, let alone rational consideration, given to social costs. This is perhaps hardly surprising when one recalls the irrationalities which have bedevilled the purely private elements of the costs of the nationalized industries. Expenditures have been loaded upon them which they would never have carried under private enterprise, nor been required to carry by rational planning. Examples of these are the losses from selling imported coal at domestic prices, the inflation of costs generally through the denial of freedom to buy their supplies from the cheapest source or to manufacture for themselves if necessary, and the burden of dead-weight debt made cumulatively heavier by the fact that the adjustment of prices to cost increases has been delayed by political fiddling. On the other hand, prices have contained inadequate provision for the replacement of assets, as the White Paper, 'The Financial and Economic Obligations of the Nationalized Industries', has admitted. In addition, arrangements for financing the extension of these assets have been such as to conceal the real cost of the capital they have appropriated. It used to be argued in favour of nationalization that it would make the raising of capital cheaper for the industries concerned by bringing them under the credit of the Government. This argument was based on the assumption that the supply of funds to the Government was infinitely elastic. This assumption has plainly turned out to be false. Increased borrowing on behalf of the nationalized industries has been an important factor pushing up the cost of the national debt, and the burden on public funds has not been sufficiently brought home to the buyers of the industries' products. To put the point another way, prudent financing in the tight conditions of the gilt-edged market would have demanded that part of the money spent on new capital assets be a charge on current revenue. There is no necessary economic reason why public enterprise should be expected to conform to the habit which private enterprise has of financing a large part of its net investment from internal sources. The correct approach is to ask what proportion of internal to external financing minimizes the total cost of capital. But the difficulties of Government borrowing in recent years would certainly suggest that the proportion of internal financing by the nationalized industries has been too low.

Thus the nationalized industries have borne certain costs which they ought not to have borne, and they have not borne certain costs which they ought to have borne. The net effect of these economic sins has almost certainly been that their prices have been lower than necessary to recover the true costs of their operations, or in other words, have been such as to subsidize the users of their products. The subsidy has not, of course, been of the explicit kind which is publicly scrutinized by Parliament before the money for it is voted. It has been awarded by allowing the nationalized industries to drift into financial difficulties which make them into a convenient Aunt Sally for the doctrinaire proponents of private enterprise.

These irrationalities in the treatment of private costs in the nationalized industries, and their unconcern over social costs, will have to change if they are to play a part in planning in the first sense that I have given it. What about the second sense? In this we are concerned that certain purposes and certain groups of people should get more of the social product than they would if its distribution were determined by planning in the first sense only. In working to this quasi-moral end, much of the stage is occupied by the Government itself, central and local, which ensures that more education and more medical services, for example, and less roads and less liquor, are provided than would be the case if the task were left to entrepreneurs seeking a certain profit, or to a balancing of social revenue and social cost. The Government does this partly by itself providing what it thinks there should be more of, partly by subsidizing its production by others; and it can do this because it can command its revenues. Does this leave any room for public enterprise as distinct from Government – that is, for a provider which is not in a position to command its revenues, but must elicit them in the form of payment for what it has provided? Public enterprises in Britain can and do, by virtue of their size, produce a pattern of output which is different from that which considerations of profit would determine. That is, they run part of their activities at a loss, which they aim to recoup from profits made on other parts. The history of this cross-subsidization did not start with nationalization. It was known on the railways and in road passenger transport long before nationalization. It is still found in privately-owned sections of the latter, and instances could no doubt be turned up in other parts of private industry. But cross-subsidization was usually enforced in the past through legislation (such as the Coal-mines Act, 1930) or through licensing systems established by legislation (such as the Road Traffic Act, 1930). Furthermore, for reasons which I shall outline later, it was a contributory cause of their nationalization. For the same reason, where it exists in private enterprise, it is likely to be a precarious feature which will not survive for long when profits are under pressure. By contrast, it is built into the operations of public enterprise, and is the point of which their spokesmen make the most when they are explaining to the public or to investigating committees why they are not as other industries are.

We should also observe that the case for cross-subsidization as a permanent and developing feature of public enterprise is underlined by the difficulties of achieving an equal income distribution. The Utopian solution to the problem of distributing the national product might be to divide incomes equally and then let everyone buy at cost whatever he wanted, including health, education and such like. The Utopian solution would leave unsatisfied some genuine but inarticulate wants, and neglect such economies as there are in providing certain things on a national scale. But the absence of the practical possibility of equal incomes makes much more important what we can do through cross-subsidization to rectify the pattern of production resulting from the interplay of the profit motive and an unequal income distribution.

It does not follow that because the nationalized industries are accustomed to 'take the rough with the smooth' in a way which would not long be allowed under private operation, they are therefore doing right. Anything which is done by custom should be suspect to Fabians. It should rouse us to ask what social purpose is served by charging coal consumers in the East Midlands more than the cost of getting it to them, and consumers in Scotland and all consumers of anthracite less; by subventing rural rides and peak-hour travel; by allowing free use of costly road space to owners of motor cars for parking, while because of the resulting congestion the costs of public transport and the fares its users pay mount steadily; by selling electricity cheap for space-heating and dear for other purposes; and so on. To be fair, the extent of cross-subsidization has in many cases only become apparent in recent years as knowledge of the behaviour of costs has grown, so that where it persists with little apparent social justification, the lapse of time may be enough to extinguish it. It will also be contended that when we speak of one consumer subsidizing another, we mostly do not mean that the two pay different prices for the same product, but that they pay the same price although the costs differ. This may seem to alter the case; in fact it does not. In whatever form the relation between prices and costs appears, it remains true that someone who pays less for a product than it cost to make is receiving a free gift of the nation's resources, and that if more must be paid for it than it cost, someone is denied the opportunity of having it to whom it is more valuable than the resources it contains. Such giving of gifts and exaction of sacrifices cannot be justified, like prefects' privileges and the duties of fags in a public school, on the grounds that they have always been so. Responsible planning requires a closer examination than that.

Thus when we examine the cross-subsidization policy of the National Coal Board, we can see that if the board were to allow the price of each pit's coal to be adjusted to its cost of production, it would be condemning many of them to rapid extinction. While this would benefit a wide range of coal consumers, it is clear that the extra amount of satisfaction diffused over a large number of them would be nothing like as intense as the misery conferred on the displaced miners, given that collieries are often in areas where they are the dominant source of employment and that the average age in the industry is high. At the same time, miners are not immortal, and the closing down of uneconomic pits can take place gradually by stopping recruitment. Also many pits are close to alternative employment, as many ex-miners have themselves demonstrated. Thus this aspect of the Coal Board's policy is justified as a humane way of handling a problem of transition.[1] Whether any social justification can be claimed for other aspects of its policy, such as the relation between the prices of different types of coal, and of coal sold to different types of consumer, is much more doubtful.

There is also a convincing social argument for cross-subsidization where otherwise people would be denied facilities because they

---

[1] An alternative would be for the Coal Board or some other organization to bring in new work for the displaced miners to go to – Editor.

live in certain places.[1] This applies to rural electricity development and to transport facilities in sparsely-populated areas, including those by air and sea to such outlying areas as the Western Isles, the Channel Islands and the Isle of Man. The economic purist would oppose this on the grounds that resources would be saved if those concerned moved elsewhere to enjoy the facilities where they could be provided at lower cost; and that the subsidy may attract new economic activities to uneconomic locations. The factors which affect location decisions are so complex and unpredictable that it is difficult to be persuaded by the latter argument; and great doubt is cast on the former when one remembers the enormous social costs of urban congestion, which would not be collected from those who did make the decision to move. But at the same time that one accepts the equalization of facilities between more and less densely populated areas as a valid social objective, it should not be stretched to require the maintenance of whatever facilities happen to exist. Provision of rural transport is a socialist principle; maintenance of rural railway lines is not, when a similar and less uneconomic service can be provided by road.[2]

But should we be ready to do battle on behalf of the peak-hour traveller and consumer of electricity? Admittedly, what most causes one to question the subsidy to them is its enormous cost. Rural transport and electricity are some burden on the nation's resources, but this does not compare with what could be saved, in terms of generating and passenger-carrying capacity, if the public could be persuaded to spread out the times at which they call on these. We ought not to flinch at the cost if we are convinced that some vital social purpose is served by the concentration of demand for these services within limited periods of each day; but can we really search our socialist conscience and say that it is? In one way our conscience should be positively offended by it; for one thing that inflates the demand for road space is the practice of commuting by private car, which has been encouraged (though the trend may now be against it) by a virtual subsidy in the form of free use

[1] This does not necessarily mean, of course, that the nationalized corporation is the inevitable source of funds for such social purposes – Editor.

[2] It must be admitted that the provision of the road alternative has sometimes been prevented by statutory restrictions on the expansion of publicly-owned passenger transport services by road.

of the public highway for parking. Although in electricity too the tide may be turning, with the introduction of cheap rates for power at night, not much progress has been made; and off-peak price reductions will have nothing like the effect of increases at the peak. I suspect that it is the deep conservatism of the public, and the vested interest of part of it, that explains our reluctance to husband our national resources by flattening out the peak in these two industries, and not any legitimate aspiration to supersede the cost-price criterion for a genuine socialist purpose.

Something which demands particularly searching examination is the appearance of uneconomic competition *between* nationalized industries. The emphasis here is heavily on the word 'uneconomic'. There is no reason to frown on competition as such when it occurs between two nationalized industries. If the gas industry develops some better method of meeting a need which has hitherto been met by electricity, it must be not merely allowed but encouraged to offer it to the public, and it is difficult to see who but the public itself can judge whether it is better. For Government to interfere in such a case would not be planning, but its perversion. But there are cases where, because of the prevalence of cross-subsidization in nationalized industries, uneconomic competition between them can arise. Such a case is that of the competition between B.E.A. and British Railways on the London–Glasgow route. Here is a route which involves fairly dense and regular traffic over a long haul, so that the railway comes into its own and its costs are low; but not so its fares, because these conform to the general average and must contribute to uneconomic services elsewhere. B.E.A.'s fares, on the other hand, only just cover those of their costs which are allocable to the route, and make a negligible contribution to their other costs compared with what their international routes contribute. This must result in some people going by air when at equal convenience to themselves and a smaller cost to the country, they could go by train. Others, of course, would still go by air even if the train fare were reduced to reflect costs. This is entirely legitimate. What is wrong is that B.E.A. should take traffic from the railways which the railways would retain if they were not committed to the principle of cross-subsidization.[1] In another sphere it is the railways who are threatening to be the aggressors,

[1] See also Chapter 3, p. 68 – Editor.

by exploiting their greater opportunities to choose which goods traffics shall carry their unallocable, overhead costs, against road hauliers (including British Road Services) who have no such choice. The competition between gas and electricity has been marred by similar absurdities, chiefly in the realm of space-heating. While the real cost of supplying gas and coke has been below that of supplying electricity, the price that the householder has had to pay has been higher; and the margins are not negligible either. What has enabled the price of electricity to be set so low in this case is its monopoly of other uses, namely lighting and small power units, on which ample profits can be reaped. Once again the effect has been to delude the public into wasteful choice. However, it is not the choice that we should be against, but the waste, when it is incurred for no convincing social purpose.

Thus the first ingredient of a positive policy for public enterprise must be a critical examination of the cross-subsidization which is so prevalent within it. Such an examination must seek to disentangle those instances of cross-subsidization which are rooted in conservatism, inertia and plain vested interests, from those which are expressions of a valid social purpose, the means of planning a pattern of production which is more socially desirable than that which results from the operation of the test 'will it pay?'. But the purpose of this should be wider than that of tidying up what exists. It should look forward to new and higher conceptions of the social aims of economic activity, in the realization of which public enterprise – and probably only public enterprise – can be a leading agent. This is the second ingredient of a positive policy. An illustration of what this might mean lies to hand in the evolution of the 'public service' principle in transport, which has introduced the conception of regular, scheduled services of known and minimum frequency, and indeed made it so familiar that we are no longer thankful for it. But the effect of it has been to provide us with a service of a higher standard than one which only runs when the load factor ensures a profit. There are surely many other ways in which the quality of our economic life could be improved, but only if their sponsor were prepared to stand losses. For example, it would be heartening to see the jungle of the advertising agencies invaded by some missionary enterprise which set itself a high standard of truthfulness and candour. There might be shops that provided crèches and consumer advice bureaux, and pubs that made special provision for the old, and free rooms for serious discussion. A desirable social purpose which is under-served today is provision for large families, and, particularly in housing, there is room for extension of the principle of cross-subsidization to them. The breaking down of class divisions in our cultural life urgently requires that the enormous business of entertainment should be liberated from the commercial principle. We shall get the point wrong here if our approach is one of going with high purpose into the field with cheap culture for the unenlightened. Whether Cliff Richard's fans subsidize Callas's or bingo pays for ballet is secondary to the principle that all forms of leisure-time occupation should be provided in more equal measure than answers the criterion, 'will it pay?'. Perhaps the most important sphere in which we should look forward to the supersession of this criterion by something better is the renewal and revitalization of our urban life. There is certainly no more striking illustration of the limits of the commercial principle than the drab and rambling British city. We must not, of course, lose sight of the fact that a city is also a place of economic machinery – coming into existence, as Aristotle observed, not merely that men might live, but that they might live well – but in the good society which we should be building the wealth that cities create should surely carry much that does not pay for itself: parks and gardens, public buildings which satisfy civic pride rather than fiscal meanness, and a range of provision for physical and cultural activity which surpasses our present achievement as much as our wealth does that of the Greeks.

The catalogue of aspiration could be continued indefinitely. There are many things we want provided that the commercial criterion will not provide. But as we let our imagination ramble, we come back to the question: is this a task for public enterprise as distinct from Government? Government commands the resources it needs; public enterprise must persuade people to buy what it sells. This faces public enterprise with a formidable difficulty when it sets out to act as an agent of redistribution in the ways I have outlined. For within the overall balancing of the accounts, any public enterprise which offers some of its products to the public at less than cost must inevitably charge more than cost for the others. In the supply of the latter, therefore, a fertile field is immediately opened up for cultivation by private firms recognizing no obligation to 'take the rough with the smooth'. Since there is nothing to compel them to make other products (or provide other services) which do not pay, they are in a strong position to undercut public enterprise weighed down by its social burden of losses elsewhere. The problem is not just one of financial difficulties for public enterprise, but of real waste of economic resources; for the private firms, where they are competing with public enterprise, will be quoting prices below the latter's, even though it may actually be costing them more – in terms of labour, capital and materials used – to meet the demand they have thus created. Thus there are people and firms in the East Midlands, for example, who could be supplied with coal from local pits at a smaller cost to the nation than that of imported oil; but the oil comes in because the East Midlands has to support the loss-making pits of Scotland, Wales and elsewhere. In city transport the subsidization of peak-hour travel and the resulting concentration of demand generally inflate the capacity required and so the fares of the public transport system; but they also have the effect of making travel at other times by public transport seem more expensive than it really is, thus opening the way to the uneconomic use of private cars.[1] In inter-city transport the fares of express trains must be kept high in relation to costs to meet the losses on stopping services and cross-country routes; and so again there is an invitation to private competitors. Of these the owners of private cars are now the dominant class, but as we have seen, they have recently been joined by another public enterprise, B.E.A.

Looking from the present towards new fields that we have suggested public enterprise might enter, it is not difficult to foresee similar problems. Suppose there were created some municipal enterprises which aimed to provide, preferably within the same physical location, a wide range of leisure activities from the

[1] Although this has opened the way to the uneconomic use of private cars in cities, it may not be the most important factor which has brought them flooding in. Certainly experiments in reducing off-peak fares have shown no signs of having power to cure the malady, whereas economic charges for parking may. I can see no socialist purpose which is served by failure to enforce these, i.e. by the maintenance of a subsidy to parking. But this is not relevant to the argument here about the difficulties of maintaining a cross-subsidizing enterprise in the face of competition.

'popular' to the 'serious'. If they were to meet the losses on their theatres from the profits on their dance-halls, they would risk losing their dancing clientele to private dance-halls which are not hindered by serious drama in fixing their charges. If we imagine the reconstruction of our cities, or of parts of them, being undertaken by public enterprises committed to high standards of amenity and design, the meeting of these standards will impose their financial burden on the rentable part of the redevelopment property. Rents will have to be high, and tenants will be driven elsewhere; perhaps to other parts of the city, perhaps to other cities. In either case the financial solvency of the public enterprise, and the success of the social policy to which it is dedicated, are threatened.

What is the moral? It is that public enterprise, in so far as it is deliberately pursuing a valid social purpose – that is, aiming at a pattern of production which is socially preferable to that determined by the criterion 'will it pay?' – inevitably stands in need of protection against private competition. There is no point in evading the issue. But it is worth emphasizing the qualification. It is not public enterprise as such that ought to be protected, unless we adopt the mystical view that the fact that it is public makes it holy. Its claim to protection rests upon the validity of the social purpose it pursues. This leads to the important distinction between 'fair' and 'unfair' competition. We must not fall, as some socialists do, into the attitude of children who complain that the game was unfair because they lost it. It is no way unfair that public enterprise should be expected, other things being equal, to hold its own against private enterprise in meeting the requirements of the public; or, to put it another way, it is perfectly fair that the public should call in private enterprise to satisfy its requirements if public enterprise fails to do so. If public enterprise loses in competition, we may be sorry or disappointed, but we should not be indignant except when we can identify an inequality in the conditions of the competition which works against public enterprise. When it must carry social obligations of which private enterprise is free, then the conditions are not equal, the competition is 'unfair'. But when this is so, we do not have to choose a method of correcting the inequality which excludes competition altogether. We should be chary of rushing in with outright bans and restrictions against competition, even when the objective is the correct and legitimate one of preventing it from hamstringing the social purposes laid upon public enterprise. Thus, while the humane, long-term transformation of the coal industry demands that in the interim its low-cost pits should carry its unprofitable ones, and therefore be protected against the competition of imported fuels, it does not justify a ban on these. My reason for saying this is partly an ideological one: that any measure to prevent people doing things they want to do, although it may turn out to be necessary, should be approached with suspicion in a democratic society. But it is also the case that, although competition may often be an inaccurate judge of efficiency, it is at least a sanction against serious departures from it. And it is not inaccurate enough to make it worth taking the risk of throwing it overboard altogether. Quite apart from this, there are significantly large areas where the problem of competition arises in which it would be quite impossible to ban it. These areas are ones in which public enterprise is in competition not so much with private enterprise as with private individuals. The main threat to regular passenger transport, for example, comes not from private bus companies but from the private car. Except in comparatively limited areas in the centre of cities, it would be politically inconceivable for any government to prohibit the use of private cars; and the same would apply, to a lesser but significant extent, to the use of private commercial transport by 'C' licensees, who pose as great a competitive problem for British Railways as the non-nationalized road haulage companies. Salvation by order restricting competition with public enterprise may be as unattainable in practice as it is undesirable in principle.

How, then, should we protect the social purposes of public enterprise from competition which is unfair but irrepressible? One way, of course, which has been mentioned more than once in earlier chapters is by means of subsidies expressly given by the Government. Where social policy demands that the full cost of producing a good or of providing a service should not be extracted from a user, the balance should be met from Government funds, so that it will not weigh down the public enterprise concerned in its struggle elsewhere to meet the competition of private companies or private individuals. Thus the losses of uneconomic pits, of rural electricity and transport services maintained at uneconomic charges, and of other socially desirable departures from the commercial principle, would become a direct charge upon the exchequer. This would be in many ways an attractive arrangement; indeed, I have advocated it myself as part of a solution of the problem of the co-ordination of transport in the United Kingdom. It brings out into the open the cost of the uneconomic services which are maintained. It enables them to be measured one against another, and subjects them to public scrutiny and discussion. It also means that the managers of the nationalized industries are furnished with a clear-cut, commercial objective to work to; that is, to provide the public with those things which it will buy, for a price which covers the cost of providing them. There are, of course, well-known difficulties of identifying costs of individual products or services; partly because of the presence of social costs which the producer does not have to bear (such as that of smoke pollution caused by coal), and partly because of costs jointly incurred in the production of several services (such as the maintenance of railway track and signalling systems). But even if one concedes more to these difficulties than I would be prepared to, one must surely allow that the task of the nationalized industries would be eased if their managers' price and output decisions were freed of a further complication: namely, the obligation to maintain services which are commercially unsound. This increase of freedom would be gained if the suggestion for specific subsidies were adopted.

But this is not the only way of protecting public enterprise from the penalties of carrying loss-making activities in a competitive setting. Alternatively the conditions of competition can be equalized by imposing a special tax on those private competitors who do not labour under the non-commercial obligations that public enterprise may have. This justifies, for example, the duty laid on imported fuel oil by the Budget of April 1961. A similar expedient in the transport field would be to differentiate between 'public service' operators, who accept the obligation to run unremunerative services, and 'freelance' operators, who would include private motorists, 'C' licensees and other private road users unwilling to accept such an obligation; and to charge the latter a licence fee for using the roads from which the former would be exempt. The case for tax rather than a subsidy as a protective device will generally be based on administrative convenience; for none of the theoretical advantages of a subsidy, described above, are attached to it. It is a very general form of protection, with no specific reference to the particular goods or services which it is thought socially desirable to supply below cost. Consequently, the proper level at which to fix it is highly uncertain; we can say little more than that some tax is better than none. The public enterprise, though benefiting from the protection of the tax, is left with the problem of juggling social and commercial considerations in deciding its prices and output; and the public is not clearly informed of the cost of preferring the former to the latter. Moreover, the revenue which flows in from the tax may well cause it to outlive its economic justification; for example, as the gradual transformation of the coal industry is completed, by means of the socially responsible closure of uneconomic pits, it may be difficult to persuade the Chancellor of the Exchequer that the duty on imported fuel oil has served its purpose.

The best form of protection in each case cannot be deduced from general arguments, any more than it can neglect them. At the same time the really important thing is that protection should be given; the means is secondary. But where does this leave us in our inquiry about the particular role that public enterprise is to play in the mixed economy? We find that once a public enterprise begins to interweave certain social purposes with its trading activities – so that some people have more, some less than under purely commercial operation – it runs into financial difficulties unless it receives protection from the state. If it does not receive protection from the state, it can look forward only to decay, unless, like electricity supply, it enjoys an unusually buoyant demand. But if it does receive protection, its role is in effect reduced to that of carrying out the social decisions of the Government; for it is the Government which provides the subsidy or fixes the protective tax. The public enterprise is not an arbiter of social policy, but only an agent; and as such it is in a position indistinguishable from that of a privately-owned industry, like farming, which is protected on similar grounds of public policy. This tempts us to draw two conclusions. The first is that public ownership is irrelevant to social policy; for trading organizations, whether they are public or private enterprises, are equally incapable of bearing the burdens of social policy without aid from the state, and equally capable of sustaining them with it. The second conclusion follows on : namely, that if public enterprise is not able to make an independent contribution to social policy, we should stop pretending that it can and accept the doctrine which has been established (as Mr Albu reminds us) by the Select Committee, that commercial principle should determine the operation of the nationalized industries unless the Government specifically directs otherwise. To this conclusion we should add – as Mr Albu would, but the Select Committee might not – that when Government wills the end, in the form of non-commercial operation, it should also will the means, in the form of protection against commercial competition.

I would be reluctant to draw these conclusions. In the first place, I would recall the principle mentioned above that it is undesirable to pay subsidies from public funds (or otherwise give protection) to industries which are not publicly accountable in the fullest sense. If this is so – and I believe that it is – and if, in order to bring about a pattern of production which is socially preferable to what we would otherwise get, we have to subsidize certain goods or services, or protect others, then there is a strong case for public participation. But unless we adopt the mystical view of public ownership, it enters in as an implication of our social policy and of a responsible attitude to the use of public funds, and not as an end in itself.

More important than this, however, is the fact that to accept the above conclusions is also to accept an over-narrow circumscription of social policy, in so far as the latter is concerned to ameliorate the pattern of production drawn by the brash hand of profit. We may say that all non-commercial decisions should be taken by Government and should be accompanied by the necessary subsidies or protection in favour of the public enterprise concerned ; what we mean is that such decisions should be limited in number and extent. We may say that the maintenance of uneconomic pits, of rural transport and electricity, of cheap commuter services, and so on, should be made like the maintenance of the National Health Service, of education and of the road system, and so be met directly from public funds ; what we mean is that the former should be restrained, as the latter are, by the difficulties of raising taxes. We have suggested that some of the non-commercial operations of the nationalized industries are overdue for public scrutiny, so that a reform which restricted them need cause no socialist heart to bleed. But important as it is to disentangle vested interest from social purpose in these non-commercial operations, to purge the former and sustain the latter, we must not think of them only as they are. There are surely ways yet unexplored in which a good society would wish to reorder the priorities of profit-seeking enterprise, to give more to some purposes and less to others than would be given if each must recover its costs from what the public will pay for it. But if in every case we can do this only in a manner which involves adding to taxation, we shall be greatly hampered. Suppose rural transport and electricity services had never been supplied below cost, and that it were proposed to raise taxes in order to subsidize them. The resistance would be intense; certainly no less intense than that which now greets any proposal to remove the existing subsidy. Although the problem would be alleviated if more rapidly rising national income were to increase the buoyancy of the revenue, to rely solely on subsidies from taxation to twist the pattern of production in the socially desirable direction is to set out for Paradise in leaden boots.

Can the revenues required to pay for uneconomic but socially desirable production be raised in any other way? As an alternative to the Government commanding them through its power of taxation, are there any fields in which public enterprise can be set to earn these revenues? We have seen that public enterprises are unlikely to earn them unless they are protected against the competition of private enterprise; and that the necessity of protecting public enterprises, if it is to be done through subsidies and taxes, is likely to restrict their scope. This dilemma leads us to conclude that the fields in which public enterprise is most likely to flower are those in which it enjoys a natural monopoly over at least some part of what it produces. For this averts the danger that there will be a flight from those services of the public enterprise whose charges are raised above cost for the purpose of subsidizing other services. There must be present, in addition to the conditions of a natural monopoly, general public assent to its being exploited in this way, to what those who lose by it would be quick to call (as indeed it would be) a 'discriminatory pricing policy'.[1] It seems likely to me that it will be in local and municipal rather than national enterprise that a pricing policy of this kind can be developed to support the expansion of socially desirable services below their economic cost. With the increasing urgency of tackling the problem of urban renewal, there is here a fertile field for municipal enterprise to cultivate. For by taking over derelict and decaying areas in and around the centres of cities, municipal enterprises have an opportunity to exploit the scarcity values which attach for commercial purposes to such sites, and thus to gain the revenues which will enable them to provide below cost (and therefore for wider enjoyment) those amenities of a civilized urban life which have been so neglected by the working of the commercial principle. There are, of course, limits to the extent to which the scarcity value of central sites can or should be exploited by municipal enterprise; over-exploitation will only swell the drift to the suburbs or to areas outside municipal ownership, and thus create diseconomies of its own. But the monopolistic position of municipal enterprise has elements of natural strength which public enterprise on a national scale will often lack. It takes a good deal more to cause a firm with central offices to move to the suburbs than it does to persuade its employees to abandon public transport in favour of their cars for the journey to work. Moreover, the extent of any flight from high rents in economically valuable areas can be minimized now that local control of the use of land is accepted as a social necessity; and within the local setting those who suffer from the high rents will also benefit from the urban amenities which these rents are intended to finance. Since the reconstruction of our cities is as urgent in itself as it is favourable to public enterprise, we should hope to see the question whether public enterprise has a positive and independent part to play in the economy answered in bricks, mortar, steel, glass and concrete, without delay.

---

[1] I have myself attacked the proposal of the railways to make fuller use of such a discriminatory pricing system. But there the argument is complicated by other factors, particularly the structure of road taxation. There is no inconsistency in disapproving of discrimination on the railways and approving of it in other cases where circumstances are different.

# CHAPTER SIXTEEN

# THE FRONTIERS OF PUBLIC ENTERPRISE

THIS chapter considers the general question of where, and how, the boundaries of the nationalized industries should be drawn. In practice this is not one question, but two. The first is chiefly concerned with the size of the main nationalized industries, fuel and transport, and with the contribution that may be expected of these industries in a situation where the nationalized concerns are competing with the private sector. This is one sense in which we can ask about the frontiers of the nationalized industries: has anything like a strategy which assigns to these industries some defined task in the economy been developed?

The second main question concerns not the total contribution from these industries, and how it is being or ought to be determined, but their scope and ramifications – their ability, in short, to extend or alter the frontier of the activities they inherited on nationalization.

If, for example, these two broad questions were to be applied to the coal industry, the first would be: what task is envisaged for the industry as a supplier of primary energy in relation to oil and, in the future, nuclear power? It means asking what progress has been made towards a coherent, rational fuel policy, which takes into account the characteristics of the industries concerned. The second question would be: should the coal industry diversify or expand its activities to take advantage of technological changes and new markets; what principles should determine the boundaries of the industry?

## Policies for Fuel and Transport

In the discussion about competition among nationalized industries, and about the decision that they should show a profit,[1] it was shown that profit had quite a different significance for

[1] See Chapter 8.

nationalized and for private industry. For private industry, profit is the objective, and the level of profitability is the measure of success; but public industry may be required to break even or show a certain loss, and this would be quite consistent with its objective of serving the national interest. It would therefore be mistaken to believe that because the nationalized industries are now required to show a profit, they will in some way find the right level or size for their operations; that requiring them to show a profit of a given size automatically puts them on a 'sounder' basis, from the standpoint of serving the public interest, than if they made no profit. There are indeed good reasons why it is preferable that the public industries should show a profit – but there is nothing to suggest that showing a given profit will automatically lead the nationalized industries to become of the 'right' size.

A decision therefore that these industries should show a profit is no substitute for a policy. There are, of course, circumstances under which the requirement to show a profit would have only slight effects. Probably at any time in the decade up to 1956, the coal industry could have been made very highly profitable by raising prices. But today, under highly competitive conditions, the same requirement may lead to a contraction of the industry which might, on strategic or balance of payments grounds, be damaging to the national economy. Under highly competitive conditions, if the decision that a profit must be made by coal and transport weakens their competitive positions, it drives home the fact that the responsibility for the size and the contribution to be made by these industries in their respective fields, is a responsibility of Government.

Governments have been unwilling to accept this responsibility. Yet one might have expected that public ownership of these industries in Britain would be welcomed by any administration. Their basic economic problems do not, after all, arise from nationalization. No major railway system privately or publicly owned in any Western country pays its way. The road/rail problem antedates public ownership in Britain. There is no major European coal industry which can be adjusted, easily and without long-term effects, to meet market conditions arising from rapid changes in industrial production or changes in the world oil supply situation. It is idle to pretend, as some still do, that it is only necessary to create conditions which are as nearly as possible those under which private industry operates, for the problems of coal and transport to disappear.

More prevalent is the tendency to arrive at decisions about coal and transport on the basis of arguments which treat these industries as if they were manufacturing firms, whereas one is a basic extractive industry and the other a basic service industry. Both have characteristics – technical, geographical and social – which make them relatively inflexible in their response to changing market conditions. Both have to meet competition from products – oil and private road transport – which have the advantage, from the standpoint of the individual consumer, of convenience and very often also of cost. But the cumulative effect of consumer decisions, each decision a rational economic one from the standpoint of getting the best bargain the market has to offer, may produce a total effect which is the reverse of rational and economic.

For example, the economic effect of individual consumer decisions to use private in place of public transport, is to necessitate very much greater total investment by the community. It may, of course, be objected that the results are not the same: that people switch to private transport to get the convenience of door-to-door delivery. The basic question then is: how much is this convenience worth, not only to the user but to society as a whole? The real cost does not of course end with the much greater investment (in road and motor vehicles) required in comparison with public services; it includes also road congestion, the toll of accidents, and the impoverished quality of life of those who do not have private transport. There is no evidence of any real attempt to balance the investment costs involved in new road programmes against the net benefits (that is, taking into account social costs) that may accrue from them; yet it is this sort of comparison that must be made when investment in road and rail are being compared.[1]

The consumer who is looking for the cheapest and most convenient way of moving himself and his goods (assuming that the private motorist puts a very high price on door-to-door convenience) can hardly be expected to calculate costs of which he is not aware and which may not be borne to any large extent by him.

[1] For a valuable discussion of this aspect of road use, see P.E.P., 'The Cost of Roads', *Planning*, May 15th, 1961.

It may also be true that all the costs are not calculable with great precision. But it does not follow that Governments should be as unwittingly irresponsible as the consumer. A rational transport policy would undoubtedly include a large programme of road improvements, but it would not be undertaken without any clear idea of the total real costs involved in relation to the expected benefits, for without a reasonable idea of these, how can rational judgments be made about the public transport system? If the real costs of the alternative have not been assessed, how could it be argued that a public transport system is more expensive? It is true, of course, that there are aspects of a public service which do not lend themselves to precise economic evaluation. How much is it worth to the community at large to prevent some, even quite small, sections of it from being deprived of public transport? How much is it worth to promote diversification of industry? Yet parallel questions in the field of education and other communal services have been answered more or less satisfactorily. A rational transport policy would not pretend that such questions did not exist. Where the benefits cannot be calculated, the judgments still have to be made.

A more rational approach would, first, take into account the real costs attached to an ever-greater 'private motorization' of the transport system; and secondly, it would consider what method of recovering costs from consumers is appropriate to a public transport *service*.

There are three possible ways of meeting the costs of a service. The first is to recover total costs from users, on the basis of charging each user the full cost of the service he gets, each time he uses it. This is the method used by, say, garages for car repairs. Generally speaking, it is appropriate where the service is of a personal, non-standard character.

The second is the familiar two-part tariff method used for telephones, for example, and electricity; a fixed charge is made, irrespective of the number of occasions of use. This represents the high fixed costs of installation and the availability of the service to the user. Thereafter, through the second part of the tariff, the consumer pays according to use.

The third method is the equally familiar one employed for running the social services, where all or most of the cost of the service is met by a fixed charge and no attempt is made (with some exceptions) to recover from the user of the service even part of the cost of providing it on each occasion. The fixed charge in this case is, of course, part of general taxation, the services themselves representing ways of achieving various social objectives, some of which, such as education, would hardly be met if every family were required to pay the full cost of providing it with this service. In other instances, such as the industrial injuries scheme, the costs could obviously not be recovered at all from the 'users'. This is, in short, the method of communal provision for services that are available to all.

A rational transport policy would be one which recognized that the first of these methods, which is the one imposed upon the railways, is inappropriate to a transport service. It does not, for example, take account of the social and economic benefits derived by communities throughout the country from the availability of the service. It is surely obvious that the benefit of the service is not restricted to the actual user on each occasion of use. The beneficiaries may never actually travel or transport anything. The 'user' is, in fact, the entire community. Why then should we attempt to recover the total cost from each user each time he uses the service? For this is to treat transport as if it were a manufactured product, a once-for-all transaction. The third method, at the other extreme, would fail to recognize the benefit to users on each occasion of use. Accordingly it should be recognized that the appropriate method of recovering the costs of a transport system would be a national two-part tariff system: since the service is available to all communities, the fixed part of the tariff could be derived from taxation (though of course more complicated methods, such as charging a 'rent' to each area served, could be devised). The direct cost of the service would then remain to be covered by the passenger and freight rates charged for each occasion of use.

It might be argued, of course, that this offers no simple yardstick, such as profit, for deciding how far the service should be extended. Does this not offer a limitless 'subsidy' to public transport? But if it is recognized that the user of a transport service is not simply the individual who is concerned with one particular transaction, but the community which benefits in ways which cannot be reflected in the charge made to individual users, then the word 'subsidy' in this connection becomes meaningless. In what sense is the fixed tariff for the telephone service a 'subsidy'?[1] Once that is recognized, the question of how far the service should be extended is seen to be comparable with other questions to which answers are being found: the question of how much education the nation requires, or the amount of protection that it is appropriate for the armed services or police to provide, or the amount of food which should be grown at home irrespective of world prices. Certainly, in these and similar matters there is room for disagreement; the real point is that they *can* be considered in terms of national needs. By recognizing that there is a large public service element in the transport system, it becomes possible to consider the system in terms of national needs. But this is not possible if the public transport system is required to operate as if it were run for private profit.[2] In the case of transport the need to make a deliberate national choice, not to allow a high-cost system of private transport to oust a lower-cost system of public transport, is obscured by the fact that private motoring has become a symbol of higher living standards to which everyone aspires.

The need for a rational fuel policy, however, is more obvious, if only because the consequences of 'leaving it to the market' can have implications for the balance of payments which cannot be ignored. There are voices briskly advocating 'low-cost energy policies' based on cheap oil and American coal. But there are also the voices of oil industry spokesmen explaining that present oil prices do not reflect the long-run supply problems of the oil industry. And there is the knowledge that Atlantic freight rates can make all the difference between cheap, and very expensive, American coal. There is, above all, the growing realization that to allow temporary market forces to impose an irreversible contraction of the coal industry would be an irresponsible gamble.

[1] If a particular service could not meet the direct costs of providing it (the 'inescapable' costs being met by the national block tariff, i.e. taxation) it might then be decided on social or other grounds (e.g. distribution of industry) to keep it going from public funds. In that event it might be more legitimate to use the term 'subsidy' to describe the *additional* funds provided by taxation.

[2] A system of public transport based on the two-part tariff idea would not, of course, mean that all railway services would remain; some public services could no doubt be run more efficiently by road.

Unless and until it is established that the country's energy in the future – our long-term requirements – can be met more economically from other sources, a rational fuel policy for Britain is a policy designed to avoid the permanent, irreversible contraction of the coal industry. What constitutes irreversible decisions? Those which involve the abandonment of substantial coal reserves or of our ability to get coal. This could happen if collieries have to be closed long before their reserves have been worked out – these reserves could only be worked again at prodigious expense, if at all. Equally, the disbanding of a mining labour force which could not be re-assembled is an irreversible decision. Such decisions can be avoided by ordering economic life in such a way as not to subject the coal industry to rapid fluctuations; by minimizing short-term fluctuations in the demand for coal. A rational fuel policy would, in short, assign to the coal industry the task of providing the base-load, as it were, of the nation's energy requirements. Oil, and later nuclear power, would increasingly have to carry the burden of economic fluctuation and expansion.

Such a policy would start from the assumption that the nation requires reasonable security and permanence of fuel supplies. Since we are dealing with fuel, the basis of industry itself, the time-span to be considered is not a matter of five or ten years – although even ten years from now, to sustain a total fuel consumption which will certainly be well over 300,000,000 tons of coal equivalent would require oil imports up to sixty per cent greater than in 1960, a substantial contribution from nuclear power, and a coal industry no smaller than it is now. If we take a view over the next three or four decades – a period well within the life-span of children now at school – an annual energy consumption for Britain of some 500,000,000 tons is not an extravagant assumption, in the context of a total world fuel use increasing to nearly four times its present volume; an annual supply of at least 200,000,000 tons of British coal could become a minimum guarantee of industrial security.

Obviously, during periods of world surplus, relatively small quantities of oil, natural gas and foreign coal can be offered to fuel users in Britain and Europe at prices with which the coal industries of these countries could not compete. During such periods the coal industry could be forced into rapid contraction, involving widespread closures of mines and the dispersal of large numbers of miners: actions which are irreversible for geological and sociological reasons. A rational fuel policy would take into account both the longer-term fuel requirements of the country and the characteristics of the coal industry.

It is sometimes argued that the coal industry resists violent contraction simply because the industry has vested interests, that it is naturally reluctant to give way to superior alternatives. This is an unfounded assumption. The social consequences of contraction would not present insurmountable difficulties; nor has the industry private property to defend, or private profit to cling to. What is involved is not a sectional interest but the national interest. At present, there are hopes about the future of atomic energy as a supplier of primary fuel for producing electricity; but they are not more than hopes. Nor is there any assurance forthcoming that even for the next three or four decades, enough oil will be discovered and made available at reasonable prices to meet the world's energy needs – quite apart from Britain's problem of paying for them by exports even if they are available. Under these conditions, it is not defending a sectional interest to maintain that the country should not recklessly abandon coal reserves, or its power to exploit them, because of temporary fluctuations in the world fuel market.

The fundamental question which must be answered about both the nationalized coal and transport industries is clearly – though unintentionally – brought out by those who advocate that the country's fuel supplies should be exposed to the free play of the market: those who suggest that under present conditions of world oil surplus, the coal industry should be allowed to diminish to 150,000,000 or even 120,000,000 tons a year, at which size it is said the industry would be highly profitable. They may be right about the profitability, provided that sufficiently large amounts of capital were written off. But since the coal industry cannot be turned off and on as if it were a tap, Governments have to take a more responsible view. Under highly competitive conditions, it would be impossible for coal and public transport to attain whatever financial objective is set for them by the Government without drastically curtailing their services and reducing the scale of their operations. If, however, the Government felt that it was not in the national interest to allow certain activities to be eliminated, it can relax the requirements of profitability. In other words Government will be making deliberate decisions about the contribution that is expected from these industries.

Investment in coal and public transport is long-term investment in national assets. A responsible attitude towards them would be reflected in policies which assigned to each industry clearly defined national objectives, to be pursued 'until further notice', and created the conditions in which these objectives could be attained.

### Room for manœuvre

The second of the two questions posed at the start of this chapter, namely, the ability of the nationalized industries to meet changing circumstances, will also be looked at in terms of general principles, for unless these are agreed, or at least discerned, a great deal of pointless discussion can take place.

As to whether the nationalized industries should be enabled to change their scope and the range of their activities, there can be little room for argument. No industrial organization is likely to be efficient, whether it is publicly or privately owned, unless it can adapt itself to changes, whether these are devised by itself – in the form of new technologies or systems of management – or imposed by external circumstances.

There can be no justification for statutory restrictions such as those imposed upon the powers of the electricity and nationalized transport undertakings not to engage in manufacture. Such restrictions exist to protect private interests. Private industry, which is subject only to minimal public accountability, is free to pursue the private appropriation of wealth by altering its financial structure, integrating or diversifying. Nationalized industries, extensively accountable to the community for their financial and economic policies, and with the public not the private interest as their objective, should at least not be inhibited by statute from extending the range and scope of their activities.

The two principal nationalized industries, coal and transport, both inherited a variety of ancillary industries or services. They participate in many different industries. Thus the National Coal Board owns more than twenty coke oven plants, and is the largest producer in the country of crude benzole and crude tar; it is the country's second largest producer of bricks, operating more than sixty brickworks; it owns and maintains 140,000 houses and operates 210,000 acres of farmland. In contrast with some of these, its share of the retail coal market is small – about three per cent of house coal is retailed by the board. Public transport also has many ramifications, including, for example, the manufacture of rolling stock and the very substantial ownership of property. The boundaries of both industries are fairly arbitrary. But all the nationalized industries and services draw upon supplying industries and serve certain markets. What should determine, to take an example, whether the coal industry should itself develop the manufacture of new fuels, new chemical derivatives; or develop its ancillaries such as brickworks, or expand its share of the market in coal distribution?

It is not surprising that no clear-cut answers to such questions speedily emerged. The nationalized industries are vast enterprises which are still evolving the forms of organization appropriate for their tasks. But it is high time that these questions should be asked, and answered, now.

The central problem of any large-scale administration, irrespective of whether it is publicly or privately owned, is to reconcile the two opposites of central control and local autonomy. Too much of one or the other tends to throttle effective administration. While it is impossible to expect that a final theoretical solution to this problem of reconciliation exists, there are certain techniques which can be employed to attain a large element of local freedom and satisfaction in work, without diminishing effective central control.

One very effective technique is to employ profit as an instrument of control. But there is a major stumbling block in the way of doing this, which springs from the well-established confusion between profit for private appropriation, and profit as an indicator of success in performing a particular job. Profit in the first sense gave rise to nationalization, which is a practical expression of a decision that economic activity should be conducted for the value of the work done and not simply for the enrichment of owners. The notion that pervades laissez-faire economics, that what is profitable for owners is necessarily in the public interest, provided there is competition, did not bear objective scrutiny and was constantly belied by events. Nationalization meant conducting industries in the public, not the private, interest, and there is no private appropriation of wealth in the process. The elimination of private greed and of the scramble for private enrichment makes it possible for the industry to engage in comprehensive rational planning, to obtain not only economic but also social and human benefits which competitive private enterprise could not pursue, or pursue only by abrogating the sanctity of the profit motive: by conceding that the variety of human needs could not be met by the simple criterion of profit for private enrichment.[1]

Because the private profit motive occupies a central position in the dogma of capitalism, the word profit itself has become identified with the evils of that system. But this is surely a confusion. There can be no valid criticism of the notion of profit as such, for it means nothing more than this: that what has come out of a particular activity is more valuable than what went into it. As a measurement of real wealth created by work it is an indicator simply of the success with which real resources are used.[2]

This confusion of thought, based upon the association of 'profit' with private greed, has had far-reaching effects. In part, at least, it was responsible for the feeling that nationalized industries should not aim at making profits but should let the consumer have the benefit of lower prices. At the same time, it was inevitable that the absence of profits was and still is being taken as a decisive sign of failure, by those who cannot perceive the difference between private gain and public profit.

However, this abolition of the profit motive extended into the industries themselves. The absence of the *private* profit motive was not felt as a shortcoming – indeed it is one of the principal advantages of public ownership. But there has been at the same time an implicit rejection of the use of profit as a measure of success. No one would seriously argue that the private profit motive is essential for an industry to be efficient, flexible and

[1] For a detailed discussion of this issue, see E. F. Sutor, 'Is the Ownership Debate Closed', *Socialist Commentary*, Feb. 1959.

[2] Subject to what has been said on pp. 272–3. Where costs are not recovered from users on each occasion of use, profit cannot of course be used as an indicator of efficiency.

progressive – for this motive in any case exists only at the very top of large-scale private enterprise. But at certain levels, which for present purposes can be defined as the levels of general management, profit – the excess of income over expenditure – is a comprehensive and valuable measure of success. In other words, profit, stripped of its historical associations, can become an instrument of control of operations at the same time as giving a high degree of creative freedom to general management in different branches of the industry. Employed in this way, as a measure of success and an instrument of accountability, profit ascertainment, of course, becomes merely an internal accounting device to promote efficient administration and efficient use of resources. This is so whatever may be the financial objective which the industry as a whole is given: whether it is required to show a profit, or to break even.

The use of profit as an instrument of accountability implies that certain clearly defined operational units, which may be selected on a functional or geographical basis, would be set up with their own accounting arrangements. This procedure need not be limited to such activities of nationalized industries as are quite clearly ancillary to its main functions: it is a technique of administration that can be employed at key levels throughout the industry. But it is particularly appropriate for activities which are offshoots, so to speak, from the main stream of the industries' operations, for at such points the difficulty of reconciling central control with local freedom is especially marked, if only because the specialist knowledge at the operational levels is not easy to fit into the chain of command to the central organization.

What this amounts to is the establishment of certain units *as if* they were firms, as 'quasi-firms'. Each clearly identifiable activity can be given a separate identity to the extent of setting it up with its own balance sheet and accounts – and not necessarily more than that. National policy would continue to be formulated by the parent body to which the 'quasi-firm' would remain responsible – the National Coal Board in the case of the coal industry – and the 'quasi-firm' would continue to draw upon central services and centralized functions where appropriate. At the same time, its general management would have a yardstick of success in the form of profit and loss account. Subject to considerations of national policy, profitable 'quasi-firms' would expand and unprofitable ones either be made profitable or contract.[1]

In practice, the method of creating 'executives' for the administration of certain activities, such as opencast mining and underground gasification, broke the ground for the development of the 'quasi-firm' in the case of the coal industry, and the recent creation of a Brickworks Executive has given further expression to the idea. (The regrouping of the activities formerly covered by the Transport Commission, on the other hand, goes too far towards making each major activity into a 'firm' rather than a 'quasi-firm'.)

The establishment of 'quasi-firms' is justified wholly on the grounds of more effective administration. But it can at the same time provide a simple and effective guide to the question: should nationalized industries expand their existing ancillary activities, and start up new ventures? The answer is that in principle they should be free to extend their activities wherever it is profitable to do so – and that the establishment of 'quasi-firms' would provide the necessary organizational structure.

Does this mean reintroducing the private profit motive under a new guise? It does not. The ascertainment of profitability in order to maximize it – to use profitability as an objective measure of the efficiency with which real resources are used, and as a means of distributing responsibilities – does not introduce the private profit motive, for in public ownership there is no private enrichment involved. But the difference goes far beyond this. The *private* profit motive is to maximize that part of real wealth creation which can be taken for private enrichment (that is, that part of the real wealth created by work which is left over after contractual obligations of production, wages and capital charges have been met) – to maximize private gain. But the *public* profit motive is to maximize the real wealth created; in other words, to maximize the efficiency with which resources are used. This does not imply that the particular activity should aim for maximum profits shown as a surplus available for disposal, nor even that any profit at all should be shown. The public interest may be best served by reducing prices, or improving services to consumers,

[1] When, as in the case of the coal-mines themselves, overall pricing policy necessitates units working at a loss, this can be recognized by devising 'rents and subsidies' so that all 'accounting units' start off on an equal footing.

and as a consequence, profit as an available surplus may not appear.[1] The point is that such a choice exists, whereas activity undertaken for private profit offers no choice of that kind. Nor does the ascertainment of profitability imply that only those activities which are capable of revealing profits should be pursued, again for reasons founded upon the public interest – that is, reasons which are explained and publicly accepted (the maintenance of production from so-called 'uneconomic' mines being a case in point). Thus, for a publicly-owned industry to aim at maximum profitability is simply to aim at the most efficient use of resources. There is no predetermined allocation of the real wealth created. Where expansion can take place on the basis of profitability thus defined, it should take place unless there are reasons, justifiable on grounds of the public interest, why it should not.

---

[1] Whether a surplus is to be shown, and, if it is, how it should be distributed become matters of deliberate choice.

# CHAPTER SEVENTEEN

# LESSONS FROM ABROAD

*by*

## PETER LOWELL

T O D R A W valid lessons from foreign experience one must compare like with like. First, which countries are sufficiently similar to the industrial economy and political democracy of the U.K. to enable comparisons of nationalization to be drawn? They are in the main the Common Market and E.F.T.A. countries, Portugal excepted.

Secondly, which nationalized industries or public enterprises in these different countries should be compared? Enterprises may be classified into productive, financial and cultural groups. There are in the different countries examples of cultural public enterprises such as broadcasting stations, or financial ones such as banks and insurance companies, or productive ones such as railways, coal-mines and manufacturing units. It would, however, not appear instructive to compare except within one of these groups. Comparison will therefore be restricted to productive public enterprises which by definition include any enterprises marketing some measurable physical commodity or service.

The extent of productive public enterprises in Western European countries is considerable. But quantitative information is inadequate, and no comparative analysis exists. The following table was specially compiled but leaves large gaps, particularly for Italy and Western Germany. Yet a general picture emerges of the coverage, investment and degree of monopoly of nationalized industries in nine Western European countries.

The comparative table demonstrates the significance of the public sector in Western Europe. In the United Kingdom this sector – which includes, broadly speaking, nationalized industries and local authorities, but excludes the central Government – accounts for nearly a third of the national gross fixed investment.

PUBLIC ENTERPRISES IN WESTERN EUROPE:
Relative size per country, breakdown of investment, degree of monopoly.

| | U.K. | | AUSTRIA | | ITALY | | FRANCE | |
|---|---|---|---|---|---|---|---|---|
| Share in National Gross Fixed Investment: | 32% | | 27% | | 27% | | 25% | |
| BRANCH OF INDUSTRY | Inv. % | Mon. % | Inv. % | Mon. % | Inv. % | Mon. % | Inv. % | Mon. % |
| Postal/Telecommunications | ⎫ 28 | 100 | | 100 | | 100 | (?) | 100 |
| Transport (excl. road transport) | ⎭ | 100 +inland water-ways | | 100 | | 100 | rail 15 | 100 |
| Energy (excl. oil) | 64 | 100 | coal 11 | 85 | gas 100 elec. 25 | | 43 | ca. 100 |
| Iron and Steel | 2 | 10–15 | 52 | ca. 100 | over 50 | | ⎫ 42 | |
| Other | 6 e.g. oil aircraft | ? ? | 37 e.g. mining oil + chemicals food electrical textiles paper | 86 74 40 34 14 12 | e.g. shipyards 75 electrical 52 oil refining 24 motor vehics 11 | | ⎭ e.g. chemical aircraft motor vehics cigarettes matches | ? ? ? ? ? |
| | 100 | | 100 | | | | 100 | |

284

Sources; *United Nation's* 1959 *Economic Survey of Europe*
*Annals of Collective Economy, vol. XXXI, nos.* 1, 4.

| WEST GERMANY (author's estimate:) (15%–20%) | | SWEDEN 15% | | NORWAY 14% | | NETHERLANDS 13% | | BELGIUM 10% | |
|---|---|---|---|---|---|---|---|---|---|
| Inv. % | Mon. % | Inv. % | Mon. % | Inv. % | Mon. % | Inv. % | Mon. % | Inv. % | Mon.% |
| | 100 | 16 | 100 | 11 | 100 excl. some t/phone | } 26 | 100 | 18 incl. broad-casting | ca. 100 |
| | 100 | 27 | 100 | 26 | 100 | } 26 | excl. some air | 53 | ca. 100 |
| gas 91 elec. 62 coal 25 iron- | | 47 | elec. 50 | 40 | ca. 67 | 51 | 100 | (?) | elec. + gas ca. 100 |
| ore 37 steel 5 | | (?) | ? 50 | (?) | 67 | (?) | ? | } 29 | |
| e.g. | 10 | | 23 | e.g. | 23 | e.g. | | | |
| spirits | 100 | tobacco | 100 | road transport | ? | oil | ? | | |
| matches | 100 | forests | 25 | mining | ? | mining | ? | | |
| aluminium | 70 | road transport | ? | | | salt | ? | | |
| motor vehicles | 40 | mining | ? | | | | | | |
| shipyards | 18 | | | | | | | | |
| | | 100 | | 100 | | 100 | | 100 | |

In the Common Market the share is roughly one-fifth and in the Scandinavian countries about one-seventh.

The table shows great variety in the nature and degree of monopoly of productive public enterprises in the different countries. But common features emerge for enterprises in the basic sectors of postal-telecommunications, transport and energy. The *common* features of productive public enterprises in the basic sectors and the *varied* features of the rest suggest this question: do productive public enterprises divide into two separate groups which are so different as not to permit useful comparison? One group covers those basic industries which constitute the economic infrastructure of a country. The other group is a heterogeneous collection of public enterprises nationalized *ad hoc*, that is, for different reasons and in different ways. The two groups of productive public enterprises – infrastructure nationalization and *ad hoc* nationalization – should therefore be compared and considered separately.

*Infrastructure nationalization*

Infrastructure may be defined as those basic facilities which are necessary to establish and expand a structure, be it military, social or economic. It is generally agreed that postal-telecommunications, transport and energy are basic to a modern economy. They may therefore be said to constitute the whole or major part of a country's economic infrastructure.

Just as the industrial economies of Western European countries show a very similar pattern, so the story of infrastructure nationalization is strikingly similar. First, there is the extent. In the United Kingdom it constitutes ninety-two per cent of all nationalization investment. The equivalent figures are lower for other countries. But this is largely due to the greater proportion of infrastructure in the British economy. With the exception of road transport and oil, infrastructure nationalization has a virtual monopoly in most Western European countries. Secondly, the history of this nationalization abroad goes back many decades and is largely non-socialist. Throughout Western Europe the extension of public ownership over postal/telecommunications, transport, and energy has proceeded gradually and continuously with the introduction

286

and expansion of these services. Thirdly, the organizational trend has been to make postal services Government departments, to municipalize gas and electricity and to nationalize railways by stages. Fourthly, the purpose has been the same for capitalist as for socialist Governments: the primacy of public interest with regard to infrastructure industries. Nationalization was motivated by the dangers of price exploitation by private monopoly and the demands of 'social service', such as in servicing outlying areas.

A classic example is the nationalization of the German railways. Some nationalization had been effected by some German states as early as 1850. Advocates of the nationalization of road haulage will be interested to know that after 1850 some denationalization took place, but that re-nationalization started about 1875. Bismarck, the hero of railway nationalization, decided to operate the railways 'in the general interest'. Uniform charges were introduced on the Prussian State Railway in 1880, but lower rates were applied to agricultural supplies, such as fertilizer, to certain areas, to certain imports needed by German industry, and to certain ports to make German harbours more competitive. It was about this time that the concept of 'social service' (*gemeinwirtschaft*) appeared in German literature. After the first world war the German railways operated profitably, and under the Nazis were forced to finance motorways. During the inter-war years the German Railway Undertaking was formed as an independent legal body, in many ways the forerunner of the public corporation in this country. In 1951 federal legislation required the railways to work 'in accordance with commercial principles while safeguarding the interests of the German economy'.

Much discussion has recently proceeded in Western Germany on how to reconcile commercial principles and social service. For example, the Scientific Advisory Committee of the Transport Ministry in its 1953 report called for 'equal services in economically strong or weak areas on the basis of equalities of tariffs and adequate services'. In France *service publique* is clearly defined in French administrative law. In Germany, France, Italy, Sweden and Switzerland considerable social service charges have been transferred by law to the state budget. It has been calculated that German, French and Italian railways would in fact be profitable if all social service charges were taken on by the state. Such charges embrace numerous items of expenditure, including special pensions, which the public enterprise would not take on if it were guided only by commercial considerations. The following table is based on 'Economic Problems of Railways of Member Countries of European Conference of Ministers of Transport', International Union of Railways, July 1961:

SOCIAL SERVICE SUBSIDIES: RAILWAYS 1959

Operating results before and after the normalization of accounts
Ratio of expenditure to receipts

|  | Excluding state subsidies Monetary Units | Including state subsidies Monetary Units | % of estimated total social service charges that were actually granted % | Operating results on assumption that total social service charges were fully granted Monetary Units |
|---|---|---|---|---|
| Germany | 109 | 105 | 16 | 91 |
| France | 119 | 104 | 71 | 98 |
| Italy | 140 | 114 | 55 | 98 |
| Holland | 98 | 98 | 0 | 95 |

In the United Kingdom the Parliamentary Select Committee on Nationalized Industries has recommended the Government to take over social service expenditure as subsidies and subject to Parliamentary discussion. 'Social service' in infrastructure industries thus raises problems of subsidies from the Government, or cross-subsidies within the industry, or commercial losses. And this same problem is encountered in much the same form throughout most of Western Europe.

But what social service is in fact required: a railway service or a transport service? An electricity service or an energy service? Complementary to the social service problems are those of integrating, or at least co-ordinating, investment. Integration is required to maximize service and minimize investment and costs. But integration is complicated by the private competition of road transport and oil. In the U.K. both are better placed than the public sector to concentrate on profitable operations or to cross-subsidize internally. In many countries abroad there is either more integration with, or more restriction of competition from, the private sector. Austrian railway and motorway investment are co-ordinated and one-third of the passengers carried by the Austrian 'Federal Railways' do not in fact travel by rail. The Swiss Post Office (P.T.T.) operate rural bus services. Their number and frequency are relatively high. Every village with a sub-post office or on a mail-carrying route enjoys at least two return journeys a day to the nearest town. The decision as to which services should be run, and how frequently, lies with the postal administration which has to be satisfied that the journey is justified on grounds of need. The P.T.T. seems, however, to have a flexible rather than a rigid standard of adequacy and to some extent bargains with local people. Villages which want a higher standard of service than the P.T.T. is prepared to provide can obtain it by making a financial contribution themselves; eighty out of some seven thousand five hundred villages do so. But the P.T.T. has never entirely withdrawn a bus route and would be unlikely to do so even if only three or four people were using it. In Germany and France road haulage and buses are subject to many more restrictions than in the U.K. over weight, volume, distance and publication of prices.

The story of energy is similar to that of transport. The private sector, pipelines and oil, is more subject to state intervention on the Continent than here. It appears from the above that the problems of social service, integration and investment versus commercial management are characteristic of infrastructure industries and not of nationalization or 'the public corporation'. These problems do apply to a different institution of the same public enterprise abroad, such as the French coal industry *Charbonnages de France*. They do not apply to the same institution of a different enterprise such as the B.B.C. Similarly, the controversy over Government intervention on finance, prices and wages reflects the size and special role of these industries, not the fact of nationalization.

The economic impact of infrastructure industries marks them out as the 'commanding heights'. But when we compare Labour Party legislation with other countries the verdict is that nationalization of transport and energy allowed us little more than to catch up with similar measures of capitalist Western Europe. True, different organizational forms were chosen and larger-scale industries were created. But this was the product of a later time and later industrial experience rather than socialist doctrine.

We are in fact late-comers in the field of infrastructure nationalization as well as modernization. Thus two confusions have arisen: first, public opinion in Britain identifies nationalization with the present public corporations of infrastructure industries. Secondly, socialists are in danger of ignoring the distinctions between this group and *ad hoc* nationalization, and of applying the theory and practice of the present nationalized group to some future general group. The idea of a British Sugar Corporation typifies this state of mind.

## Ad Hoc Nationalization

In contrast to infrastructure, the story of the second group of nationalized industries is strikingly different between each country and each industry. Only in France, and to a small extent in Austria, did political and ideological reasons for nationalization obtain. In Italy, Germany and Austria there was a spurt of nationalization during the 'thirties. It arose out of the Fascist Governments' draconian economic measures to overcome depression and prepare for war. The aftermath of war provided a further fillip to *ad hoc* nationalization. In France, Germany, Italy and Austria the state found itself the owner of big industrial assets belonging to former Nazis, fascists and Vichy *collaborateurs*. In the Scandinavian countries and the Netherlands, by contrast, public ownership has grown primarily in response to economic and practical requirements.

A variety of industries has been nationalized in whole or in part. Iron and steel may be regarded as a border-line case between *ad hoc* and infrastructure nationalization. There is an historical curiosity about the nationalization of salt, alcohol, tobacco and matches in many countries, and there is a certain recurrence in the case of mining. Beyond this, it is hard to discern a common pattern.

French *ad hoc* nationalization covers enterprises as different as potassium, films, aircraft and motor vehicles. The case of Renault demonstrates French concern to make *ad hoc* nationalization pay.

A special top management organization structure was created and is discussed below. The onus upon the very independent head of the firm is to act in accordance with the profit motive.

In Italy fifty per cent of steel and seventy-two per cent of shipyard production are examples of *ad hoc* nationalization. But this is nationalization by share acquisition, not by legislation. An interesting case is that of the Italian E.N.I. state enterprise. It is one of the more important oil companies of the Middle East and has the monopoly of oil and natural gas supply in Italy. The company is not subject to any form of administrative regulation other than that applicable to all commercial companies. Large surpluses have been earned and the late head, Signor Mattei, acquired a world-wide reputation as a highly individual tycoon. The bigger Italian public enterprise is I.R.I., founded by Mussolini in 1933. I.R.I. has majority and minority holdings in a vast number of small and large operating companies. The growth rate of I.R.I. has been larger than that of the Italian economy as a whole; its investment portfolio is divided roughly equally between public utilities and manufacturing. The company plays an important part in matters of national importance such as rationalizing the Italian shipyards and developing southern Italy. Its operations are highly profitable. In Germany, Volkswagen has been the most successful of all public enterprises, operating on an almost totally autonomous basis. In 1962 the company clashed publicly with the Federal German Government on pricing policy – and won.[1]

Sweden provides the classic example of treating a public enterprise *ad hoc*. Swedish forests, twenty-five per cent nationalized, are directly administered by a Government department and thus subject to very detailed Parliamentary control. But as they compete with private enterprise, they are allowed considerable freedom of price determination. Other public enterprises, such as in the catering trade, are joint stock companies with Parliamentary control restricted to share capital. Prices are only dictated by Government in the case of public monopolies, such as tobacco and liquor. In Norway local authorities own public enterprises outside the infrastructure.

To conclude, foreign nationalization outside the infrastructure is widespread but *ad hoc*. It is usually organized in the form of

[1] Volkswagen was recently partially denationalized.

joint stock companies. The managing directors are fêted rather than obstructed. As a rule, they make and retain large profits. The state is major shareholder, but acts no differently than other major shareholders would act. Public accountability and in certain cases particular national interests are secured without abandoning the profit motive and without state aid, protection or interference.

What is the value of this lesson? There are many different reasons for and forms of public enterprises. The public corporation does not necessarily apply to all. Each future project of nationalization outside the infrastructure should therefore be considered entirely on its own merits.

### Two-tier Boards and Ministerial Interference

Infrastructure industries are increasingly nationalized and will have to learn to live with the state. The state is increasingly engaged in economic planning and thus tempted to intervene. So far this has resulted in the U.K. in ministerial interference rather than public accountability and planning. It is fashionable to blame the minister. But is it fair? The minister is first and foremost a member of the Government with political aims and subject to collective Cabinet responsibility. If in doubt, politics come before public corporation. The result is collision of interests. But there is no organizational framework to cushion the clash and help reconcile the different parties. Chairmen of public corporations work under the Damocles' sword of ministerial appointment, dismissal and power to direct. This turns weekly ministerial advice into verbal command. In short, there is a problem of top management organization. Are there any organizational lessons from abroad to help solve this problem?

French experiments in public enterprise organization show two extremes: one is Air France, i.e. infrastructure nationalization, the other Renault, i.e. *ad hoc* nationalization. Air France is headed by a mixed board (*Conseil d'Administration*) of sixteen members. Four are civil servants, two chosen by the Minister of Public Works and Transport, one by the Minister of Finance and Economic Affairs and one by the Minister of Overseas France. Four are personalities outside the civil service, but chosen by the Minister of Public Works and Transport, two of whom must come from the Chambers of Commerce. Four are employee representatives and four represent private shareholders. This mixed board has decision-making powers and has been strongly criticized as a brake on commercial management.

Renault, on the other hand, is directed by a President Director General appointed by the Minister of Industrial Production, with the advice of the Minister of Finance and Economic Affairs. He is assisted by a *Conseil d'Administration* as well as a *Comité Central d'Entreprise*. Of the *Conseil's* fifteen members, seven are appointed by the Minister of Industrial Production, six are employee representatives and two consumer representatives.

In Germany the law requires every public company to be headed by a two-tier board: the supervisory board (*Aufsichtsrat*) and the executive board (*Vorstand*). The supervisory board consists of non-executive members appointed by the shareholders to safeguard their interests. It appoints the executive board, approves share issues and annual accounts, and may call for any reports on the affairs of the company. It is supervisory but strictly non-executive, keeps informed but does not interfere directly or in detail. The managing director and executive board are full-time executive directors. They cannot be members of the supervisory board although they may be called in to meetings. The supervisory board thus acts as the shareholders' watchdog without in any way infringing on the entrepreneurial role of the managing director.

The Germans are very proud of their entrepreneurs (*Unternehmer*). But it is always the managing director as head of the executive board who is referred to as the entrepreneur, and not the chairman of the supervisory board. The relations between the two boards are fixed by law in very general terms. Frequently bankers sit on the supervisory board and thus maintain a very close liaison with industry to their mutual advantage. This applies particularly in a rapidly growing economy, hungry for finance. Employee representatives sit on the supervisory board in the iron and steel industry as a matter of law, and in many other industries voluntarily. The two-tier board thus serves as the basis of the German co-determination experiment, which is – at least on paper – a more ambitious exercise in socialism than any form of industrial democracy attempted in this country. Volkswagen is a typical example of a nationalized industry (although by now sixty per cent of its shares are in private hands) where the two-tier board has allowed state supervision and employee representation without interference in management.

British company law, by contrast, provides for only one board. But as a rule, the board comprises executive and non-executive directors. In many of the larger companies the managing director sets up a separate executive committee. These committees have no legal status and the managing director is member of both board and committee. But the organization resembles that in German companies. There is also the example of the holding company where the relations between the board and its subsidiaries are somewhat analogous to the German system. There are thus pointers even in ordinary company organization in this country, towards the need for an organizational device clearly distinguishing more general and supervisory responsibilities from those of executive management.

But the two-tier board is perhaps most relevant to the public corporation. Austria has experimented in this respect. A supervisory board could be created to comprise the Ministry, the Treasury, bankers, industrialists, trade union officials, employees and consumers. The supervisory board could even be given special power over specific matters like long-term investment and finance. The minister would appoint most of the members of the supervisory board. He could be chairman himself. But he would be compelled to formalize his relations with the chief executive and to justify his policy to the supervisory board. The appointment of the chief executive would be by the supervisory board, not by the minister. Thus a two-tier board might be a means of maintaining public accountability without direct ministerial interference in management.

## Economic Planning and Control

Throughout Western Europe the state is assuming a more active role in the national economy. Government influence and intervention have been considerable even in 'free enterprise' Western Germany. In fact, continental governments have tended, if anything, to be more interventionist than in the United Kingdom.

Since the war the range of governmental economic instruments has been greatly refined; but the role of public enterprises has tended to remain confused and unsatisfactory.

Partly this is the result of temptation. The public enterprise sector represents a significant share of gross national expenditure, as indicated in the comparative table above. Added to Government expenditure, it greatly increases the power of the state to spend and invest more or less, in other words to turn the tap on and off. Most Western European Governments have repeatedly used public enterprise investment and pricing as an instrument of counter-cyclical policy: examples are Sweden in 1954, the Netherlands in 1957, Belgium on several occasions. On the whole, this policy has failed abroad, as it has in Britain. The time-lag between investment decision and national stabilization is too great. It is easier to speed up investment than to slow it down. Another aspect of temptation is the key role of infrastructure nationalization. The United Kingdom in particular has endeavoured to stabilize or restrain prices and wages in the transport and energy sectors. But again, restraint has either been ineffective or too short-lived. The story is very similar abroad, with notable exceptions such as in Germany.

The other and more important reason why public enterprises as economic instruments are unsatisfactory lies in the effect on the public enterprises themselves. Infrastructure nationalization needs to be shielded rather than exposed, as the railways problem demonstrates throughout Western Europe. *Ad hoc* nationalization is expected to make profits and therefore needs to be left alone. In the United Kingdom we are beginning to learn from our own mistakes. It is perhaps comforting to find that the Continent has made the same mistakes.

Yet there are lessons to be learned from abroad on how to make the economy grow. The first comes from Western Germany. In this emphatically capitalist country the Government has never hesitated to intervene. But the accent has been on specific positive measures regardless of whether the industry was dominated by public or private enterprises. The Government has directly assisted private enterprise housing and public enterprise energy, private and public enterprise shipyards and private enterprise heavy industry. Another important lesson derives from France, and the special form of planning which has come to be known as 'Monnet planning', after its great pioneer and practitioner M. Jean Monnet. Monnet planning commenced in France as modernization planning. Two characteristics of all Monnet schemes are that he gets the three important parties together at one table, that is employers, trade unions and Government. And secondly, that he discusses, publicizes and popularizes all issues as much and as openly as possible. He has led and inspired first France and then the Common Market as the prophet of modernization. Results have followed, and the snowball effect of this modernization mentality has changed the economic map of France and the Common Market.

The permanent secretariat of Monnet planning is the *Commissariat Général du Plan,* numbering some one hundred and forty permanent staff including office boys. The actual planning work is, however, carried out by commissions representing different sectors of activity such as agriculture, manufacturing or housing, while other commissions deal with problems common to all sectors such as labour, finance and regional plans.

In these commissions, representatives of industry, trade organizations, trade unions and other interests work out targets for growth, investment and pricing. The people who have to work the plans draw them up. The *Commissariat Général* comes under the Minister of Finance and Economic Affairs, but is confined, however active and persuasive, to proposing, advising and estimating. Plans have been drawn up in full knowledge of other plans, bottle-necks can be avoided and the very self-commitment to achieve a plan appears sufficient obligation to implement it. Monnet planning is, in fact, self-planning. By making economic interdependence explicit, targets are set, publicized, adjusted and maintained. The emphasis is away from specific industries. Our lesson is that as planning increases, specific ministerial interference should be confined to long-term plans and pre-arranged short-term adjustments.

The importance of the Plan for public enterprises is that Monnet planning does not distinguish between public and private enterprises. Each enterprise remains solely responsible for carrying out its own programme. In Monnet planning the infrastructure receives full attention. There is a specific commission on post/

telecommunications, one on transport and another on energy. But these commissions operate in the same way as those of mixed public and private enterprises such as manufacturing and agriculture.

There are Government sanctions, such as control of capital issues and prices, and in public enterprises the state does exert direct influence. But Monnet planning allows the state to achieve its directives of full employment, growth and stability without singling out public enterprises as counter-cyclical instruments. It is also significant that in France the key nationalized industries like coal and the railways have not been expected to pay their way. Modernization has proceeded on a basis of heavy annual deficits and state subsidies, without noticeably alarming or out-raging French public opinion.

## Nationalization and the Common Market

So far, nationalization has taken place within the framework of the nation-state. How will it be affected by the Common Market?

*Ad hoc* nationalization need not be affected as such, though the trading position of some public enterprises will be affected as their monopoly privileges or tariff protection cease in the Common Market. The Common Market will, however, make a strong impact on infrastructure nationalization. Post/telecommunications and air transport on an international basis and railways on a continental basis are already subject to extra-national control and co-ordination.

In the energy field, Euratom was created by the Treaty of Rome as the first Common Market public enterprise. It was set up for new tasks rather than to take over old ones. Euratom was designed to control nuclear materials and to own key nuclear plants, but at present it operates rather as a co-operative research station. Nuclear development is likely to prove slower and less profitable than at first anticipated. But in time, Euratom may highlight the problems of relationship and demarcation between public enter-prises of the Common Market and their counterparts in member countries, such as the Atomic Energy Authority of the U.K.

More specific problems will arise when we join the Coal and Steel Community. This was founded by the Treaty of Paris with the object of achieving a common market with free flow of goods and competition, but no monopoly, in coal and steel. Post-war British policy for coal, steel and their transport has rather been to accept monopolies, but to make them accountable to Parliament. As a result, E.C.S.C. pricing methods are practically the opposite of those hitherto in force in the U.K. They do not permit price discrimination between customers; but we have, both in transport and (less markedly) in coal. They distinguish steel and coal prices at given basing points, i.e. ex factory or mine, from transport charges; but we have not. They allow producers to 'align a price' to meet competition, but require 'basing point' prices and transport charges to users to be published separately; we have not. As members of the E.C.S.C. we shall have to adapt our practices in these respects to the Six, and we have started to do so.

The Six have until recently made little or no progress in evolving a common policy on energy, or – outside the field of coal and steel – on transport. Harmonization of transport policy is however included in the provisions of the Rome Treaty, and this is likely to be one of the next major tasks of the Common Market Commission in Brussels.

Work on a common energy policy for the Six has been hampered partly by organizational difficulties. All three executive organs of the European Economic Community are involved – the E.C.S.C. for coal, Euratom for nuclear energy, the Common Market Commission for oil, gas and electricity. More fundamentally, the Community has been split between the coal producers – Germany and Belgium – and the consumers – Italy and Luxembourg; France and the Netherlands, with interests in coal, oil and natural gas, have a foot in both camps. It now looks, however, as if the negotiations which have been going on in the special inter-executive energy committee of the Community are beginning to yield results. The outlines of a possible energy policy are beginning to emerge, and it seems clear that it will be based on the principle of cheap energy – which means greater reliance on oil and coal from outside Europe, and a planned run-down of Europe's own coal industries. At the time of writing, this policy exists only in the vaguest outline, and the details still have to be argued. As a member of the E.E.C., Britain will play her part in working out the policy. Whether a member or not, we would obviously have to take account of Europe's energy policy in framing our own, since a large margin between our energy costs and those of our Continental competitors would weaken our ability to quote competitive prices on world markets.

*Conclusion*

The present chapter has been devoted to a comparative analysis. On the Continent there has been more eagerness to learn from neighbouring countries than there has in our hitherto secluded island. We now live closer to our neighbours than in the past and it is imperative that we compare closely.

The experience of nationalization among our Western European neighbours points to several important lessons. The main lesson is that the British debate on the problems of nationalization is really a debate on the problems of the economic infrastructure. In future the E.E.C. is likely to play a major role in solving these problems. Continental nationalization outside the infrastructure is *ad hoc* and made to pay. Another lesson is that the German two-tier boards offer a possible organizational contribution to solving the vexed problems of ministerial interference. Finally, problems of economic planning and control have been tackled more successfully by Monnet planning than by Morrison nationalization. It remains to be seen whether the National Economic Development Council will have the same success in Britain. To this last lesson must be added the fact that economic development and efficiency abroad have been more affected by the general growth climate than by public ownership and enterprise.

CHAPTER EIGHTEEN

# THE FUTURE OF PUBLIC ENTERPRISE[1]

THIS book has not been about *nationalization* so much as about *nationalized industries*. It has been concerned not with the principles of public ownership, but with the performance of those industries taken into public ownership in post-war Britain. This is an important distinction. We have been dealing with one small corner of a vast field, and the lessons to be learned from studying this corner are not necessarily applicable to the whole. We should be extremely chary about generalizing from the experience of the nationalized industries in post-war Britain to public ownership as such – as the previous chapter has demonstrated.

The record of Britain's nationalized industries is in any case, as previous chapters have shown, inconclusive. While there have been many fine and impressive achievements, there have also been missed opportunities; the ideals of the public corporation have too often been marred by faulty execution, whether through lack of imagination or resources, or through a conflict of objectives. One has the impression that the Labour Party, having occupied the commanding heights of the economy, did not know what use to make of them. Like the Austrian generals in the Napoleonic Wars, it deployed its troops in their bright uniforms in full view of the enemy and within range of his artillery – and was surprised and distressed at the resulting carnage. Terrain is useless without a plan of campaign.

It is to be hoped that this book will have gone some way to providing such a plan – or at least some principles on which a plan could be based. The central lesson is that nationalization by itself solves nothing. What it does is to create the conditions in which changes can be made, and fundamental reforms carried out. But this it can only do if the nationalized industries are run intel-

[1] In preparing this chapter I have received invaluable assistance from Miss Margaret Reid – Editor.

ligently and efficiently, and also – which may not be at all the same thing – in circumstances which allow them a reasonable chance of success.

Public ownership is not, and cannot be, an end in itself. It is a means whereby great ends can, with wisdom, be achieved. And there are many paths to public ownership, of which the Morrisonian public corporation – the nationalized industry as we know it in modern Britain – is only one. It does not follow, therefore, that by criticizing British Railways one is denigrating public ownership. One might as well say that in criticizing *Titus Andronicus* one is denying Shakespeare's claim to be a playwright!

What are the arguments, in Britain in 1962, for seeking further extensions of public ownership? There is, first of all, the moral argument of socialism – namely, that in the good society no man should be in a position to exploit his fellows by ownership of the means of production; and further, that it is better that a man should work directly for the community rather than to maximize the profits of shareholders. Indeed, as the role of the shareholder becomes more and more residual and functionless, it becomes increasingly clear that, at least in large-scale industry, it is private enterprise that needs to make a moral case for itself and not public enterprise.

The divorce between ownership and control in modern large-scale industry, pointed out by James Burnham in *The Managerial Revolution* two decades ago, has become increasingly apparent in the post-war trend towards larger and larger units. In such organizations the role of the shareholder is not to determine or even to influence policy (except when there is a threat of a take-over, and management finds it necessary to persuade its shareholders not to 'vote with their feet'!), but rather to act as a passive, functionless bondholder. To say that I.C.I., for example, is in any real sense 'owned' by its shareholders, is to employ an archaic and misleading terminology.

The growth of the management-run corporation, in fact, makes much of the passion with which the argument between public and private ownership is commonly conducted in the Anglo-Saxon world outmoded and irrelevant. There is normally much more in common between the giant private corporation and the public corporation than there is between the giant private corporation and the small privately-run enterprise where ownership and control are in the same hands. Indeed, it may be that in the long sweep of history the giant private corporation may be seen simply as a stepping-stone from private to public enterprise.

An important landmark in this transitory process is of course reached when the giant corporation achieves a monopoly in its chosen field; for with the disappearance of effective competition the biggest single argument against public control also vanishes. And the trend of modern industrial organization is increasingly towards monopoly.

Moreover, public ownership – as J. R. Sargent points out in Chapter 15 – enables national resources to be redistributed according to different principles from those imposed by the profit motive; and this is a benefit of great potential significance. Not only can the public corporation allocate its services and products to different classes of customers on the principle of cross-subsidization, it can also distinguish between the claims of its customers and employees, and transform the human relationships within its labour force on to a saner and more civilized basis. These benefits will not flow automatically from the act of nationalization. This, as we saw in Chapter 1, was one of the mistakes of the nationalizers after 1945. But, wisely operated, public ownership should be able to achieve a transformation in industrial relations and in the status of labour, as well as in the morale of both labour and management. Freedom from the tyranny of the profit motive should extend the range of choice in decision-making, and make it possible to create new values and new techniques in industry. These opportunites are as yet largely unexplored.

These are general arguments for public ownership. They do not, however, help one to determine either the priorities for nationalization, or the form that it should take. These can perhaps be made clearer by a brief summary of some of the more specific arguments for public ownership.

First, there is the argument of *power* – that the state should control the commanding heights of the economy, that great accumulations of industrial power should be publicly accountable and publicly controlled.

Second, there is the argument of *planning*. It is now accepted on all sides that modern society functions best on a basis of planning, and it may well be argued further that planning is facilitated by, though it does not absolutely require, public ownership. In any event, the more closely industrial management becomes integrated into a planning system, and the more widely the requirements of the planners come to be accepted as determining industrial policy, the more shadowy becomes the policy-making role of the share-holder.

This shades into a third argument for public ownership: the Galbraithian argument on *priorities*. This is the argument that modern capitalist society suffers from a serious distortion in its allocation of resources between the private sector and the public – the latter being starved in order that the former may be surfeited, so that private affluence battens on public squalor.

This again shades into a fourth argument – the argument of *equality*. Through all the controversies and heart-searchings over the future of socialism in Britain, nobody has so far seriously questioned the proposition that, however the term be defined, the main objective of socialism is greater equality. Clearly, there is a strong prima facie case for saying that the transfer of big industrial assets from private to public hands could in certain circumstances be an important means to greater equality.

Fifth, there is the argument of *efficiency*. Clearly, if private enter-prise can be shown to be 'failing the nation' – by charging too much for its products, by failing to achieve reasonable rates of productivity, by persistently bad labour relations or export records, by lagging in research and development, by technological backwardness – and if it cannot be brought to reform itself either by exhortation or competition, then there is a prima facie case for transferring it to public ownership. Again, if there are important opportunities for expansion in the economy which private enter-prise is unwilling or unable to finance, then the state has an obliga-tion to fill the gap.

Lastly, there is the argument of *equity* – namely, that when the Government provides money for private industry, whether it be loans for a new steel strip mill, or a new Cunarder, or grants for re-equipment of a cotton mill, it has an obligation to the taxpayer to see that the money is being used to good effect; and the best way of doing this is by buying a share in ownership with its money.

'No taxation without representation' should be the motto when public money is being put into private industry.

No doubt other arguments also could be advanced, but this brief catalogue in itself surely indicates that there is a powerful case for further selective extensions of public ownership, and that this case does not rest on the performance of the mixed bag of assets taken into public ownership since 1945. But the case which has been made out is for public ownership as such, not necessarily for the public corporation *à la* Morrison. The various arguments which have been put forward above manifestly do not all call for a single form of public ownership. Since the objects to be achieved are different, the means employed need to be different too.

Where one is dealing with a natural monopoly the public corporation does have obvious attractions. But if one is primarily concerned with limiting the *power* of big business and with imposing the will of the state on industry, there are many other ways of doing it. One obvious way is to develop a more effective system of planning, buttressed by the ultimate deterrent of the Chancellor's power of acquiring compulsorily a controlling interest in any company which refused to play its part. Elaborate controls on industry would not be needed if the Government had the power, which could be conferred by a simple Enabling Bill in Parliament, to make a compulsory take-over bid for any firm which was not co-operating in the national plan, or which after a full public examination could be shown to be in any way 'failing the nation'.

A great deal could also be done through the planning mechanism to make private industry more publicly accountable. One way would be to set up planning councils in each industry, financed by a levy on firms in the industry, with powers to ascertain and if necessary to publish the sort of information which seldom finds its way into the Press today – information on the market shares of the different firms, the rate of profit earned in various sectors of their operations, and so on.

The Government could also do much to improve standards in expanding the National Research and Development Council into a fully-fledged National Development Board which would promote research, develop patents and so on. The board could let out work on development contracts to private or public firms, and might be encouraged to acquire shares in private industry. It could be a channel whereby state intervention would go into capital-hungry firms, in return for a state share in ownership and control.

On the Galbraithian argument, it is worth pointing out that a great deal could be done to improve the existing public services of this country without taking a single private asset into public ownership. This is not so much an argument for transferring resources from private to public hands, as for spending more on those already in public hands. These two issues tend sometimes to get confused in current Labour thinking.

The argument for equality would seem to have two main policy implications. First, it implies that the existing nationalized concerns should be encouraged to make profits rather than simply break even. It is worth pointing out that nationalization in Britain so far has *not* led to a more even distribution of the nation's wealth between the public and private sector. The form of compensation to private owners, and the nature of the relations with private industry outlined by John Hughes in Chapter 7, have meant that, if anything, the effect has been in the other direction.

Second, the best way of using public ownership to achieve a more equal distribution of income would appear to be by buying shares in the more profitable sections of private industry, either by investing the proceeds of a National Superannuation Fund or by some other means. The aim here would be to get the rewards of ownership, without necessarily exercising control – though the two would not always be distinct.

We come next to the argument for public enterprise as a means of improving industrial efficiency, or filling gaps left in the structure of the economy by private enterprise. Here the intervention of the state could take many forms. In areas of heavy unemployment, or where there is a particular felt need which private enterprise will not fill, there is an obvious case for a national or regional development board – in conjunction perhaps with local authorities, or even trade unions or co-operatives – to set up in business as a public enterprise. In this case, public ownership would not mean the forced transfer of assets from existing owners, but the utilization of unused resources to create public assets which did not exist before. It would be seen by all to be fulfilling a social need, and the element of expropriation or 'grab', with all its emotive implications, would be mercifully absent.

These do not exhaust the possibilities of public enterprise. The range of alternatives is in fact enormous. The public entrepreneur need not be the state. Local authorities, trade unions, co-ops and existing public corporations could between them do a great deal to extend the frontiers of public ownership, without incurring the dangers – real or imagined – of 'bureaucratic over-centralization' and 'the dead hand of Whitehall'. And the participation of the state itself could range all the way through a minority shareholding in a large profitable concern, to an active partnership, control of one or more competing firms in a given industry, or the industry-wide concentration into a single ownership represented by the public corporation. The method chosen must vary with the nature of the particular problem. But there are two necessary ingredients for success. First, the frontier between public and private enterprise needs to become less rigid. The 'mixed economy' needs to become yet more mixed if it is to prosper. Second, public enterprise must not only be more flexible in its forms; it must also be efficient in its operation, and be seen to be so. The opposition which will be bound to come from private industry when public enterprise starts to extend its frontiers can only be countered if public opinion generally supports the aims and objectives of public ownership. This is very far from being the case today.

Within the galaxy of different kinds of public enterprise in the future, the Morrisonian public corporation obviously will have a part – though probably not a major part – to play. The advantage of the public corporation as we have known it since 1945, as compared with other possible forms of public enterprise, lies in the benefits of large-scale operation and the rationalization of production methods which it facilitates. As against this, there is one major disadvantage – in addition to those previously mentioned – about the piecemeal extension of nationalization as it took place between 1945 and 1951, on the basis of full compensation for existing owners. This is the danger of disturbance to the capital market and diminished incentive to efficiency and investment in industries fearing nationalization.

The problem of the capital market is simply this. If the Government is to float a constant succession of bond issues as compensation for bought-out shareholders in nationalized industries, bond values on the gilt-edged market are liable to fall as a result of glut and investors are going to be deterred from lending to the state except at steeply rising yields, which means higher interest rates on any new borrowing by the state or public industries. This will not only make a cheap-money policy extremely difficult; it will also impose a mounting financial burden on the nationalized industries, requiring a correspondingly greater financial surplus on operations to offset it. Ordinary share prices in private industry are liable to rise steeply in value as they become more scarce – a trend which offers rich opportunities for capital gains for big private shareholders. This can hardly be regarded as an important socialist objective!

At the same time, there are obvious disincentives to a private employer who has reason to fear total expropriation. He will become less eager to accept the strains and the risks of expansion, or to undertake new capital investment. These disincentives become less serious to the extent that the state becomes a partner rather than an expropriator of private industry. They would cease to operate at all if nationalization, in the sense of expropriation, came to be recognized as a penalty for failure and sloth, rather than as the reward for success and profitability!

This argument hardly applies in the case of a private monopoly, where profitability may have only a very tenuous connection with efficiency. The more nearly a private firm approaches to the position of a monopolist, the easier the process of nationalization becomes, and the more appropriate as a form of organization the Morrisonian corporation is. This country is badly in need of an effective body of anti-trust legislation. There is no reason why nationalization, or the threat of nationalization, should not be used as one weapon in the armoury. But it should not be the only one. When a firm establishes itself as a private monopoly, we should not be reduced to the alternative of leaving it untouched or turning it into a public one.

The danger of undermining the gilt-edged market by flooding it with compensation issues could be avoided if the Government found some way to sell the financial interest in companies taken over, while retaining the voting rights. On certain conditions, this might be done through the creation of state unit trusts.

The Government might for example take power to require
companies of a given kind to make new share issues for cash to the
Treasury, giving it fifty-and-a-half per cent of the enlarged capital
at a price equal to fifty-and-a-half per cent of the original share
capital's total market value at a determined date. The firm would
have to distribute the cash to its shareholders pro rata. The
acquired shares would then be formed into a unit trust, and the
public (whose total resources would have been raised by the cash
distribution) would be offered units reflecting the financial
benefits of the underlying shareholdings, though without voting
rights. Government representatives would sit on the company
boards with power to use the controlling votes, but the character,
structure and policies of firms would not change more than the
public interest demanded.

Under this system, the state could hope to recoup by sales of
units the initial cash outlay on taking up new shares. Whether
recovery could be complete would depend on several things,
including the phasing of the sale programme and, above all, the
profit-making policy to be aimed at by the state-controlled concerns. Only if the companies taken over were allowed to follow a
reasonably profitable course would the unit offers succeed and the
'minority' shareholders receive a fair deal. Profitability, of course,
would inevitably fluctuate, but this whole method would probably
not be suitable for firms embracing low-earning or loss-making
projects in the public interest. Another question concerns the
setting up of a market in the units. This could probably be done,
but there might be difficulty in an unrestricted right to resell units
to the state, since the latter could hardly realize the underlying
securities, as an ordinary unit trust would do.

Variations on this theme would no doubt be possible; for
instance, companies might in some cases be taken over in full. The
approach, which is untried, would clearly need refinement. But it
could be a supplement, or alternative, to straight share-buying by
means of a National Superannuation Fund or National Development Board. No doubt other and better methods could be devised.

The mechanics, however, are comparatively unimportant. What
is important is that the aims which public ownership is to achieve
should be carefully thought out and fully explained to the public,
that the form of public ownership chosen should reflect those aims,

and that once established, public enterprises should be operated and directed in such a way that they are enabled to succeed. A great deal of thought needs to be given, for example, to the question of where the new managers of an expanding public sector are to come from. It is simply no good for the Labour Party to draw up new 'shopping lists' for nationalization until these basic exercises have been done. The party should start by examining the situation in the existing nationalized industries. It should recognize frankly that while some nationalized industries are working well, others are not. It should stop trying to pretend that everything in the public sector garden is lovely – or would be if only the Government stopped interfering – and that British Railways in its pre-Beeching state represents the full flowering of the socialist dream (too many Tory voters believe this already!).

'The mixed economy' is an unlovely phrase. It is not the sort of cry that will send men to die on the barricades. But it expresses a vital truth about modern Britain – that in our sort of society there is a place for both public and private enterprise, and for varying forms of each. It is surely time that in our industrial life we moved out of the era of Stalinist cold war and into an era of competitive co-existence. In such an era the first requirement of the public sector is, quite simply, that it should be seen to *work*. Then, and only then, can it be made to *grow*. The requirements of the national economy, and the interests of socialism, demand alike a dynamic, efficient system of public enterprise in Britain.

# SELECT BIBLIOGRAPHY ON THE
# NATIONALIZED INDUSTRIES

U P-TO-DATE literature on the nationalized industries is
scanty, whether one is looking for well arranged facts or
informed and creative comment.

By far the best accounts and discussions of the most important
aspects of each industry are contained in the series of *Reports of the
House of Commons Select Committee on Nationalized Industries*. Reports
have so far been issued on the following:

H.C.     304     Ministerial responsibility generally and
the North of Scotland Hydro-Electric
Board, October 1957.
H.C. 187–1     Coal, April 1958.
H.C.     213     The Air Corporations, May 1959.
H.C. 254–1     British Railways, July 1960.
H.C.     280     The Gas Industry, July 1961.

The Annual Reports and Accounts of each of the nationalized
industries contain a mine of interesting and detailed information,
although some are distinctly more informative and more readable
than others. The account in the first two or three reports of the
National Coal Board of the setting-up of its organization is
particularly interesting. In general, all the Reports and Accounts
give more information than can be obtained from the published
accounts of most privately owned companies.

In addition to the Parliamentary inquiries, the Coal, Electricity
Supply and London Transport industries have been the subject of
reports by specially appointed committees, as follows:

*Report of the Committee of Inquiry into the Electricity Supply Industry*
(The Herbert Report), January 1956, Cmd. 9672.
National Coal Board: *Report of the Advisory Committee on Organization*
(The Fleck Report), 1955.
*Report of the Committee of Inquiry into London Transport.* (The
Chambers Report), Ministry of Transport publication, 1955.
*Electricity in Scotland.* (The Mackenzie Report), 1962.

The first two of these reports are of historic importance, and offer some very interesting contrasts; the third is somewhat pedestrian.

The only comprehensive and nearly up to date account of all the nationalized industries is Professor W. A. Robson's monumental *Nationalized Industry and Public Ownership*, George Allen & Unwin, 1960, which reproduces and discusses virtually all the hitherto published information and trends of informed opinion about the present state and future of nationalized industries generally. It can be taken as virtually completely reliable, and is a well-nigh indispensable guide to the subject. A selection of further literature is as follows. In each case particular note should be taken of the dates of publication, because of the frequent organizational and economic changes which most of the industries have undergone.

A. H. Hanson (ed.), *Nationalization: A Book of Readings*, Allen & Unwin for Royal Institute of Public Administration, 1963.

A. H. Hanson, *Parliament and Public Ownership*, Cassell, for the Hansard Society, 1961.

Sir Henry Self and E. M. Watson, *Electricity Supply in Great Britain*, George Allen & Unwin, 1952.

*Coal: The First Ten Years*, The Colliery Guardian, 1957. (Composite authorship, mainly by members and officials of the N.C.B.)

R. Kelf-Cohen, *Nationalization in Britain*, Macmillan, 1958. (Extremely critical of practically every aspect of nationalization in both theory and practice.)

J. F. Sleeman, *British Public Utilities*, Pitman, 1953.

W. A. Robson (ed.), *Problems of Nationalized Industry*, George Allen & Unwin, 1952.

*Fuel and Power Industries in the United Kingdom.* Central Office of Information, 1961.

R. J. S. Baker, *The Management of Capital Projects*, Bell for London School of Economics, 1963.

J. R. Sargent, *British Transport Policy*, O.U.P., 1958.

Professor P. Sargant Florence, *Industry and the State*, Hutchinson, 1957.

D. N. Chester, *The Nationalized Industries – an Analysis of the*

*Statutory Provisions*, Royal Institute of Public Administration, 1951.

Royal Institute of Public Administration Research Group (chairman R. S. Edwards), *Budgeting in Public Authorities*, George Allen & Unwin, 1959.

Lord Simon of Wythenshawe, *The Boards of Nationalized Industries*, Longmans, 1957.

H. A. Clegg and D. N. Chester, 'The North of Scotland Hydro-Electric Board' in *Public Administration*, Autumn 1953.

Anthony Lines, *Concerns of State*, Bow Group, 1961.

An important statement of Government policy is contained in the White Paper:

*The Financial and Economic Obligations of the Nationalized Industries*, Cmnd. 1337, 1961.

Fabian Society Pamphlets:

John Hughes, *Nationalized Industries in the Mixed Economy*, 1960.
John Hughes, *Plan for Steel Re-Nationalization*, 1958.

The fuel and power industries have published various long-term plans as follows:

National Coal Board: *Plan for Coal*, 1950.
*Investing in Coal*, 1956.
*Revised Plan for Coal*, 1959.

The Gas Council: *Fuel for the Nation*, 1954.
*Gas Looks Ahead*, 1958.

British Electricity Authority: *Power and Prosperity*, 1954.
The Electricity Council: *Power for the Future*, 1958.
North of Scotland Hydro-Electric Board and South of Scotland Electricity Board (jointly): *Scottish Electricity: Plans for the Future*, 1958.

For a study of the origins of the present nationalized public corporations the most important material can be found in the independent reports made on the industries concerned before nationalization. For the fuel and power industries see the reports of the following committees (appointed by Coalition or Conservative Governments):

*Report of the Committee on Electricity Distribution* (The McGowan Report), Ministry of Transport, 1937.

*Coal-Mining: Report of the Technical Advisory Committee* (The Reid Report), Cmd. 6610, 1945.

*The Gas Industry: Report of the Committee of Inquiry* (The Heyworth Report), Cmd. 6699, 1945.

Two of the most important books embodying the development of the idea of national public corporations are:

Herbert Morrison, *Socialization and Transport*, Constable, 1933.

W. A. Robson (ed.), *Public Enterprise*, George Allen & Unwin, 1937.

The following are the principal Acts of Parliament which set up public corporations of an industrial character, and national as distinct from local in their scope, or which substantially amended their constitutions:

Electricity (Supply) Act, 1926.
British Overseas Airways Act, 1939.
Hydro-Electric Development (Scotland) Act, 1943.
Coal Industry Nationalization Act, 1946.
Civil Aviation Act, 1946.
Cotton (Central Buying) Act, 1947.
Transport Act, 1947.
Electricity Act, 1947.
Gas Act, 1948.
Iron and Steel Act, 1949.
Iron and Steel Act, 1953.
Transport Act, 1953.
Atomic Energy Act, 1954.
Cotton Act, 1954.
Electricity Reorganization (Scotland) Act, 1954.
Electricity Act, 1957.
Transport Act, 1962.